Administering
the School Reading Program

WAYNE OTTO · RICHARD J. SMITH

University of Wisconsin

Houghton Mifflin Company · Boston

New York · Atlanta · Geneva, Ill. · Dallas · Palo Alto

*Preparation of the statement of skills and objectives for
elementary reading given in Chapter 2 was undertaken and
published as a project of the Wisconsin Research and Development Center for Cognitive Learning at the University of
Wisconsin, Madison, Wisconsin. The Wisconsin Research and
Development Center for Cognitive Learning is supported in
part as a research and development center by funds from the
United States Office of Education, Department of Health,
Education and Welfare. The opinions expressed in the statement
do not necessarily reflect the position or policy of the
Office of Education and no official endorsement by the Office
of Education should be inferred.*

*To
Eleni,
Jeannine,
Karen,
Shirley,
Suzanne,
Theresa
and
Tony*

PREFACE

In choosing a title for this book we were torn between *Administering the School Reading Program* and *Improving the School Reading Program*. An important focus of the book is upon the administrative acts that are requisite to the creation and guidance of a balanced school-wide reading program. Yet we were concerned that by stressing the *administering* we might be misdirecting attention from the goal, which is an *improved* program. We decided finally that use of *administering* would highlight the importance of the administrative role in improving the school reading program. Our hope is that administrators will assume that a book directed to them must have as its ultimate concern the improvement of the program.

This book is for superintendents, principals, curriculum specialists, reading consultants — all school personnel who are in a position to make administrative decisions regarding the reading program. We have attempted to provide what we feel is essential background information on the reading act and the reader for those who are not specialists in reading; perhaps it will serve as a serendipitous review for those who are. From a consideration of the reader as a person we have gone on to consider the components of a balanced reading program, the relationship of reading to the other language arts, steps toward program improvement and the establishment of public relations, the selection of personnel, and the operation and function of in-service education in the bettering of reading instruction. We have tried not to dictate or prescribe the steps toward or components of program development. Our intent, instead, has been to examine and explore appropriate steps and components in order to establish guidelines for local program development. Adequate reading programs are not created by administrative fiat. They are built with administrative guidance.

This book is also for classroom teachers. School-wide reading programs stand or fall on the participation and support of classroom teachers. Those who have a feeling for the direction and operation of a total program will be enthusiastic supporters of the program.

And, of course, this book is for reading specialists and school administrators in preparation. As a primary or supplementary text it can underscore the administrative responsibilities of reading specialists and the need for commitment to the development of the reading program by school administrators.

We are indebted for many of the ideas expressed and positions taken to our experiences in two specific roles: as principal investigator in the Reading Project at the Wisconsin Research and Development Center for Cognitive Learning

(Wayne Otto) and as assistant curriculum director for reading development, Madison, Wisconsin, Public Schools (Richard Smith). Needless to say, we are indebted, too, to many people for the ideas they have shared with us in these and other contexts.

WAYNE OTTO
RICHARD J. SMITH

CONTENTS

PART ONE

The Reading Program: An Overview

Part One, the first four chapters, of this book is devoted to a consideration of the reading program: its focus and scope, its component skills and their development, and its relationship to the other language arts. The emphasis is upon matters that we feel must be of concern not only to everyone who has administrative responsibility for building the program but to everyone who has an interest in supporting efforts expended toward that end. There is information for those whose specialty is not in reading and, we hope, a review of critical points for reading specialists. The concern is not with the specifics of instruction — adequate presentations can be found elsewhere — but with providing a framework within which efficient reading instruction can be carried on.

Chapter 1 is long but it is basic, for it represents an attempt to establish a proper perspective for viewing the person in the reading program. The measurement and correction of reading ability, the components of an adequate reading program, and guidelines for implementing a person-oriented program are considered.

In Chapter 2 the focus is upon specific reading skills that can provide both a framework for the program at the elementary level and a foundation for the development of reading competence at all levels. Chapter 3 deals with the acquisition of reading maturity and the characteristics of mature readers. Taken together, the contents of the two chapters show that the development of reading maturity continues throughout the school experience. In Chapter 4 the relationship of reading to the other language arts and the possibilities for mutual reinforcement by the activities in the several areas are examined.

Part One lays the groundwork for the presentation of specific steps toward improving the reading program in Part Two.

CHAPTER 1

The Person in
the Reading Program

Individuals are unique. Their rates of physical development vary; they are exposed to and shaped by an almost limitless variety of experiences; their styles and paces of learning differ; and they appear to be capable of learning different things to different levels of mastery. No single concept from psychology is more widely accepted by educators than that of individual differences, and no single aspect of education is receiving more attention from educators than schemes for individualizing instruction in the schools. Yet acceptance of the concepts of individual psychology and individualized instruction have not led to the solution of all — or even many — of the instructional problems attendant on individual uniqueness. Much of the labeling, categorizing, filing, profiling, and cross-filing that has been done is little more than a tentative step in what appears now to be the right direction. Furthermore, in our zealous attempts to understand and to provide for the individual we tend often to forget about the person.

Macdonald (1965) has discussed the individual-person paradox: "The *person* . . . in contrast with the individual, is not prized for his uniqueness. . . . The person is valued because of what he shares in common with all other persons: the human condition. . . . It is not the uniqueness of the individual in terms of his personal perceptions, idiosyncratic needs, desires and motives that make him of value, but his common human status." And he concludes, "To treat persons as individuals (in the psychological sense) is in essence to treat them as objects for our study and control."

Mounier (1952, p. 23), too, has spoken to the point regarding the person as a *subject* and as an object:

> If I treat another person as though he were not present, or as a repository of information for my use, an instrument at my disposal; or when I set him down in a list without right of appeal — in such a case I am behaving towards him as though he were an object, which means in effect, despairing of him. But if I treat him as a subject, as a presence — which is to recognize that I am unable to classify him, that he is inexhaustible, filled with hopes upon which he alone can act — that is to give him credit. To despair of anyone is to make him desperate; whereas the credit that generosity extends regenerates his own confidence.

The intent here is not to justify a chapter title or to add another slogan to the literature of reading instruction but to focus upon a dichotomy that ought to be kept in mind when readers and reading instruction are discussed. Individuals are indeed unique, and they do indeed seem to respond to instruction that is sensitive to their idiosyncratic strengths and weaknesses. Ultimately, though, the acceptance of these facts can — and often does — cause students to be treated as if they were little more than "objects for our study and control," as Macdonald put it. In this case, what began as a sound and desirable attempt to personalize instruction becomes an extremely impersonal complex of procedures and categories. We ought not to lose sight of the person as we focus upon the individual. The individual may be classified as a disabled reader and referred for remedial instruction because of his unique problems, but the person must continue to operate in the classroom because of his common human status. The individual may be assessed in terms of his reading skill development, categorized according to his strengths and weaknesses, and taught according to his own characteristics; but the person must remain unclassified, free to strive and to attain according to his own efforts and hopes.

In the pages that follow, much has to do with the individual, but we have made an earnest attempt not to lose sight of the person. To lay a foundation for a consideration of the person in the reading program the reading abilities of individuals and groups are first considered, then the program and its components, and finally the person in the program.

The Reading Ability of Individuals and Groups

Hundreds of studies of the reading abilities of individuals and groups have been reported. From all of these studies, two things are clear: (1) the acquisition of reading skills is a highly personal process that is sensitive to many interacting factors, and (2) it is difficult, for a number of reasons, to generalize about the reading ability of groups of children. While these generalizations may be disconcertingly nonspecific, they do point up the need to look with caution at groups and with extreme care at individuals. The discussion here is limited to a number of issues that merit particular attention when the reading abilities of individuals and groups are considered. We shall proceed from general reading ability to individual reading ability and finally to correlates of reading ability.

General Reading Ability

The focus with regard to general reading ability is upon (1) the importance of defining functional literacy in personal terms, (2) the inadequacies of standardized tests as measures of reading achievement, and (3) the need for a broad-based approach to the study of general reading ability.

Functional Literacy. A fact to be considered by everyone who is concerned about the development of reading ability is this: In our affluent, supposedly highly literate nation millions of adults have not reached an acceptable minimum level of functional literacy and millions more have not reached an optimum level of functional literacy. Fixing the blame is less important than recognizing the problem and accepting the fact that the schools are in a position to provide assistance in dealing with the problem. Much more important, the schools must be willing to go beyond existing definitions of minimal literacy to a definition that is stated in terms of personal abilities and aspirations. Let us consider some current definitions and a proposed definition.

"Basic literacy" has been operationally defined by the Census Bureau: Persons ten years old or over who respond negatively to the question "Can you read and write?" are classed as illiterates, the implication being that they can neither read nor write a simple message in English or any other language. Such a restricted definition has limited usefulness, for the demands of a complex society go far beyond the ability to encode and/or decode simple messages.

The concept of "functional literacy" promises to be more meaningful, but operational definitions tend to be arbitrary. A common practice is to equate educational attainment with number of years of school completed. Persons who are, say, twenty-five years of age or older and have completed fewer than four, six, or eight years of schooling can then be designated illiterate. The problem is that completion of a given number of years of schooling insures neither reading skill development nor general educational attainment at that level; moreover, failure to complete a given number of years of schooling does not necessarily impose a ceiling on educational development.

Fox (1964) defined illiteracy by example:

> The illiterate adult in American society is that individual who does not have the necessary reading skills to make him eligible for vocational training when his marginal job in the labor market is discontinued. His lack of reading skill serves to make him and keep him unemployable. His functional reading may be on a number of levels, varying from preprimer to that of the word-by-word reader who does not comprehend what he reads. He may well be of that 25 per cent of the population which is trainable but below average in intelligence . . . or he may be of average intelligence but of the unfortunate group of individuals who have been educationally deprived.

Fox's definition, which is tied to the ability to read well enough to respond to basic vocational training, reflects the main concern of recent programs designed to reach the chronically unemployed. A specific definition can serve a purpose in a given, limited context, but in the general context of society today such a definition is not adequate.

Otto and Ford (1967, p. 3) concluded that

> Functional literacy . . . is perhaps most realistically defined in terms of the needs of both individuals and the society of which they are a part. Whereas the ability to decipher simple messages may have been adequate as a functional skill in the past, this is no longer so in most situations. Individuals who cannot read fluently are not only likely to be unable to function effectively on the job; they are quite likely to be unable even to apply for new jobs. But certainly all jobs do not require the same level of reading skill: functional skill in one area may be far from functional in another. Clearly, there is need for a sliding scale in defining functional literacy.

The essential point here is that "functional literacy" must realistically be conceived to cover a vast range of levels of reading competence. For a newly literate adult about to enter the world of work, a basic ability to decode printed symbols may, at least temporarily, be adequate, but it will not be adequate as he seeks advancement in his work and/or the cultural enrichment that the ability to read makes available to him. Likewise, what constitutes functional literacy will differ greatly for, say, a farm laborer, a draftsman, a graduate student in anthropology, and a literary critic. Functional literacy can be defined specifically only in terms of the intellectual capacity and the aspirations of the person. Acceptance of such a definition will mean that school personnel can no longer derive much satisfaction from knowing that on the average their pupils meet or exceed local or national norms: The success of the reading program must then be judged by the extent to which it meets the personal needs of each student.

Measurement of Reading Achievement. How great is the gap between the desired goal of functional literacy stated in terms of personal attributes and aspirations and actual reading ability? The question is basic, for in order to consider how to get from where we are to where we want to be we ought to be able to consider how what we have differs from what we want. Unfortunately, there is no straightforward answer to the question. The elusiveness of a general description of the goal because of the personal nature of functional literacy has already been noted. Furthermore, surveys of actual reading performance — status studies — are complicated not only by the elusiveness of criteria but also by limitations of the available measuring instruments.

Standardized reading achievement tests, the most commonly used measuring instruments in status studies, typically share some severe limitations as measures of both group and individual reading performance. The following is an elaboration of some points Eisenberg (1966) has made about the limitations of standardized tests.

1. The tests are "standardized" in terms of administration and scoring by observing the results obtained from samples of children from presumably representative communities throughout the nation. Yet many widely used tests have been shown repeatedly to be inappropriate for use with certain subpopulations: The norms tend to be unrealistic, and specific items are misplaced or meaningless. (Parenthetically, it is only fair to say that the desirability of local norms is pointed out in many test manuals. Perhaps local adaptations in the test items should also be encouraged; then local norms could be derived from tests that are locally meaningful.)

2. A survey achievement test must be brief enough not only to insure that children will not become overly fatigued as they take it but also to appeal to school administrators beset with scheduling problems. The quest for brevity typically causes the test maker to choose between depth and breadth — or to stop short of acquiring either — in sampling from the reading skills. Time limits — which are imposed in the name of standardization as well as brevity — also place severe restrictions upon the confidence with which scores can be treated: The score of, say, a child who works very slowly but with accuracy and understanding will be meaningless.

3. Also in deference to practical considerations, the tests are constructed to be administered to groups of children. Group administration — again combined with the demands imposed by standardization — makes it necessary to give directions and, once they are understood, no further information. Thus the behaviors actually sampled can turn out to be different from the behaviors intended to be sampled. For example, the child who does not know one or more words in the stem of an item will not get to the point of responding to the item itself; and a child who is unable for any reason to work efficiently in a group will do badly. The person quickly becomes lost in the group.

4. Again in deference to practical considerations, the tests must permit not only extremely straightforward but also extremely rapid scoring. As a result most of the items are of the multiple-choice type whether or not the content to be tested lends itself to multiple-choice testing. The trend toward machine scoring has tended to impose more rather than fewer restrictions upon test content in the name of scoring ease. A cynic might observe that the more rapidly tests can be scored the less useful it becomes to score them at all. On the other hand, a realist might say that busy people should get all possible assistance. Perhaps it is more the misuse than the use of rapid-scoring items and techniques that causes problems. If the person is kept clearly in mind, such abuses are likely to be kept to a minimum.

5. The tests designed for use in the upper grades assume competence in reading at the lower levels. That is, a pupil can attain a better-than-zero score by merely signing his name to the answer sheet. Further, because in most instances there is no adjustment for guessing, the pupil who works rapidly is likely to receive an inflated score simply because he takes more chances. Reading specialists typically report that functional reading levels based upon informal inventories or other individual tests are a year or more lower than functional reading levels based upon group tests.

6. The tests designed for use in the lower elementary grades are devoted largely to the word attack skills whereas at the upper levels the comprehension, study, and interpretive skills are given most of the attention. It follows, then, that the upper-level tests draw much more heavily upon general vocabulary, reasoning ability, and general intellectual ability. As a result, lack of experiential-intellectual stimulation extracts an increasingly higher penalty as grade level increases.

The standardized reading achievement tests in common use are gross measures of reading ability. While it may be legitimate to point out that they are intended to be nothing more than gross measures of group performance, the fact remains that several of the limitations discussed hold even when the tests are used with certain groups. An individual's score on a particular test is, at best, a realistic indication of where that individual stands in relation to the norm group for the particular test. Even so, there is no assurance that the reading behaviors sampled by the test reflect the reading demands encountered most often by that individual or that he might not have performed quite differently had other behaviors been sampled. At worst, an individual's score may reflect nothing more than rapid but lucky guessing or an inability to cope with the constraints and demands imposed by the test and/or the testing situation.

Are we, then, to abandon all attempts to examine group reading achievement? Of course not. But as limitations of the test are recognized, perhaps there will be fewer generalizations based upon group test results. Taken together, the points made regarding the personal nature of functional literacy and the limitations of the standardized reading tests demonstrate the difficulties encountered in attempting to assess general reading ability. With these difficulties in mind, it will be useful to examine the contribution that can be made by broad-based, epidemiological studies.

Epidemiological Studies. Many of the studies of reading ability and disability reported in the literature have been done with limited samples of pupils from general school populations or with captive groups of pupils in clinical settings. The results obtained from such groups must be interpreted with caution, for they are likely to reflect little more than instruction-based biases or, with clinical groups, selection biases. Fortunately, more researchers are now taking an epidemiological approach to the study of reading ability and disability. The approach is to gather extensive data from an entire population — say, the pupils of a city school system — in order to look broadly at reading behavior. We shall review two epidemiological studies. Together, they explicate some important points about reading ability and the study of reading ability.

Eisenberg (1966) reported and compared reading achievement test data from three distinct populations: the entire sixth-grade population, excluding pupils in special classes for the retarded, in (1) the public schools of a large urban center ("Metropolis"), (2) the public schools in a county immediately outside Metropolis ("Suburbia"), and (3) the private ("Independent") schools in Metropolis. The results are summarized in Figure 1, which is reproduced from Eisenberg's discussion.

The median grade equivalency for each group should, by definition, be 6.5. Inspection of Figure 1, however, reveals that the median for each of the three groups is quite different: approximately 5.2 for Metropolis, approximately 7.2 for Suburbia, and approximately 10.0 for Independent. While the Independent group might be expected to rate somewhat high because entrance examinations could serve to exclude certain low achievers, the fact remains that the differences among the three groups are substantial and of greater magnitude than could legitimately be expected on the basis of differences in intelligence. Furthermore, the incidence of reading disability as it is commonly defined — i.e., reading performance two or more years below grade placement (Otto and McMenemy, 1966, pp. 35–40) — is substantially different for each group.

Obviously a survey based upon group test results is limited because no differential information is available regarding common scores: Ten scores that place performance at, say, the 4.8 level may be derived from completely different combinations of correct items, but there is no provision for differential analysis. Yet one of three conclusions — or some compromise combination — can be drawn: (1) General reading ability is greatly influenced by where children grow up and where they go to school; (2) general reading ability is a product of why children go to school where they do; (3) general reading ability is little more than the product of test bias. Regardless of which conclusion is accepted, the data base is sufficiently

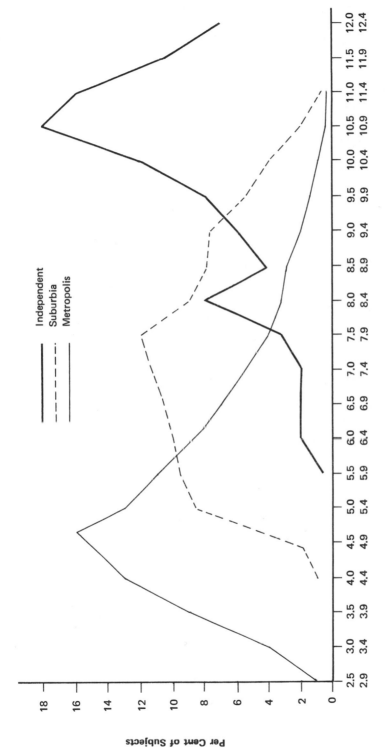

FIGURE 1: Reading levels in 1964 for sixth-grade children in Metropolis, Suburbia, and Independent. Number of subjects: 12,000 for Metropolis, 8,000 for Suburbia, and 200 for Independent. Expected mean based on national sample is 6.5 (five months into the sixth grade).

broad to lend credibility to the score distribution for each group and to the demonstrated differences among groups.

Belmont and Birch (1966) took an epidemiological approach in studying the intellectual profiles — as revealed by the Wechsler Intelligence Scale for Children (WISC) — of disabled readers. They pointed out specific limitations — all of which merit consideration in any study of disabled readers' attributes — of many of the earlier WISC profile studies:

1. The subjects are not drawn from a definable population: They comprise small samples with a wide age range and an unknown composition by sex and other characteristics known to be significantly related to reading ability.

2. The subjects are often drawn from clinical populations. When this is so, the results obtained reflect selection biases of the clinic rather than the characteristics of the general population.

3. The sample composition by sex is not always noted explicitly. This may result in distortion of the results because it is possible that boys and girls differ in reading disability patterns and it is known that boys and girls do differ in intellectual organization at certain ages.

4. The "normal" group to which the "disabled" group is compared is seldom drawn from the same population as the latter. Any demonstration of differences under such circumstances is likely to be meaningless.

The Belmont and Birch study was conducted with the total population of school children in Aberdeen, Scotland, born between 1951 and 1955. The children were given four reading tests in December, 1962. The specific study of WISC profiles was limited to boys born in 1953, and 150 were chosen at random from the 173 whose raw scores on three of the four reading tests placed them below the tenth percentile for their grade. A "normal" comparison group of 50 boys matched by birth date and school class was chosen from the total pool.

Very briefly, the results were as follows:

1. The groups differed in total WISC IQs, with the poor readers scoring lower; but the poor readers were disproportionately lower on the Verbal Scale.

2. When only the poor readers with IQs of 90 and above were included, the normal readers scored higher on the Verbal than on the Performance Scale and the poor readers scored higher on the Performance than on the Verbal Scale; and the proportion of normal readers scoring higher on the Verbal than on the Performance Scale was greater than for poor readers.

3. The poorest readers were superior in Performance Scale scores but inferior in Verbal Scale scores to the normal readers.

The salient conclusion drawn by the authors was that deficiency in language functioning rather than deficiency in perceptual and manipulative skills most clearly sets poor readers apart from normal readers. This finding, which has been replicated in other epidemiological studies, is the opposite of the finding in many studies with clinical groups and a striking demonstration of a contribution to be made by broad-based studies.

We have attempted to make three points about general reading ability. First, functional reading ability *can* be arbitrarily defined, but the ultimate definition must be in terms of the capacity and aspirations of each person. Achievement at the twelfth-grade level might, for example, be designated as the criterion for functional literacy among high school graduates, but the criterion will be beyond the grasp of some and beneath the aspirations of others. The success of a reading program cannot be measured exclusively in terms of norms exceeded or general criteria attained. Second, standardized reading achievement tests are not likely to yield adequate or even accurate information about the reading behavior of individuals. They are constructed with no tolerance for idiosyncratic behavior and little sensitivity to local conditions. Instructional practices based upon standardized test results are probably only grossly in line with personal needs. Third, the epidemiological approach to the study of reading ability promises to help clear up some of the distortions of small-sample studies. A broad-based approach will be useful in arriving at more adequate descriptions of general reading ability, but individual reading ability will always be best approached through a consideration of the person.

Individual Reading Ability

Most experienced teachers and administrators would agree that even in a single, homogeneously grouped classroom the individual pupils are likely to show considerable variance in reading abilities. Yet many of these same people are quick to defend the status quo in their classrooms and schools because their pupils exceed local or national norms on group achievement tests. The fact of the matter is that the greatest single deterrent to a serious consideration of the person in the reading program is the tendency of responsible individuals to be satisfied when grade norms are being attained or exceeded by the group. The paradox that confronts us is that while there is little reluctance to acknowledge the existence of individual differences in reading ability there is much reluctance to question group test results when the group appears to be performing well. When grade norms are not being attained, of course, there is much more willingness to examine current practices and to seek new approaches.

One very straightforward way to get back to the reality of individual reading performance is to take a careful look at the reading performance of the individuals in a single classroom. Typically, such an examination will not only demonstrate once again the wide range of reading abilities in a classroom but make clear the fallacy involved in deriving satisfaction from "grade level" performance by the group. The examination could be expanded to an entire class or school population, but in the present context the procedure would become unwieldy and in a larger context some of the immediate impact for classroom teachers would be lost. Furthermore, the basic points can usually be adequately made with scores for a single classroom.

As an example, reading and related data from an actual seventh-grade classroom are presented in Table I. Scores from identical or similar tests are routinely available for analysis from all-school testing programs. Tests from which the scores in Table I are derived were given at the beginning of the school year, and four of the thirty-six pupils represented were subsequently transferred to another classroom to equalize class size. The data in Table I were originally presented by Otto and McMenemy (1966, pp. 113–120) to demonstrate an approach to classroom screening for the purpose of identifying pupils in need of special help in reading.

The columns in Table I present: (1) *Chronological Age* (CA) expressed in years and months; (2) *Mental Age* (MA), derived by computing CA × IQ to establish an *expectancy* or *general capacity* criterion age; (3) *Reading Age* (RA), established by adding five to the achievement grade level attained on a group test; (4) *Arithmetic Age* (AA), established by adding five to the achievement grade level attained on the computation subtest of a group arithmetic test; (5) a com-

TABLE I: Comparisons of Chronological, Mental, Reading, and Arithmetic Ages of Seventh-Grade Pupils*

Pupil	Chrono-logical Age (CA)	Mental Age (MA)	Reading Age (RA)	Arithmetic Age (AA)	Difference Between MA and AA	Difference Between MA and RA
1	12.0	14.3	15.0	13.2	−1.1	+0.9
2	11.11	15.0	15.0	13.2	−1.10	—
3	12.5	16.1	15.0	14.8	−1.5	−1.1
4	12.2	14.9	15.0	13.9	−1.0.	+0.3
5	12.4	15.2	15.0	14.1	−1.1	+0.2
6	12.0	17.1	15.0	14.2	−2.11	−2.1
7	12.0	14.8	15.0	14.5	−0.3	+0.4
8	11.2	14.3	14.6	14.0	−0.3	+0.3
9	12.1	14.8	14.6	13.7	−1.1	−0.2
10	11.9	16.7	14.6	14.5	−2.2	−2.1
11	11.6	14.0	13.9	13.9	−0.3	−0.3
12	12.3	13.7	13.4	14.2	+0.7	−0.3
13	11.7	13.7	13.3	12.2	−1.5	−0.4
14	12.5	13.1	14.2	14.4	+1.3	+1.1
15	12.1	12.11	13.2	12.3	−0.8	+0.3
16	11.7	12.3	12.6	13.0	+0.9	+0.3
17	11.11	12.0	12.6	14.4	+2.4	+0.6
18	12.1	11.4	12.4	12.1	+0.9	+1.0
19	12.3	11.8	12.3	12.5	+0.9	+0.7
20	12.9	12.0	11.6	11.4	−0.8	−0.6
21	11.7	11.7	11.3	12.3	+0.8	−0.4
22	12.6	12.0	10.9	11.9	−0.3	−1.3
23	12.4	12.3	10.7	11.9	−0.6	−1.8
24	12.1	12.9	10.7	12.5	−0.4	−2.2
25	11.11	11.0	10.6	13.8	+2.8	−0.6
26	12.6	10.8	10.4	11.1	+0.5	−0.4
27	12.4	10.9	10.2	12.0	+1.3	−0.7
28	12.2	10.8	10.1	10.7	−0.1	−0.7
29	12.0	10.6	9.9	10.6	—	−0.9
30	13.3	10.5	9.9	11.2	+0.9	−0.8
31	12.7	10.4	9.8	11.7	+1.3	−0.8
32	13.2	10.6	9.5	12.8	+2.2	−1.1
33	13.3	10.3	9.3	12.1	+1.10	−1.0
34	12.1	9.7	9.2	11.0	+1.5	−0.5
35	11.8	12.0	9.1	11.2	−0.10	−2.11
36	13.0	10.4	9.0	10.7	+0.3	−1.4
Range	13.3–11.2	17.1–9.7	15.0–9.0	14.8–10.6		
Mean	12.2	12.9	12.8	12.8		

* All ages are in years and months.

parison between each child's mental age and arithmetic age; and (6) a comparison between each child's mental age and reading age. Again, the scores are from group tests routinely given at the seventh-grade level to provide assessments of intelligence and achievement. All scores are converted to age equivalencies to permit direct comparisons between scores. Five years were added to the reading and arithmetic achievement grade scores to establish age equivalencies for performance in each area; e.g., assuming school entry at age 6.0, $RA = 1$ (grade placement) + 5, which is the constant. Arithmetic computation scores are included to provide a check on performance that is not dependent upon reading ability.

Mean (average) scores are given in the last row in each of the first four columns in Table I. Inspection of the mean scores, in the absence of other data, would suggest that the group represented is about average in chronological age (i.e., the expected age of beginning seventh-graders would be 12.0 if they began first grade when they were 6.0) and somewhat above average in intelligence and in reading and arithmetic achievement. On the basis of mean scores, one might argue that the class is doing about as well as can be expected and, therefore, that present practices are appropriate and adequate. But closer examination of the data shows how deceptive mean scores can be.

The range of the age scores in each of the first four columns in Table I is given in the second-to-last row in each column. The CAs range from 13.3 to 11.2, a two-year range, which is not uncommon by seventh grade. The MAs range from 17.1 to 9.7, which means that the pupils' IQs range from over 150 to less than 70. Even when all the limitations of group intelligence tests are considered, the fact remains that the individuals in the class differ greatly in verbal intelligence, as measured by the group test employed, and in potential ability to achieve in reading. The RA range, limited by the fact that the test used has a tenth-grade-level ceiling, is from 15.0 to 9.0, or from fourth- to tenth-grade level. The AA range is almost as great as the RA range. The frequency distributions in Table II show how different the picture derived from inspection of score ranges is from that derived from a simple inspection of means: The pupils are not generally achieving at their capacity levels in spite of the fact that the mean scores for mental age are comparable.

TABLE II: Frequency Distribution of Chronological, Mental, Reading, and Arithmetic Ages of Seventh-Grade Pupils

Age in Years and Months (midpoint)	Chronological Age	Mental Age	Reading Age	Arithmetic Age
17.0		2	—	—
16.0		1	—	—
15.0		5	7	1
14.0		5	4	12
13.0	6	3	4	4
12.0	28	8	4	11
11.0	2	5	5	7
10.0		7	7	1
9.0		—	5	—

The careful analysis of group scores from a single classroom, then, serves to put mean scores into perspective and to underscore the need to look at individual scores if the person is to be kept in focus. In subsequent sections of Chapter 1 we shall consider the components of a comprehensive school reading program designed to provide administratively for each person in the program. While explicit suggestions for placing each person in the program are given there, it is appropriate to examine now individual scores in Table I to identify pupils who appear to be having problems in reading. Again, if satisfaction with group scores precludes such an analysis, individuals are likely to be lost in the crowd.

A comparison of each pupil's mental age (MA) and reading age (RA) is given in Table I: The smaller the *plus* or *minus* quantity, the closer achievement is to ability; the larger the quantity, the more likely it is that there is either a reading problem or an erroneous test score. Because with group tests the possibility of substantially erroneous scores is great, the comparison in the second-to-last column in Table I is included. There the mental age–achievement comparison is restricted to the non-reading-dependent skill of computation in arithmetic; thus, discrepancies between the quantities in the arithmetic and the reading achievement comparison columns give cause for cautious interpretation. For example, *Pupil 17* shows up in the reading column with a +0.6 and in the arithmetic column with a +2.4. While the +0.6 in the reading column suggests that the child's reading ability is in line with his mental ability, the substantial +2.4 gap in the arithmetic column suggests that he is doing considerably better in the nonreading area. The most straightforward interpretation is that the mental age assessment appears to be in error and in need of rechecking. The IQs and MAs derived from group tests of mental ability are, of course, delimited in the examples given by the fact that the verbal test of mental ability requires reading ability, so an individually administered, nonreading type of test would be most useful. In each examination of individual data, limitations of the tests used must be considered.

Considering *Pupil 6,* the −2.1 in the reading column suggests a reading disability; but the reading achievement test has a ceiling of Grade 10 (RA = 15.0). Since Pupil 6 performed to the ceiling of the test, there is no way to tell how he might have done without the ceiling. In view of the −2.11 in the arithmetic column, some further testing would be desirable: The child is obviously bright (IQ above 140) and in spite of his above-grade-level achievement he might be performing substantially below his potential. Likewise, *Pupil 10* appears to have an IQ above 150, and he too is performing substantially above grade level — 14.6, or 2.6 above grade level in reading — but more than two years below his potential in both reading and arithmetic. While test scores that approach the ceiling of a test must be interpreted with caution, chances are that Pupil 10 would profit from enrichment activities and come closer to realizing his potential for achievement.

Pupils 30, 31, 34, and *36* appear, on the basis of the $\frac{MA}{CA}$ conversion, to have IQs in the 75 to 85 range. In each case, AA is somewhat higher than MA, and RA is somewhat lower than MA. This means that the MA scores are probably minimal and in need of further checking; but if they are substantiated the pupils would no doubt benefit most from instruction adapted to their limited abilities. In the case of *Pupils 17* and *25*, the AAs are more than two years above the MAs. Chances are that the mental ability test scores are in error.

Pupil 24 appears to have a specific problem in reading, with a −2.2 lag in RA and only a −0.4 lag in AA. He would probably benefit from remedial instruction. *Pupils 32, 33,* and *35* also appear to have specific problems in reading.

The analysis of the individual data in Table I could be extended or modified, depending on the specific purpose. Again, the essential point is that satisfaction with mean scores can produce a false sense of security about the adequacy of reading instruction in a given program. A more realistic approach is to inspect the range of scores and individual scores. The procedure suggested is a straightforward way to focus upon individual performance; as such it can be a worthwhile first step toward the improvement of reading instruction.

Factors Related to Reading Ability

One does not need to go beyond a single classroom to be struck by the wide range of reading abilities among pupils of approximately the same age and with similar exposure — at least in terms of years in school — to reading instruction. Individuals differ greatly in reading ability. Furthermore, as demonstrated by the epidemiological data reported by Eisenberg (1966), entire groups of individuals may differ greatly in reading ability. Literally hundreds of studies have been done to identify causes for the differences; but, as already pointed out, the main generalization to be derived from the results is that reading ability is affected by many interacting factors that differ from person to person. This is not the place for a comprehensive survey of specific causal factors, but a review of general categories is relevant to a consideration of the reading abilities of individuals and groups.

Assumptions Regarding Etiology. Studies of the etiology (causation) of reading ability or disability often reflect the biases or the basic assumptions of the workers who design and execute them. That is, workers with, say, a medical orientation have tended to look for and to find physical factors whereas educational psychologists have looked for and found psychological and educational factors to be related to success in reading. Furthermore, Wiener and Cromer (1967) pointed out that proceeding from different sets of assumptions leads not only to the identification of different factors but also to markedly different implications regarding the appropriate approach to the remediation of difficulties. They identified four assumptions that are used to account for difficulties in reading: (1) the assumption of defect, (2) the assumption of deficiency, (3) the assumption of disruption, and (4) the assumption of difference. Concern for the person requires an awareness of each.

Implicit in the *assumption of defect* is the belief that reading difficulties are caused by certain malfunctions — typically attributed to sensory-physical impairment — that preclude the person's benefiting from his experiences. A literal interpretation of the assumption, which appears to be accepted by some investigators, would suggest that for every reading disability there is a specific, identifiable defect. The suggestion, too, would be that remediation can proceed only through elimination of the defect (e.g., brain surgery, corneal transplant) or through an unimpaired modality (e.g., the tactual modality in the case of a blind person). In certain instances a visual, auditory, neurological, or other sensory-physical defect can indeed be identified, but more often than not such an identification cannot be made.

Investigators who operate with an *assumption of deficiency* appear to be convinced that difficulty in reading is attributable to the absence of certain functions, such as adequate language development, basic word attack skills, or essential study skills. Presumably the missing function(s) must be added in order to clear up the difficulty. Unlike the assumption of defect, the implication is that the difficulty can be reversed through remedial teaching. Needless to say, most school-centered remedial teaching efforts proceed from the assumption-of-deficiency orientation, but most remedial teachers would agree that their efforts have not met with unequivocal success in all cases. While an absence-of-function explanation for reading difficulties is both straightforward and adequate in many cases, it is an oversimplification in many others.

With the *assumption of disruption* the conclusion is that the presence of certain factors or functions interferes with reading development, and that these must be eliminated before the difficulty can be eliminated. Investigations of anxiety, personal-social conflicts, emotional maladjustments, and "neurotic learning disability" all proceed from an assumption of disruption. The suggestion is that remediation can proceed efficiently only after the source of disruption has been removed; e.g., only after intense anxiety has been brought under control will the pupil be receptive to tutorial help designed to overcome skill deficiencies. Again, there are many cases in which interfering factors appear to be present, but it is doubtful that significant interfering factors are present in all, or even a majority of, cases.

With the *assumption of difference,* investigators attribute reading difficulty to differences between typical and appropriate modes of responding. The suggestion is that (1) the pupil would read adequately if the material were consistent with his behavior patterns and (2) remediation amounts to changing either the material or the behavior pattern. An example of a mismatch given by Wiener and Cromer (p. 630) is personified by a lower-class child who speaks neighborhood slang: The child is unable to respond to reading tests written for middle-class children because the reading material and his typical pattern of responding are out of phase. Thus, the child has a language problem rather than a reading problem as such. Another example is, say, a psychologist who attempts to read a physics text: He reads more slowly, makes more errors, and has less comprehension than when he reads in his own field. With an extreme interpretation, all reading difficulties could be attributed to the existence of differences between the material to be read and the ability of the reader. This, of course, is not the intent. The focus is upon differences between typical and appropriate modes for responding, which merit much more attention than has been given in the past.

The essential point here is that when investigators proceed from different assumptions they are likely to come up with different suggestions regarding appropriate approaches to efficient reading instruction. While there is some movement toward more interdisciplinary work, for the foreseeable future practitioners who wish to take a broader view in dealing with the development of reading ability will have to continue to do their own line crossing. Realistically, our knowledge of the etiology of reading ability or disability is not yet so definitive as to permit us to take anything but the broad view.

The avoidance of a narrow focus regarding etiology can help to insure that important approaches to the remediation of reading difficulties will not be overlooked. Too often, though, the discussion of factors related to reading ability is limited to an examination of the causes of difficulties and nothing is said about normal development. The discussions take on needlessly negative overtones, for the same factors that can cause problems at one end of a continuum often can lead to optimum growth at the other end. We need to be as willing to make maximum use of the positive as we are to expend remedial efforts to minimize the negative.

General Categories. By examining general categories or clusters of factors often considered in relation to reading ability we can sample from the variety of interacting factors involved and point out some concerns that are relevant when the focus is upon the person. Any categorization of factors related to reading ability must be arbitrary. Intelligence, for example, has a biological base, but that there are social-psychological-cultural overtones is accepted by almost everyone. In this discussion we have chosen three major categories: physical, psychological, and environmental. Both the choice of categories and the placement of factors within them is admittedly arbitrary.

1. Physical. In this category *general health* is an important but relatively seldom discussed or investigated factor. Vernon (1957), in her excellent review of factors related to reading difficulty, is one of the few writers to mention it at all, and she cites only a few relevant studies. Perhaps the neglect is due to the nonspecificity and ambiguity necessarily involved. Not only is it difficult to specify the exact nature and degree of debility that is likely to make a critical difference in a child's reading development; it is equally difficult, particularly after a child begins school, to say whether it is his sickness or his resultant nonparticipation in developmental activities that causes problems. Nevertheless, it stands to reason that a healthy, well-nourished child is usually a more receptive learner and a more successful reader than a child who is not physically up to par. Eisenberg (1966, p. 13) has recommended a thorough pediatric examination as the first step in the evaluation of any child with a learning failure. We must take care not to become so involved with the esoterica of etiology that we forget something so mundane as general health.

In the area of esoterica, *cerebral dominance* has received much attention from investigators. A. J. Harris (1961) captured the general mood when he wrote, "One of the most puzzling and most controversial issues in the whole field of reading is the significance of lateral dominance" (p. 249). In the simplest terms, cerebral (or lateral) dominance amounts to the preference of use and dominance of function of one side of the body over the other. Many workers have contended that children who are not right-dominant — that is, those who have either a consistent left-side preference or a mixed or converted dominance — are disposed to reading disability. While the results of studies have tended to be somewhat inconsistent, the fact is — at least with clinical groups — that groups of poor readers tend generally to include disproportionately many individuals with dominance problems. That all poorly lateralized children are not poor readers has been the source of some embarrassment to certain investigators, but Zangwill (1962) has suggested that perhaps poorly developed laterality results in reading difficulty only in combination with another factor (e.g., cerebral lesion, constitutional weakness in maturation, extreme anxiety).

After a thorough review of the literature Zangwill concluded, "It is difficult to arrive at a very clear-cut conclusion. . . . [However] fuller understanding of reading and its disorders must presuppose fuller understanding of the ways in which asymmetrical functions become established in the human brain" (p. 113). With regard to present approaches to the treatment of reading disability on the basis of current knowledge of cerebral dominance (e.g., Delacato, 1959), Money (1962) concluded in 1962 that "Scientifically speaking, it is far too premature to be applying hypotheses of cerebral dominance to methods of treatment. What these hypotheses need, above all else, is to be tested experimentally, and in controlled observation, for validity" (p. 28). No support has been forthcoming, and Robbins (1967) is only representative of those who have issued further indictments. For the practitioner with more concern for persons than panaceas, the message seems to be: Proceed with caution.

Brain injury, too, has received much attention as a possible causal factor in reading disability. There seems to be little doubt that children with significant impairment are likely to have learning problems, but the specifics of causality are by no means clear. Exactly what constitutes *"significant* impairment" is not precisely known: There is no straightforward relationship between amount or locus of damage and ultimate academic achievement. Furthermore, neurological examinations are not always sensitive enough to pick up subtle but significant dysfunctions (Thelander *et al.,* 1958); and dysfunction may become critical only at higher levels of skill development in basic academic areas like reading, writing, and spelling (Pasamanick and Knobloch, 1960).

The issue is further clouded by the tendency of some workers to lump together "brain injury," "minimal cerebral dysfunction," "diffuse brain damage," "word blindness," "dyslexia," "strephosymbolia," and "specific reading disability" as if they all meant the same thing. Since the designations can and often do — depending, apparently, upon the investigator's fancy — describe quite different conditions, confusion is rampant. The reader is referred to two excellent books edited by John Money (1962, 1966) for clarification. A point essential to consideration of the person has been suggested by Eisenberg (1966, p. 14): Some children with sufficient brain damage to result in moderate mental deficiency are able, in the elementary grades, to attain better than average fluency in oral reading, but they can comprehend little of what they read. That this is the case serves both to demonstrate a subtle manifestation of brain damage and to underscore the need for careful reading diagnosis in conjunction with an adequate physical examination.

Finally, the *sensory bases* of reading, vision and hearing, have received deserved attention. Many studies of the relationship of visual factors and reading ability have been reported, and there is little question that certain visual anomalies occur more frequently among poor readers than among good readers. Yet one need not jump to conclusions regarding the relationship, because (a) defects must go beyond critical levels of severity to become significant causal factors, and critical levels appear to differ from person to person, and (b) visual defects may become critical only in combination with other factors.

Irvine (1941) concluded that visual defects cause reading problems only when acuity is reduced by half or more. Robinson (1946, p. 19), in her classic study, judged that "among the visual difficulties most frequently linked with reading inability and apparently in need of more careful investigation are hyperopia, hyperopic astigmatism, binocular inco-ordination, visual fields, and aniseikonia if younger children are being studied." Years later, Smith and Dechant (1961, p. 132) reviewed the literature and said, "In searching for possible relationships between visual defects and reading achievement, we must consider the likelihood of multiple causation. In many cases an eye defect alone might not reduce reading efficiency, yet the same defect combined with other factors might do so. And it is quite possible that certain eye defects affect reading performance only when their severity is beyond certain critical points." Harris (1961, p. 239) reached the conclusion that is most relevant for the teacher of reading: "No matter how complete the vision test in a school may be, no teacher, nurse or psychologist should attempt to prescribe treatment for eye defects. The school's function is to find those who are in need of expert attention; children who are found or suspected to have defective vision should be sent to an eye specialist."

Perhaps still another word of caution is in order: In some circles various forms of visual training — visual-motor, visual-perceptual, etc. — are not only fashionable but aggressively pushed. These approaches offer some promise, and further study is certainly warranted, but at the present time any wide-scale adoption by practitioners is premature. Any assumed transfer of training remains, generally, to be demonstrated.

With regard to auditory factors, Goetzinger, Dirks, and Baer (1960) reported that there is increasing evidence that children with normal pure-tone auditory thresholds may have difficulty in discriminating speech sounds. The point is an important one for it underscores the need to look beyond the gross level in assessing the relationship of auditory factors and reading performance. Hearing is, of course, important both before and after formal reading instruction begins. Carhart (1947, p. 302) put it very well: "Any substantial loss of hearing which exists at birth or occurs soon thereafter will hinder both language development and the establishment of adequate speech habits. Two factors are responsible. First, the hearing loss reduces sharply the number of listening experiences that the child has and thus slows up the process of learning to talk. Second, losses of certain types make it impossible for the child to distinguish some of the elements in speech. No child will learn to pronounce distinctions he does not hear, unless, of course, he has special guidance." Smith and Dechant (1961, p. 140), once again emphasizing the multiple causality of reading problems, concluded, "It may be that auditory deficiencies and reading disability are closely related only under certain circumstances: if the hearing loss is severe, if the hearing loss involves high tone deafness, and if instruction puts a premium on auditory factors."

The implication seems to be that in order to cope with limited auditory defects we can (a) de-emphasize auditory discrimination in the instructional approach (i.e., place less emphasis upon phonics and more upon other word analysis techniques) and (b) undertake training designed to make the child more aware of and more attentive to sound and to sharpen auditory discrimination. Realistically, though, whether such training — or what aspect(s) of it — actually transfers remains to be demonstrated.

2. Psychological. *Intelligence* is arbitrarily placed in this category, although it could defensibly be placed in the physiological or environmental one. Without doubt intelligence is the single factor most clearly related to reading ability; yet it is equally clear that there is far from a one-to-one relationship between reading ability and intelligence as it is now measured. As early as 1933 Durrell (1933) made the point that group intelligence tests that include a large number of reading items should be regarded as reading tests that have been inappropriately named; and the point has been made by virtually every writer on the topic since then. Poor readers are bound to do badly on reading-loaded "intelligence tests." Equally important, but not so often considered, is the fact that good readers are likely to do exceptionally well on reading-loaded intelligence tests. If the person is truly our concern, we must be as concerned about overassessment as underassessment of intelligence, for to err in either direction is to establish the basis for unrealistic expectations regarding ultimate achievement.

In general, correlations between intelligence test scores and reading achievement test scores tend to range between .40 and .60. While these are substantial correlations, as correlations go, it is quite apparent that other factors are very much involved in determining reading achievement. The correlations between individual intelligence test scores and reading scores tend to be lower (on the order of .50) than the correlations between verbal group intelligence test scores and reading scores (often .60 or higher). This finding is as might be expected in view of the fact that group intelligence tests and reading tests measure essentially the same thing: ability to read test items. When the purpose is to establish a prognosis (an estimate of rate and ultimate level of growth), the best available measure of intelligence *plus other important factors* — like motivation, experiential background, and quantity and quality of instruction — must be considered. Some highly intelligent children fail to learn to read; on the other hand, many slow learners and even moderately retarded children learn to read well enough to get along in a literate society. No person's potential can be described by a single test score.

Many investigators have reported a variety of *social-personal* factors to be related to reading achievement. Malmquist (1958), for example, reported significant positive correlations between first-graders' reading ability and the following: intelligence, concentration, persistence, self-confidence, dominance-submissiveness, emotional stability–nervousness, and social attitude (ability to make contacts). Likewise, most workers agree that poor readers often have social-emotional problems of varying degrees. Gates (1941) once estimated that personality mal-adjustment is present in about 75 per cent of reading disability cases, but estimates by others range from 10 to 100 per cent. The variance is more likely to be due to lack of agreement on a suitable definition for "maladjustment" than to lack of agreement on the symptoms observed.

The problem that confounds much of the research on social-personal factors is inherent in the fact that the data were gathered after a reading difficulty was already well established. It becomes extremely difficult then to determine whether the reading difficulty is the result or the cause of social-personal problems. Learn-ing to read is the most important single developmental task encountered by the child in the school setting. Children who are overly aggressive, defiant, or reluctant to grow up will have powerful negative motivation when they come to learning to read. Furthermore, children with severe emotional problems are not likely to be in a position to devote the needed concentration and attentiveness to reading instruction. On the other hand, children who come to the reading task without emotional hang-ups but fail for other reasons are almost bound to become emotionally involved with their failure. To fail at such a basic task, where quality of performance is constantly open to the scrutiny of teachers, parents, and peers, is to deviate substantially and obviously from the expectations of important others. The problem of extricating cause and effect when reading difficulties and an emotional problem coexist is a thorny one for the researcher.

For the practitioner, it is less important to decide which came first than to accept the dual nature of the problem. The child with emotional problems will not respond to instruction so long as emotional problems are more important to him than the instruction. The child who sees himself as a failure must see himself begin to succeed before he can begin to change his self-concept. To attack either the emotional problem or the reading problem in isolation would be unrealistic in view of the needs of the person.

Concern for the person requires a word of caution. In some cases social-emotional problems may lead not to reading failure but to reading excellence. Withdrawal from a real world filled with problems can take a child to a fantasy world he finds in books. The quiet kid in the corner with a book might be another Abe Lincoln — or another Lee Harvey Oswald. Every classroom does not need a psychiatrist, but it does need a sensitive teacher.

Perhaps the most nebulous, yet an extremely important, psychological factor is *motivation*. Without it, high intelligence and many other positive forces are neutralized; with it, such negative factors as certain physical defects, limited experiences, or even limited intelligence cannot block success. To some extent, motivation is shaped by the same environmental factors that give substance to basic intelligence: social class values, cultural experiences, upward striving. But to most teachers it is clear that "lack of motivation" is not limited to any social class or to any income bracket or to the so-called culturally deprived. While the extrinsic motivation of chocolate drops or plastic tokens may be sufficient to get the action started in some cases, the approach is both inadequate and a symptom of gross oversimplification in others.

Dinkmeyer and Dreikurs (1963) have addressed themselves to the problem of motivation — or encouragement, in their terminology — in a changing society. One of their premises is that with the weakening of autocratic control at all levels of our society there is much more need for inner stimulation because pressure from without has largely ceased to be a very real force. Another premise is that adults can be instrumental in nurturing inner stimulation if they will take care to provide each child with explicit encouragement. The person who encourages, then, "(1) Places value on the child as he is. (2) Shows a faith in the child that enables the child to have faith in himself. (3) Has faith in the child's ability; wins the child's confidence while building his self-respect. (4) Recognizes a job 'well done.' Gives recognition for *effort*. (5) Utilizes the group so that the child can be sure of his place in it. (6) Assists in the development of skills sequentially and psychologically paced to permit success. (7) Recognizes and focuses on strengths and assets. (8) Utilizes the interests of the child to energize instruction" (p. 50). We agree with Dinkmeyer and Dreikurs that most of us are better prepared by background and by inclination to discourage than to encourage. Genuine concern for the person is the base for acts that are encouraging and, ultimately, for motivation that is self-sustaining.

3. Environmental. In the area of environmental factors *experiential* (home) *background,* or *cognitive stimulation,* has always been considered important as a requisite to achievement in reading; but more recent and more explicit concern about the effects of "cultural deprivation" has caused workers to make more penetrating analyses of exactly what is involved, what is significant, and what can be done.

In his omnibus study of factors related to success in beginning reading, Malmquist (1958) found a significant relationship for the following home-background factors: father's income, mother's education, family social status, number of books in the home, number of rooms in the home, and child's disposal of his own room. Also investigated and found not to be significantly related (some other studies to the contrary) were: number of children in the home, child's place in the sibling constellation, attendance at nursery school, and "broken home" background. While some of the specific factors examined may seem trivial in isolation, the general message of Malmquist's results, as they represent the results of many studies in the area, is that an enriched home background pays off in terms of reading achievement.

The intent, however, is not to suggest that socioeconomic class tells the entire story. To the contrary, Durkin (1964) found that in a sample of forty-nine children who had learned to read before first grade more than half came from upper-lower-class homes. Interview data, she pointed out, showed that while the lower-class families were delighted with the early reading as a promise of better things to come, the families in the higher socioeconomic classes appeared to feel guilty and concerned that perhaps there would be interference with instruction in school. Interestingly, the most significant factor in the homes of most of the early readers appears to have been the presence of an older sibling or, less frequently, a parent who did the teaching. Again the results demonstrate a general point: The attitudes within specific homes are potent determiners of behavior.

The home environment provides the setting for the preschool cognitive stimulation that is the critical prerequisite to satisfactory growth in reading. Typically middle-class teachers are now more than ever aware of the limited backgrounds of some children when they come to school. Researchers have shown that slum children, on the average, arrive at school with severe limitations in their language development; they have not been exposed to sustained, grammatically complex speech or to an extensive range of vocabulary, and they have had little reinforcement for their own verbal efforts. As a result, they show poorly developed auditory perception, do poorly on vocabulary tests, particularly with abstract words, and do not respond well to verbal instruction in school. Lacking adequate oral language development, they are poorly prepared to tackle the more complex task of learning to read. Experientially, their world is often confined to the immediate area of their homes, and they have missed the taken-for-granted experiences of visiting the zoo or a museum or of riding the bus; a ride in the country, a day on a farm, planting a flower or climbing a tree are unknown to them. Their homes are often bereft of pencil and paper, to say nothing of books and magazines. They are not prepared to accept the constraints of the classroom because their experiences are completely alien to the classroom.

We have touched on only a few of the higher-level generalizations regarding home background. Implicit in true concern for the person is knowing and understanding the background from which he comes and to which he returns each day when school is dismissed. Often the best information and the most realistic basis for understanding can be gained through home visits. They are costly in terms of time and effort, but the price is not too high.

Unless and until sweeping changes are made in the wide-scale approach to early childhood education, the schools will continue to have little control or influence over the early experiential background of children, however desirable a systematic approach to early cognitive stimulation may be. Nevertheless, the schools do have direct and explicit control over *instructional factors* as they relate to achievement in reading once the child arrives at school. The responsibility of the school, then, is to accept the person as he is, to make no assumptions regarding his prior experiences or background, to recognize his physical, social-emotional, and intellectual strengths and weaknesses — and to teach him to read.

The popular press, the critics, the charlatans, the hucksters, and a few specially blessed professionals claim to know precisely how to get on with the job: eliminate look-say, return to *McGuffey's Readers,* cut out the nonsense, get tough, sock it to the three Rs, teach phonics, break the code, learn to creep, tutor your infant, exercise your eyeballs, and/or use Program X exactly as directed; most important of all, keep your fingers crossed. We feel that anybody who is naive or ignorant enough to claim to have all the answers regarding the teaching of reading has amply demonstrated the fact that he does not have all the answers. Across-the-board attacks on reading instruction as it is and oversimplified panaceas will contribute little or nothing that is positive. On the other hand, it is quite clear that instruction in reading is highly related to children's success in reading and that reading instruction is not always provided under the best of conditions or by teachers who are adequately prepared. There *is* room for improvement.

Time, effort, and money have been expended in seeking improvement of instruction through identification of the best materials for the most pupils. We feel that the general futility of such an approach has been made plain. Dykstra (1968), in a review of the second-grade phase of the Cooperative Research Program in primary reading, concluded that "One of the most important implications of this study is that future research should center on teacher and learning situation characteristics rather than method and materials. . . . The elements of the learning situation attributable to teachers, classrooms, schools and school systems are obviously extremely important. Reading instruction is more likely to improve as a result of improved selection and training of teachers, improved in-service training programs, and improved school learning climates, rather than from minor changes in instructional materials" (p. 66). Materials and methods are important, but it is more appropriate to examine and select them in terms of personal needs than in terms of the results of group achievement tests.

Specific Reading Disability. Having examined both basic assumptions related to etiology and general categories of factors related to reading ability or disability, we offer a word regarding specific reading disability.

Children with specific reading disability, also commonly called congenital word blindness or primary reading disability, in effect fall into a residual category for those who have failed in reading despite a strong positive prognosis for success. In a school setting the most troublesome fact about specific reading disability is its nonspecificity: A child's experiential background, physical and psychological development, motivation, effort, and instruction may all be exemplary, so when there is specific reading disability there may be no apparent specific cause for the problem. A cynic might say that the real problem, then, is that there is nobody to blame. The intent here is not to fix the blame but to recognize the problem.

Rabinovitch and Ingram (1962) have identified three diagnostic groupings for cases of reading disability that have become more or less classic:

1. Primary reading retardation. There is no evidence of brain damage, but the ability to deal with words as symbols is impaired. The assumption is that the problem reflects a basic disturbed neurological organization and that because the problem is essentially biological it is primary.

2. Brain injury with resultant reading disability. There is clear evidence of brain damage, e.g., prenatal toxicity, birth trauma or anoxia, encephalitis, or head injury, which impairs the capacity to learn to read.

3. Secondary reading disability. The capacity to learn to read is intact, but reading achievement is not up to capacity due to exogenous, or non-biological, factors, e.g., anxiety, emotional problems, psychoses, limited or inadequate instruction, etc.

Differential diagnosis is complicated by the fact that (a) there are no absolute criteria for assigning cases to Categories 1 and 3, and (b) even when secondary disability is suspected, it is difficult to rule out some degree of neurological disorganization.

Schools are, of course, best equipped, in terms of both available resources and traditional orientation, to deal with problems in the third category. As a result, there can be a tendency either to ignore the first category or to use it as a dumping ground for all cases that do not respond to the remedial teaching that is provided. Obviously, the capricious use of categories will solve no problems and may in fact preclude the confrontation of problems. Given careful consideration and skillful diagnosis, however, we feel that it is in the best interest of the person to have the primary, or specific, reading disability category available. We have known too many disabled readers who have been referred to clinic after clinic, shunted from summer program to summer program, and given massive doses of tutoring in between, all to no great good.

Early intervention in the form of expert diagnosis and intensive remedial teaching may be instrumental in helping the child with primary reading disability to reach at least a basic functional level in reading, and such help should be provided. But clearly some children need an adjusted curriculum with minimum reliance upon literacy to derive maximum benefit from their school experience. The proposed *adjusted* curriculum is not to be confused with the *adapted* curriculum that is suggested later for children who are slow learners because of limited intelligence. The focus of concern here is upon the child with average or better intelligence who appears incapable of responding to even the most carefully conceived and executed remedial teaching.

From our broad overview of reading abilities and related factors one particular implication can be derived: The school reading program that is to provide a framework for working with the range of individual differences and problems that is encountered must be broadly conceived but explicitly focused. We can turn now to the consideration of a model for such a program.

The Reading Program

In *Corrective and Remedial Teaching* (Otto and McMenemy, 1966), the senior author drew a distinction between *developmental program* and *developmental teaching:*

> The term *developmental program* generally has a broad meaning; whereas, the concept of developmental teaching usually is somewhat more restricted. Typically, a school's developmental program is designed to reach all pupils and, ultimately, to help each child to achieve near the limit of his capacity. Thus broadly conceived it encompasses the entire curriculum at all grade levels as well as special programs (adapted, accelerated, corrective, remedial) for children with particular needs. In common usage, however, the connotation of developmental teaching is usually restricted to the type of instruction given to the majority of children within the regular classroom situation.

The distinction is preserved in the present context, as is the broad definition of the developmental program.

The overall developmental reading program as we conceive it is schematically represented in Figure 2. The essential point is that there is a single, overall reading program of which the several specialized instructional programs are inter-

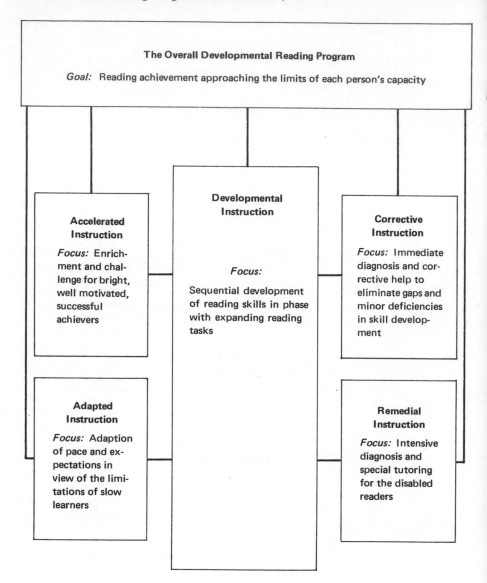

The Overall Developmental Reading Program

Goal: Reading achievement approaching the limits of each person's capacity

Accelerated Instruction

Focus: Enrichment and challenge for bright, well motivated, successful achievers

Developmental Instruction

Focus:

Sequential development of reading skills in phase with expanding reading tasks

Corrective Instruction

Focus: Immediate diagnosis and corrective help to eliminate gaps and minor deficiencies in skill development

Adapted Instruction

Focus: Adaption of pace and expectations in view of the limitations of slow learners

Remedial Instruction

Focus: Intensive diagnosis and special tutoring for the disabled readers

FIGURE 2: Schema of the Reading Program

related and contributing but subsidiary parts. We shall define and describe model subsidiary instructional programs, but local adaptations are both expected and encouraged.

The Overall Developmental Reading Program

The ultimate goal of the reading program is reading achievement that approaches the limits of *each person's* capacity. The focus is upon the person, not upon groups or grade-level performance, for, as we have shown, the mean scores of groups can be comforting but grossly misleading, and grade-level performance may be beneath the aspirations and capabilities of some individuals and beyond the grasp of others. All instructional efforts are clearly subsumed by the goal of near-capacity achievement for each individual, whether the efforts be essentially classroom-developmental or clinic-remedial. The overall program, then, must provide the master plan that includes articulation of objectives and coordination of instructional efforts. The specifics of the master plan — objectives, administrative arrangements, specialized personnel — are discussed in detail in the chapters that follow. They must, of course, be arranged in ways that are appropriate and practicable in given situations.

Regardless of the specifics, there *must* be a master plan. Without it special programs, provisions for specialized personnel, and the within-classroom developmental teaching programs are likely to be nothing more than a disorganized conglomerate of bits and pieces. Remedial teaching, for example, is only isolated drill unless it is coordinated with the person's experiences in the classroom. Likewise, second-grade reading is only an arbitrary collection of skills unless it is coordinated with first-grade and third-grade reading; and a reading coordinator is likely to be little more than a fighter of brush fires unless he has some overall guidelines for his efforts. With a well-conceived overall plan the whole can be more than a simple sum of its parts.

Keeping in mind the need for coordination we can examine some specific instructional plans within the total program. Subprograms and classification schemes do not necessarily add up to a total program, but a consideration of several aspects can help to clarify the scope of an adequate program.

Developmental Instruction

The focus of developmental instruction is upon the sequential development of reading skills in phase with expanding reading tasks. Schiffman (1966, p. 241) has stated it well:

> The developmental program involves systematic instruction at all school levels and in all content areas for those who are developing language abilities commensurate with their general capacity levels. This developmental program is the responsibility of every teacher, affects all the pupils, is provided for in the regular curriculum, and is a continuous, ongoing process. A balanced program includes instruction in the basal, curricular and recreational reading areas.

Put still another way, developmental instruction is the regular classroom teaching program that is pitched to and adequate for the normal child who moves through the skill development sequence without complications.

To say that developmental instruction is for the majority of children who progress normally and without major complications is not to imply that what goes on is unimportant or that any slapdash approach will do. To the contrary, because the developmental instruction carries the main thrust of the overall program it should receive major attention in planning and substantial support in execution. At the present time there is no definitive research to show that a particular administrative setup (e.g., graded or ungraded, inter- or intra-class grouping) or a particular instructional approach (e.g., basal, multibasal experience, self-selection) is best. Probably there never will be. The most satisfactory approach is to work continuously at offering the best possible developmental instruction with existing resources and personnel for a given situation. We believe this can and will be done if the emphasis is placed upon the person in the program.

Corrective, accelerated, adapted, and remedial instruction — which should be forthcoming in response to special problems and/or needs — must, of course, be carefully coordinated with the ongoing developmental instruction.

Corrective Instruction

Corrective instruction focuses upon the provision of immediate diagnosis and corrective teaching to eliminate gaps and minor deficiencies in skill development. Offered by the classroom teacher within the framework of regular developmental instruction, it is actually an integral part of the developmental instruction. It is differentiated from developmental instruction here mainly to underscore the need for (1) constant assessment of skill development and (2) prompt provision of additional instruction when needed. Many skill development problems can be corrected with relative ease if they are detected and corrected early, before they lead to more generalized breakdowns in the skill development process and, in turn, to the failure-frustration-failure effect that saps motivation and destroys positive self-evaluation.

Efficient corrective instruction can be provided only if there is continual, systematic assessment of individual skill development. Once-a-year achievement testing is far from adequate for spotting breakdowns in skill development. What is needed is a scheme for constant and specific skill assessment. We feel that if teachers are (1) given assistance in becoming explicitly aware of the scope and sequence of skills involved in the reading process and (2) provided with concrete bases for making judgments about pupils' skill development status, they will be able to handle the assessments required. The specifics of such a scheme are given in Chapter 2.

Corrective instruction, as already noted, is provided within the framework of regular developmental instruction. It is provided *when* the need is detected and *for* the individuals who need it. Thus, a single child might be taken aside for special help if he appears to be having a hard time with, say, three-consonant blends; or ten pupils who are experiencing difficulty in following the sequence in narrative materials might be taught as a group; or an entire class might be given a series of lessons designed to increase reading speed. Typically, the instruction will amount to reteaching or further reinforcement of skills or subskills previously introduced in developmental instruction. Actually, then, there is a double payoff for well-conceived, systematic corrective instruction: Pupils who need additional help get it; but equally important, pupils who do not need additional work on a particular skill *do not* get it. Too often we continue to bludgeon pupils with boring activities for which they have no need.

Accelerated Instruction

The last point regarding corrective instruction is extremely relevant to a consideration of accelerated instruction, where the focus is upon the provision of enrichment and challenge for bright, well-motivated, successful achievers. Every experienced teacher knows pupils who have been bored to tears or worse by having been tied to a group or to a grade level. Concern for the person must make us sensitive to the needs for accelerated as well as corrective instruction, for it is as nonsensical to repeat what has been mastered as it is not to repeat what has been missed.

Like corrective instruction, accelerated instruction should proceed from the systematic assessment of individual skill development. Given the assurance of a solid skill development base, the pace of instruction can be quickened, the scope broadened, or both, without concern that essentials are being missed or passed over too lightly.

Adapted Instruction

In the typical school setting the children who seem to fare the worst in spite of their teachers' endless concern belong to a group that we shall call *slow learners,* children whose IQs fall roughly in the 80 to 90 range. These children do not achieve at grade level in reading or any other school subject, and consequently they become a source of great concern to every school person who stubbornly clings to grade-level performance as the minimum acceptable level for each individual. Now, virtually everyone on a school staff knows and accepts the "bell-shaped curve" of normally distributed intelligence, which shows that about one-fourth of the children in school have IQs below 90. The same people know that "grade-level" performance is simply an artifact and that equal numbers of children perform above and below it. One extremely clear implication is that some children cannot and will not achieve at grade level on account of their limited intellectual ability. Yet so-called remedial reading classes are cluttered with slow learners, ostensibly with the expectation that they will "catch up"; teachers ceaselessly attempt to "motivate" their slow learners to do better; and slow learners continue to be assigned tasks they cannot handle. Apparently many of us are able to accept limited capacity as an abstract concept but not as a fact of life.

(Parenthetically, we are reminded of a Peanuts cartoon. One character asks about reading problems. The other rattles off some "causes," like strephosymbolia, poor teaching, left-handedness, etc. The first character asks, "But have you ruled out stupidity?" Being educators, we can come up with a euphemism for the word, but the message is clear!)

Children with limited ability are likely to benefit much more from adapted instruction, where the pace and long-term expectations are modified in view of their limitations, than from remedial or corrective instruction, where the expectation is that the deficit can be overcome. This is not to suggest that anyone be arbitrarily branded *slow learner* and abandoned to struggle along as best he can. On the contrary, the slow-learner category should be used only after careful assessment; but once the fact of limited capacity is established, the adaptation of subsequent instruction is a demonstration of concern for the person.

Adapted instruction is probably best provided within the regular classroom or, where classrooms are not the basic instructional units, in a generally heterogeneous context. That is, although specific teaching must realistically be individualized, slow learners should not be segregated into homogeneous groups. The materials and procedures used in adapted instruction are of less importance than the pacing of instruction. The main problem of slow learners is that they are unable to proceed in skill development as rapidly as children who have average or better intelligence; consequently, they quickly drop behind and their whole skill development sequence gets out of phase. Only when the pace of instruction is realistically adapted are the majority of slow learners able to make the most of their limited abilities. Careful, systematic assessment of skill development provides the key to realistic pacing in adapting instruction just as it provides the key to explicitly focused corrective instruction.

Remedial Instruction

Remedial instruction focuses upon intensive diagnosis and special tutoring for the disabled reader. It differs from corrective instruction in degree and from adapted instruction in expectations. Remedial instruction is reserved for pupils with disabilities so severe that they need more intensive help than can be provided through corrective instruction, but in either case the expectation is that achievement deficits will be eliminated or reduced as a result of the teaching. In adapted instruction there is no expectation of achievement at grade level or better; the instruction is simply geared to the limited abilities of the individual person.

Some modification of the administrative setup is necessary to make teacher time, adequate materials, and an optimum setting available for the provision of the intensive diagnosis and tutoring required in a remedial situation. That is, on the assumption that remedial work is to be reserved for pupils with problems too severe to be handled through developmental or corrective instruction in the classroom, it is necessary to establish a situation in which the required special help can be provided. In practice the arrangements with regard to provision of instruction range from specially staffed clinics (either centrally located, with children transported to the facility, or mobile, with the unit transported to the children) to individual remedial teachers (itinerant remedial teachers responsible to more than one school, remedial teachers assigned full time to a single school, or regular teachers with some specialized training given released time from the classroom to offer remedial instruction). There are advantages and disadvantages for each setup, and any decision as to which is best can only be made in terms of local needs and resources. Additional guidelines for making the decision are given in the pages that follow.

For a more detailed discussion of the corrective and remedial aspects of the total reading program see *Corrective and Remedial Teaching* (Otto and McMenemy, 1966, chaps. III through VII).

Several aspects of a well-rounded program have been discussed, mainly to underscore the need for each type of instruction; but, as we have said, classification schemes do not make a program. A coherent reading program is the result of careful coordination of well-conceived parts.

Two final points: First, a reading program cannot be lifted from a book or purchased, neatly packaged, from a commercial source. It must be developed, with total staff involvement, within a local context. Second, a good reading program need not be more costly than a poor one. Some of the most costly reading programs we have seen have, in fact, been the poorest. The presence of flashy hardware, shelves of materials, and specialized personnel often makes for a false sense of security. While monetary support is important, dollars alone cannot purchase a good reading program.

The Person in the Program

Given a sensitivity to personal needs and aspirations and a reading program with sufficient breadth and flexibility to provide the framework for personal development in reading, the remaining need is to consider specifically the placement of the person in the program. In this section we shall discuss (1) *who* should be considered for each of the several aspects of the program and *why*, (2) *what* types of instruction are needed and *where* each type can best be provided, and (3) *when* each type of instruction ought to be offered.

Who and Why

The person is placed in the type of reading program we have described largely on the basis of information regarding his (1) general learning capacity, (2) specific achievement in reading, and (3) estimated reading potential. Thus, the *who* and *why* of the several aspects of the program are determined on the basis of comparisons of capacity and achievement.

Learning Capacity. In considering individual reading ability, we examined the mental ages of a seventh-grade class. The mental ages were derived from group IQ test scores according to the formula CA (chronological age) $\times$ IQ = MA. In other words, a ten-year-old with an IQ of 90 would have a mental age of nine whereas a ten-year-old with an IQ of 120 would have a mental age of twelve.

To continue with the example of the two ten-year-olds, both would be in the fifth grade if they started school at the predominant beginning age of six and continued without retention. All things being equal, the child with the 90 IQ has the mental age, or capacity, of a nine-year-old, or a fourth-grader; the child with the 120 IQ has the capacity of a twelve-year-old, or a seventh-grader. On a straight MA = CAPACITY basis, the learning capacities of the two children differ substantially despite their placement in the same grade. Obviously, concern for each person would dictate that the two children be exposed to sharply differentiated instruction within the same grade level. (One would be a candidate for adapted instruction and the other a candidate for accelerated instruction according to criteria suggested in the section that follows.)

Unfortunately — or fortunately, as the case may be — all things are seldom equal, so straight MA = CAPACITY conversions are not to be taken without at least two grains of salt. First, our ten-year-olds have both existed for the same length of time and, let us assume, have been exposed to similar experiences. Assuming perfect IQ assessment (which, admittedly, is assuming a great deal), the 90 IQ child might do better than the average nine-year-old on the basis of his more than a tenth of a lifetime's additional experiences; and the 120 IQ child might be at a disadvantage in competing with twelve-year-olds because of his substantial dearth of experiences by comparison. Second, IQ scores from any source are not absolute numbers, but IQ scores from group tests are in particular need of corroboration from other sources.

An estimate of a child's learning capacity can be made in a very straightforward manner if his IQ is known. This estimate, combined with other facts and common sense, can be the basis for his tentative placement in the developmental program, but the placement must be modified in view of his actual achievement in reading.

Reading Achievement. Again, in considering individual reading achievement we noted the gap between learning capacity and reading achievement. Some children's reading achievement is below their learning capacity level. Grade level is not a realistic achievement criterion for, as noted in the cases of the hypothetical fifth-graders described above, some children are capable of doing much better and others are not capable of grade-level performance.

The main point here is that the bright child who is achieving only at grade level may need corrective help whereas the slow learner who is achieving below grade level may need adapted rather than remedial teaching. Of course, reading test scores must, like IQ test scores, be taken with a grain of salt for all of the reasons we have discussed in examining the limitations of standardized achievement tests. Both capacity and actual achievement contribute to the *why* that helps to determine *who* receives particular instructional consideration in the total developmental program.

Finally, it is probably worthwhile to consider an alternative approach to establishing capacity levels, for different formulas yield different results.

Estimated Reading Potential. Bond and Clymer (see Bond and Tinker, 1957) have suggested a formula for estimating reading potential that yields a grade level expectancy: Reading Expectancy = Years in School $\times \frac{IQ}{100} + 1.0$. As an example, take a beginning fifth-grader with an IQ of 80: 4 (years completed in school)

$\times \dfrac{80}{100} + 1.0 = 4.2$ (reading expectancy). The reasoning is that a child with an IQ of 80 develops at a rate of .8 of children with average IQs; the 1.0 year must be added to convert from years in school to a grade level. Thus, the child in the example has a grade level expectancy of 4.2 at the beginning of fifth grade. The reading expectancy level, then, is quite different from the capacity level we get from a straight MA conversion: If the beginning fifth-grader has a CA of 10.0, with an IQ of 80 his MA is 8.0 and his capacity level in terms of school grade is 3.0. The cause for the discrepancy is clear: In the former calculation the IQ factor was applied only to *years in school* whereas in the latter it was applied to the entire *chronological age*.

We shall not attempt here to resolve the problem of which type of expectancy-capacity conversion is the more realistic. Each approach has a certain amount of apparent face validity and a number of limitations. Della-Piana (1968) has pointed out the fact that the Bond-Clymer formula tends to yield underestimates of actual achievement for high-IQ groups and the MA conversion tends to yield underestimates of actual achievement for low-IQ groups and overestimates of actual achievement for high-IQ groups. (A number of other, generally more esoteric, prediction formulas have been suggested by various writers. They are not discussed here mainly because at the present time they lack both the validation and the ease of application that would make them an improvement over the formulas presented.) Our own preference is to stay with the straight MA conversion because it is extremely straightforward and because its limitations are obvious. In our experience a complicated formula is too often accepted as a substitute for common sense. The need for common sense is clear in the type of impressionistic analysis demonstrated in the discussion of individual reading ability (pp. 13–27). In any event, the perceptions of the teacher are required to keep the focus upon the person rather than the formula.

In placing persons in the program, capacity and achievement are considered in determining *who* needs differentiated instruction and *why*. We must turn now to *what* types of instruction and *where* the instruction is to be offered.

What and Where

Given reasonably accurate, reliable reading achievement and intelligence scores, it is possible to specify the particular aspect of the total developmental program that is likely to provide the most appropriate instructional focus for each child. In Figure 3 the appropriate instructional focus for three levels of IQ and three levels of reading achievement is given. The schema is not, of course, adjusted for anticipated group size. That is, the expectation is that in a normal situation the majority of pupils — with intelligence in the average (90–110) range and achievement in the grade level (grade level ± three to nine months, depending on the grade range) — would fall in the "developmental" category. With the understanding that each category is but roughly delimited in the schema, we can suggest some rules of thumb for assigning pupils.

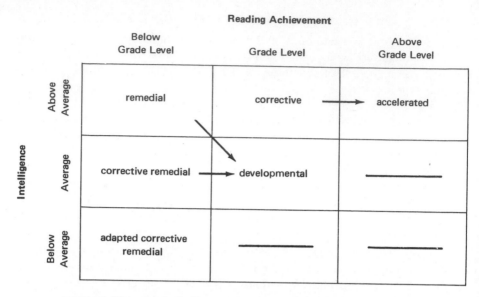

FIGURE 3: Placement in the Program Based on Intelligence and Achievement

As already noted, children with IQs and reading performance in the average range can be taught adequately in the regular developmental context as we have defined it. The average range of reading performance can be conceived as covering roughly a six-month band (grade level ± three months) by the end of first grade to an eighteen-month band by seventh-grade level and above. Teachers must, of course, remain vigilant to detect changes in performance that would signal a need for corrective or accelerated instruction.

Slow learners, children whose IQs range from 90 to 80 and below, should be given adapted instruction, where the pace and expectations are realistically modified to be in line with capacity. There is also a possibility that slow learners will perform below their expectancy level. When the gap is substantial, they should not be excluded from remedial instruction.

Remedial instruction should be reserved for children who (1) are performing substantially below their capacity levels and (2) appear to require intensive, individual diagnosis and tutoring beyond what can be provided in the developmental or corrective context. We prefer to call these children *disabled* rather than *retarded* readers, because the latter may carry a connotation of mental retardation which is not intended. In general, children in the middle elementary grades who are reading two or more years below their capacity levels (the gap must be decreased or increased for lower or higher grades) should be considered potential candidates for remedial reading. (In practice, grade level may be the criterion. In this case, bright children who read at grade level but substantially below their capacity level pose a problem inasmuch as they clearly need some additional help but are precluded from remedial reading. They should not be ignored. In the Figure 3 schema we have indicated corrective help for them. In terms of self-concepts and public relations, it would probably be troublesome to designate bright children who read at grade level "disabled," no matter how great the capacity-achievement gap.)

If remedial instruction is to serve its ultimate purpose of assisting pupils to overcome their disability and move back to full participation in developmental instruction, lines of communication must be kept open and the remedial instruction must be in phase with the developmental instruction in all areas. Too often remedial instruction is something that a child "goes to" for, say, three hours per week. Regardless of whether specialists or classroom teachers with released time provide remedial instruction, provision must be made for the transfer of what is learned to the developmental context. Because the need for communication and coordinated planning is acute, we feel that remedial teaching is, in general, better offered in each child's home school building than in a centrally located "clinic."

Corrective instruction is provided to overcome moderate skill deficiencies and to fill in gaps in skill development. Again applying a rule of thumb, one should consider provision of corrective teaching when, in the middle elementary grades, achievement is one to two years below capacity. The gap must be increased or decreased at other grade levels. Corrective teaching is provided for individuals and groups within the general context of developmental instruction. The same is true for accelerated instruction, which is offered to pupils who need additional challenge.

The question that remains is *when* each type of instruction should be offered.

When

There is but one point to be made here: When the person is given prime consideration, there can be no generalizations with regard to when certain things are to happen.

For some children the age of six is much too early to begin developmental instruction and for others it is much too late, for they may have learned to read at home or they may have grown weary of waiting. To treat as a person a child who has reached an arbitrary school entrance age is to accept him and to teach him as he is.

Remedial instruction cannot be deferred until fourth grade, as it is in some schools. It must be given when the need is recognized, before the negative overlay of failure has become thick and tough.

Adapted instruction must begin the moment the child starts to lag behind. No child should be subjected to the frustration and anxiety inherent in instruction that always moves too fast. Likewise, no child should be subjected to the boredom inherent in instruction that always moves too slowly and stops short of any challenge.

To put the focus on the person in the reading program is to remove all that is arbitrary from the program. Our intent in discussing aspects of the program has been to insure an awareness of the need for each type of instruction, not to impose more tracks and categories. If the aspects of the program we have so carefully described appear to impose arbitrary barriers, then they, too, must go.

References

Belmont, Lillian, and Herbert G. Birch. "The Intellectual Profile of Retarded Readers." *Perceptual and Motor Skills,* 1966, 22, 786–816.

Bond, G. L., and M. A. Tinker. *Reading Difficulties, Their Diagnosis and Correction.* New York: Appleton-Century-Crofts, 1957.

Carhart, Raymond. "Auditory Training" and "Conservation of Speech." In Hallowell Davis (Ed.), *Hearing and Deafness: A Guide for Laymen.* New York: Murray Hill Books, 1947, pp. 276–317.

Delacato, C. H. *The Treatment and Prevention of Reading Problems.* Springfield, Ill.: Thomas, 1959.

Della-Piana, G. M. *Reading Diagnosis and Prescription: An Introduction.* New York: Holt, Rinehart & Winston, 1968.

Dinkmeyer, Don, and Rudolph Dreikurs. *Encouraging Children to Learn: The Encouragement Process.* Englewood Cliffs, N.J.: Prentice-Hall, 1963.

Durkin, Dolores. "Children Who Read Before First Grade." In Warren G. Cutts (Ed.), *Teaching Young Children to Read,* U.S. Office of Education Bulletin No. 19. Washington: U.S. Department of Health, Education, and Welfare, 1964, pp. 78–84.

Durrell, Donald. "The Influence of Reading Ability on Intelligence Measures." *Journal of Educational Psychology,* 1933, 24, 412–416.

Dykstra, Robert. Summary of the second grade phase of the Cooperative Research Program in primary reading instruction. *Reading Research Quarterly,* 1968, 4, 49–70.

Eisenberg, Leon. "Behavioral Manifestations of Cerebral Damage in Childhood." In H. G. Birch (Ed.), *Brain Damage in Childhood.* Baltimore: Williams & Wilkins, 1964.

Eisenberg, Leon. "The Epidemiology of Reading Retardation and a Program for Preventive Intervention." In John Money (Ed.), *The Disabled Reader.* Baltimore: Johns Hopkins Press, 1966, Chap. I.

Fox, Esther. "Considerations in Constructing a Basic Reading Program for Functionally Illiterate Adults." *Adult Leadership,* 1964, 13, 7–8.

Gates, Arthur I. "The Role of Personality Maladjustment in Reading Disability." *Journal of Genetic Psychology,* 1941, 59, 77–83.

Goetzinger, C. P., D. D. Dirks, and C. J. Baer. "Auditory Discrimination and Visual Perception in Good and Poor Readers." *Annals of Otology, Rhinology and Laryngology,* 1960, 69, 121–137.

Harris, A. J. *How to Increase Reading Ability* (4th ed.). New York: McKay, 1961.

Irvine, R., *et al.* "An Ocular Policy for Public Schools." *American Journal of Ophthalmology,* 1941, 24, 779–790.

Macdonald, James B. "The Person in the Curriculum." Speech delivered at the 1965 Teachers College Curriculum Conference, Columbia University, November, 1965.

Malmquist, Eve. *Factors Related to Reading Disabilities in the First Grade of the Elementary School.* Stockholm: Almquist & Wiksell, 1958.

Money, John (Ed.). *Reading Disability.* Baltimore: Johns Hopkins Press, 1962.

Money, John (Ed.). *The Disabled Reader.* Baltimore: Johns Hopkins Press, 1966.

Mounier, E. *Personalism* (trans. P. Mairet). London: Routledge, 1952.

Otto, Wayne, and David Ford. *Teaching Adults to Read*. Boston: Houghton Mifflin, 1967.

Otto, Wayne, and Richard McMenemy. *Corrective and Remedial Teaching*. Boston: Houghton Mifflin, 1966.

Pasamanick, Benjamin, and Hilda Knobloch. "Brain Damage and Reproductive Casualty. *American Journal of Orthopsychiatry*, 1960, 30, 298–305.

Rabinovitch, Ralph D., and Winifred Ingram. "Neuropsychiatric Considerations in Reading Retardation." *Reading Teacher*, 1962, 15, 433–438.

Robbins, Melvyn P. "Test of the Deman-Delacto Rationale with Retarded Readers. *Journal of the American Medical Association*, 1967, 202, 389–393.

Robinson, Helen M. *Why Pupils Fail in Reading*. Chicago: University of Chicago Press, 1946.

Schiffman, Gilbert. "Program Administration Within a School System." In John Money (Ed.), *The Disabled Reader*. Baltimore: Johns Hopkins Press, 1966, Chap. XV.

Smith, Henry P., and Emerald V. Dechant. *Psychology in Teaching Reading*. Englewood Cliffs, N.J.: Prentice-Hall, 1961.

Thelander, H. E., Jane K. Phelps, and E. Walton Kirk. "Learning Disabilities Associated with Lesser Brain Damage." *Journal of Pediatrics*, 1958, 53, 405–409.

Vernon, M. D. *Backwardness in Reading: A Study of Its Nature and Origin*. Cambridge: Cambridge University Press, 1957.

Wiener, Morton, and Ward Cromer. "Reading and Reading Difficulty: A Conceptual Analysis." *Harvard Educational Review*, 1967, 37, 620–642.

Zangwill, O. L. "Dyslexia in Relation to Cerebral Dominance." In John Money (Ed.), *Reading Disability*. Baltimore: Johns Hopkins Press, 1962, Chap. VII.

CHAPTER 2

Foundations of
Reading Development

The focus in Chapter 2 is upon an organizational pattern of specific reading skills that can provide both a framework for the developmental program in reading at the elementary level and a foundation for reading competence at all levels. In Chapter 3 the focus is upon achieving reading maturity and on the characteristics of mature readers. The essential point here is that laying the foundation and building maturity must be conceived as complementary, not sequential. The reader who brings the full range of his thinking and feeling to the reading act is, as pointed out in Chapter 3, behaving as a mature reader. Efforts to establish such an approach to the reading act must, of course, begin early, at the very start of the learning-to-read sequence. Furthermore, they must continue even after a foundation of basic skill development has been laid.

One additional point regarding Chapter 2: The discussion of foundational skills is limited to the specifics of the developmental program for kindergarten through Grade 6. We do not mean to suggest that skill development is complete or that teaching should cease after the sixth grade. Not only do some pupils need more time to master the "elementary" reading skills, but all of them need continually to refine their skills to cope with more complex and sophisticated demands on their reading ability. Our position is that a solid foundation for the development of reading competence can and should be laid in the elementary grades. With such a foundation the way is clear for the development of true maturity in reading.

Scope and Sequence of Skills

In the literature on reading and in curriculum guides, scope and sequence statements that cover the elementary reading skills abound. The details differ, but in general there is much agreement regarding both the array of skills to be achieved and their sequential arrangement. There are differences, too, in the specificity with which the skills are stated, ranging from broad skill-objectives that guide long-term instruction to specific skill-objectives that prescribe daily instruction; but again, there is much agreement on final outcomes. For the most part, the existing scope and sequence statements reflect logical analyses of the reading task and established practice more than definitive research findings. They are the products of curriculum specialists rather than specialists in educational research.

We believe that a good scope and sequence statement can provide the focus and direction needed for teaching the foundational skills in reading. However, because there does not yet exist a skill sequence or statement of scope based on research — nor is there likely to be one in the foreseeable future — it is not possible to suggest the ultimate or even a "best" statement for use in school reading programs. The scope and sequence statement given at the end of this chapter is, therefore, suggested as a model, not as the ultimate statement. It represents consensus among teachers in several schools and it has been shown to be viable in the field; but the suggestion is that it be modified, if necessary, in local settings to reflect prevailing philosophy and practices. If a scope and sequence statement is to be used, it must first be acceptable to the people who will work with it.

Too often scope and sequence (skill) statements are treated as artifacts to be filed away in curriculum guides and, for all practical purposes, forgotten. When this is the case, we feel there are two basic reasons: First, the statement is likely to be seen as an arbitrary imposition rather than something that has been adapted and accepted by the local teaching staff. Second, the statement exists as an end product rather than the framework around which activities are organized; hence, teachers see no functional value in it. With regard to the first, we suggest that a skill statement be locally constructed and modified periodically to reflect changes in local preferences. The model given at the end of this chapter could, of course, serve as the basis for such local efforts. With regard to the second, we can suggest a number of functions that a well-conceived skill statement can serve.

Functions of a Skill Statement

Here we shall discuss the *functions* that a scope and sequence statement can serve if it is extended in a variety of ways. The statement itself is the foundation, but a structure must be added to enhance its usefulness.

First, and basically, a scope and sequence statement gets the essential skills out where teachers can see them and — if the statement is thoughtfully constructed and consensually acceptable — make plans to see that they are adequately covered in instruction. While competent teachers are undoubtedly aware of the range of skills required for mature reading, the skills tend so often to be implicit rather than explicit in instructional materials that it is easy to lose sight of them in day-to-day teaching. The advantage in having a skill statement at hand, then, is that it keeps the specifics of the developmental program prominently before teachers.

Second, the statement can provide a basis for checking on skill mastery and pacing instruction. A typical scope and sequence statement deals with skills in several categories and at sequential levels. (The model statement at the end of this chapter, for example, covers six categories of reading skills — Word Attack, Comprehension, Study Skills, Self-Directed Reading, Interpretive Skills, and Creative Skills — and five levels — kindergarten, first grade, second grade, third grade, and fourth through sixth grade.) Given the skill statement, the teacher can (1) judge whether specific skills have been mastered, (2) check to see that individuals are proceeding in each of the several categories at a reasonably even pace, and (3) check to see that specific development is proceeding sequentially, i.e., that lower-level skills are mastered before the instruction moves on to the next level. Checking procedures can be carried out informally, with teacher judgments carrying the main thrust; but assessment exercises can also be devised to focus the skill sampling and the observing that serve as a basis for making judgments. The creation of such exercises by a school staff could be a worthwhile activity in that it would cause everyone involved to consider carefully the actual behaviors called for by a particular skill. There is no question, however, that this would be a major undertaking and that substantial commitments in terms of both time and effort would be required. Such exercises have been developed at the Wisconsin Research and Development Center for Cognitive Learning (see pp. 43–44).

Third, the statement can serve as a guide for the organization of instruction and particularly of instructional materials. Teachers are sometimes reluctant to use a multi-text or multi-material approach to the teaching of reading fundamentals because they fear that by moving from one set of materials to another they may be leaving gaps in skill development or failing to provide for the sequential development of skills. With the scope and sequence of skills to be covered well in mind, teachers can be more confident that any gaps will be apparent and that they can give additional instruction as needed. Supplementary materials can be keyed to the skill statement to expedite the process of making appropriate materials readily available as needed for specific skill teaching.

The skill statement, then, can provide a basis for the assessment of the skill mastery of individuals and for the organization of materials to be brought to bear for skill development.

Fourth, the statement can lend focus to both parent-teacher and pupil-teacher conferences. With the essential reading skills clearly laid out and some notion of a pupil's skill-mastery status, the teacher is in a position to talk very specifically about where the individual stands. Both strengths and weaknesses can be discussed in the context of the total statement.

Fifth, the statement can — if restated in language appropriate for pupils at the several levels — serve as a guide to self-evaluation and self-directed study. As with teacher-guided assessment and instruction, it would be necessary to provide criterion tasks for evaluation and a guide to appropriate skill-related materials.

Focus on the Person

Agreement upon the foundational skills in reading permits explicit focusing upon the person in the program. Each individual's skill development can be examined in specific terms and his strengths as well as his weaknesses identified. Knowledge of individuals' skill development status can then become the basis for making decisions regarding materials to be used, pacing of instruction, and grouping. As we see it, grouping for skill development can be a straightforward matter once each individual's skill development status is known: Pupils with common needs are grouped for instruction and those with unique needs are taught individually. Changes in group composition can be made whenever individuals make significant progress or additional problems are identified. Most important, there can be assurance that the person is in the group — or receiving the individual instruction — that is most appropriate for him at all times.

Perhaps one implicit point should be made explicit. The examination of specific skills permits teachers to recognize strengths as well as weaknesses. Too often the focus in assessment is upon the identification of weaknesses only. There is no question that help should be provided to overcome weaknesses; but it is equally true that performance can be maximized by building upon strengths. When the skills in a particular area or at a particular level have been mastered, skill development should move along to subsequent levels and in other areas. To belabor skills already mastered is as removed from the skill development needs of the person as to slide over skills that have not been mastered.

A Model Scope and Sequence Statement

In the model scope and sequence statement at the end of this chapter behavioral objectives to parallel each skill in the areas of Word Attack, Comprehension, and Study Skills are given. We shall detail the statement of behavioral objectives in the next section of this chapter; here discussion is limited to the skill statement. The skills-objectives statement is combined simply to conserve space.

The scope and sequence statement was developed at the Wisconsin Research and Development Center for Cognitive Learning, where the senior author is a Principal Investigator. The approach was to take an existing curriculum guide (Madison Public Schools, 1964) for reading, kindergarten through Grade 6, and to revise in view of feedback from cooperating schools until there was confidence that the statement represented the consensus of teachers who had worked with it and found it viable in the field (Otto et al., 1967; Otto, 1968; Otto and Peterson, 1969).

The scope is broad: Six areas or categories of reading skills — Word Attack, Comprehension, Study Skills, Self-Directed Reading, Interpretive Skills, and Creative Skills — are included. Such a broad definition is necessary, we feel, if areas that are essential to the development of maturity in reading are to be covered. (On the other hand, we recognize that a narrower focus is advocated by certain other writers. Breadth of focus is, of course, a matter that must be worked out at the local level as a scope and sequence statement is developed or adapted. The matter is discussed further in Chapter 5.)

The skills in each of the six areas, with the exception of Word Attack, are clustered at five levels — kindergarten, first grade, second grade, third grade, and fourth through sixth grade. Word Attack is limited to the first four levels, the reasoning being that the basic word attack skills have been introduced by the end of third grade, and from there on development is mainly a matter of refining them. The decision to retain the levels of skills was made in deference to the voiced need of some teachers to have minimal guidelines regarding pacing. We suggest that the levels be ignored or eliminated as soon as teachers become comfortable with the skill arrangement, for it is individual progress, not grade placement, that is of primary importance.

The skills are stated at a relatively high level of generality. That is, they are considerably beyond the level required for, say, programmed instruction or for the writing of prescriptions for instruction. Such specificity would demand that literally hundreds more skills be stated. The intent in providing the more general statements is to establish a framework for instruction without prescribing the specifics of instruction. This approach was taken because (1) neither the *ultimate* sequential arrangement of skills nor the *best* means for teaching them is known, and (2) teachers — who know both their materials and their pupils and who know the approaches they themselves can use with the greatest comfort and proficiency — are surely in a better position than anyone else to make decisions about specific instructional procedures for specific children.

Again, the statement is given as a model, with the expectation that it will be discussed and adapted, not adopted, at the local level.

Behavioral Objectives

As already pointed out, behavioral objectives that parallel each skill in Areas I, II, and III are given in the skill statement that follows. These, too, were worked out by the Reading Project staff at the Wisconsin Research and Development Center for Cognitive Learning (Otto and Peterson, 1969). Here it is relevant to review briefly the rationale for the objectives as they are stated and for their inclusion in the present chapter.

Why Behavioral Objectives?

While there is a strong movement toward the statement of behavioral objectives in all areas of the curriculum, with the programmed instruction movement providing much of the current impetus, some writers have been rather restrained in their support. Kliebard (1968), for example, feels that we must pay much more attention to the source of these objectives, how they are stated, and what role they have in planning curriculums and in guiding teaching. Eisner (1967) has pointed out that, in general, teachers have not made wide use of behavioral objectives and there is not much empirical evidence to show that they make an important difference in teaching, learning, or curriculum construction. Atkin (1968) believes that at the moment there is no good basis for deciding whether behavioral objectives are or are not worthwhile.

The critics' points are well taken. Nevertheless, the objectives were stated initially and they are included here because we feel that (1) they are related to skills teachers are concerned about and attempting to teach, (2) they can help guide both informal skill assessment and the construction of formal assessment exercises, and (3) they can aid in the planning of instruction designed for specific skill development. There is no question, however, that empirical evidence to support them does not exist at the time of this writing. If such evidence is to be forthcoming, it will emerge most convincingly from the schools in which behavioral objectives become an integral part of the instructional program.

Levels of Generality-Specificity

Krathwohl (1965) has indicated three levels of specificity for stating objectives, depending on the purpose for which they are to be used. First, at the most abstract level, broad and general statements are appropriate for guiding program development, for identifying courses and areas to be covered, or for specifying goals toward which entire school units — i.e., elementary, junior, senior high — might strive. Second, at a more concrete level, behaviorally stated objectives are appropriate for breaking down general goals into more specific instructional goals for a unit, course, or sequence of courses. Third, ". . . there is the level needed to create instructional materials — materials which are the operational embodiment of one particular route (rarely are multiple routes included) to the achievement of a curriculum planned at the second and more abstract level, the level of detailed analysis involved in the programmed instruction movement" (p. 84).

The objectives given are at Krathwohl's second level. In line with the previous discussion regarding skills, they are intended to provide instructional goals but to stop short of dictating instructional practices. Maguire (1968) has commented on the kinds of objectives that are likely to be most useful to teachers: ". . . the kinds of objectives that the teacher makes use of in his classroom activities are the objectives of Krathwohl's second level. (This is not to say that all teachers explicitly state their objectives in this form, but it does suggest that their implicit objectives are of this level.) . . . For classroom use, level-two objectives are useful for determining the content to be covered in a unit, for selecting experiences to be arranged for students, and for guiding the construction of evaluation instruments" (pp. 68–69). These are precisely the functions intended for the present objectives.

Limitation to Areas I, II, III

Eisner (1967, p. 279) has differentiated between "open" and "closed" objectives:

> To state an objective in terms clear enough to know what it [the terminal behavior] will look like requires that the parameters of that behavior be characterized in advance. This is possible when one is working with closed concepts or closed objectives. When one is dealing with open objectives, the particular behavior cannot be defined by a preconceived standard; a judgment must be made after the fact. When educational ends are directed toward open objectives, the form and content of the pupil's behavior are identified and assessed after the educational activity concludes.

In another paper Eisner (1969, p. 20) differentiated between *instructional* objectives — with the focus upon the attainment of a specific array of behaviors — and *expressive* objectives:

> Expressive objectives differ considerably from instructional objectives. An expressive objective does not specify the behavior the student is to acquire after having engaged in one or more learning activities. An expressive objective describes an educational encounter: it identifies a situation in which children are to work, a problem with which they are to cope, a task they are to engage in — but it does not specify what from that encounter, situation, problem or task they are to learn. An expressive objective provides both the teacher and the

student with an invitation to explore, defer or focus on issues that are of particular interest or impact to the inquirer. An expressive objective is evocative rather than prescriptive.

Our feeling has been that a similar differentiation must be made between Areas I, II, and III (Word Attack, Comprehension, and Study Skills) and Areas IV, V, and VI (Self-Directed Reading, Interpretive Skills, and Creative Skills). *Instructional* or *closed* objectives can be written for the former areas, but it is virtually impossible — or, we feel, undesirable — to specify behaviors in the same way for the latter areas, which call for *open* or *expressive* objectives if, indeed, they call for objectives at all. Eisner (1969, p. 21) gives the following as examples of expressive objectives: (1) To interpret the meaning of *Paradise Lost*; (2) to examine and appraise the significance of *The Old Man and the Sea*; (3) to develop a three-dimensional form through the use of wire and wood; (4) to visit the zoo and discuss what was of interest there. We have decided, for the present, to state no objectives for Areas IV, V, and VI. Faculty groups can work together to compile suggestions as to (1) appropriate situations in which observations regarding each skill can be made, (2) particular behaviors that characterize each skill, and (3) approaches that may be used in fostering the general development of each skill.

Statement of Skills and Objectives

In the following statement of reading skills, objectives are given for the skills in Areas I, II, and III, and assessment procedures are suggested for each objective.

The statement is, of course, similar to the scope and sequence charts supplied by the publishers of certain materials for the developmental teaching of reading. The attempt in constructing the present statement was to provide a single outline of skills that would be reasonably compatible with those charts.

The statement can, we feel, be useful to the person with administrative and/or supervisory responsibilities for the reading program in the following ways.

1. The statement, or excerpts from it, can serve as the focus for grade-level in-service meetings. That is, in in-service meetings devoted to skill development at various levels, the statement can be a starting point for the consideration of the essential skills and the procedures and materials for developing them.

2. The statement, or excerpts from it, can lend specificity to conferences with individual teachers. In supervisory visits, specific skills can be isolated and reading activities examined in view of their appropriateness for developing those skills. Through systematic observations over a period of time, gaps in a skill development program can be identified.

3. It can be used in a similar manner with student teachers.

4. It can be used — with or without the accompanying behavioral objectives — to present an overview of the elementary reading program to parents and other people in the community. The presentation of the skills in an outline form can demonstrate the broad base of the total reading program.

5. The statement — or a local adaptation of it — can be used as a guide when instructional materials are ordered. Given the objectives of the skill development

program, care can be taken to see that materials adequate to cover all of the skills are made available.

Needless to say, the statement, particularly the skill outline portion, could be put into formats more appropriate for certain uses than its present book format. We have found, for example, that it is useful to have the skill outline printed on manila folders, which can then serve as individual skill development records. The statement, or excerpts therefrom, could be arranged in a variety of ways — checklists, wall charts, etc. — for other purposes. The reader should feel free to reproduce the statement of skills and objectives in any way that is useful.

Statement of Skills and Objectives for Elementary Reading

(Again, the skills are given in six areas: I, Word Attack; II, Comprehension; III, Study Skills; IV, Self-Directed Reading; V, Interpretive Skills; and VI, Creative Skills. They are tentatively grouped at five levels: A, kindergarten; B, Grade 1; C, Grade 2; D, Grade 3; and E, Grades 4 through 6.)

I. Word Attack

Level A
1. Listens for rhyming elements
   a. Words
      Objective The child is able to tell when (1) two words pronounced by the teacher (*man-pan, call-bell, when-pen*) and/or (2) the names of two objects do and do not rhyme (i.e., "sound alike").
   b. Phrases and verses
      Objectives 1. The child is able to pick out the rhyming words in traditional verses (i.e., "Little Jack Horner sat in a corner") and nonsense verses ("Wing, wong, way/Tisha, loona say") read by the teacher.
      2. The child is able to supply the missing word in a rhyming verse read by the teacher (e.g., "The big tall man/Fried eggs in a ————").
2. Notices likenesses and differences
   a. Pictures (shapes)
      Objective The child is able to match key shapes with shapes that are identical in terms of form and orientation. (e.g., △ ▽ △).
   b. Letters and numbers
      Objective The child is able to pick the letter — upper or lower case — or number in a series that is identical to a key number or letter. (The child points to the letter or number that is the same as the first letter or number in a row: P: B T P K; s: s z e c; 9: 6 0 9 8.)
   c. Words and phrases
      Objective The child is able to pick the word or phrase in a series that is identical to a key word or phrase (e.g., *down*: wand — down — bone — find; *back and forth*: bank and find — back and forth — found it).

3. Distinguishes colors

Objective   The child is able to identify colors (blue, green, black, yellow, red, orange, white, brown, purple) named by the teacher. (The child picks from four choices the color named by the teacher, e.g., key word = *blue*; color choices = *blue* and *black*. The child chooses the proper crayon to fill in boxes with the colors named by the teacher.)

4. Listens for initial consonant sounds

Objective   Given two common words pronounced by the teacher (e.g., *bird-ball, boy-take, banana-dog*), the child is able to tell when the words do and do not begin alike.

Level B

1. Has a sight word vocabulary of 50–100 words

Objective   Given a maximum three-second exposure per word, the child is able to recognize 92 Preprimer and Primer level words selected from the Dolch Basic Sight Vocabulary List of 220 words.

NOTE: The specific Preprimer and Primer words are given in the list that follows. The child should be able to recognize additional sight words that occur in instructional materials to which he has been exposed.

Breakdown of the Dolch Basic Word List by Levels

Preprimer	*Primer*	*First Grade*	*Second Grade*	*Third Grade*
1. a	1. all	1. after	1. always	1. about
2. and	2. am	2. again	2. around	2. better
3. away	3. are	3. an	3. because	3. bring
4. big	4. at	4. any	4. been	4. carry
5. blue	5. ate	5. as	5. before	5. clean
6. can	6. be	6. ask	6. best	6. cut
7. come	7. black	7. by	7. both	7. done
8. down	8. brown	8. could	8. buy	8. draw
9. find	9. but	9. every	9. call	9. drink
10. for	10. came	10. fly	10. cold	10. eight
11. funny	11. did	11. from	11. does	11. fall
12. go	12. do	12. give	12. don't	12. far
13. help	13. eat	13. going	13. fast	13. full
14. here	14. four	14. had	14. first	14. got
15. I	15. get	15. has	15. five	15. grow
16. in	16. good	16. her	16. found	16. hold
17. is	17. have	17. him	17. gave	17. hot
18. it	18. he	18. his	18. goes	18. hurt
19. jump	19. into	19. how	19. green	19. if
20. little	20. like	20. just	20. its	20. keep
21. look	21. must	21. know	21. made	21. kind
22. make	22. new	22. let	22. many	22. laugh
23. me	23. no	23. live	23. off	23. light
24. my	24. now	24. may	24. or	24. long
25. not	25. on	25. of	25. pull	25. much
26. one	26. our	26. old	26. read	26. myself
27. play	27. out	27. once	27. right	27. never
28. red	28. please	28. open	28. sing	28. only

29. run	29. pretty	29. over	29. sit	29. own
30. said	30. ran	30. put	30. sleep	30. pick
31. see	31. ride	31. round	31. tell	31. seven
32. the	32. saw	32. some	32. their	32. shall
33. three	33. say	33. stop	33. these	33. show
34. to	34. she	34. take	34. those	34. six
35. two	35. so	35. thank	35. upon	35. small
36. up	36. soon	36. them	36. us	36. start
37. we	37. that	37. then	37. use	37. ten
38. where	38. there	38. think	38. very	38. today
39. yellow	39. they	39. walk	39. wash	39. together
40. you	40. this	40. were	40. which	40. try
	41. too	41. when	41. why	41. warm
	42. under		42. wish	
	43. want		43. work	
	44. was		44. would	
	45. well		45. write	
	46. went		46. your	
	47. what			
	48. white			
	49. who			
	50. will			
	51. with			
	52. yes			

2. Follows left-to-right sequence

   Objective The child reacts to number, letter, or word stimuli in a left-to-right sequence. (The child names the letters or numbers presented in rows

N	C	H	P
c	o	e	g
4	7	1	2

   in a left-to-right sequence.)

3. Has phonic analysis skills

   a. Consonant sounds

      1) Beginning

      Objectives 1. Given two common words pronounced by the teacher (e.g., *man-pet, ball-boy*), the child is able to tell when the words begin alike. (Review.)

      2. Given a real or nonsense word pronounced by the teacher, the child is able to give the letter that makes the initial sound.

      3. Given a word pronounced by the teacher, the child is able to give another word that begins with the same sound.

      2) Ending

      Objectives 1. Given two common words pronounced by the teacher (e.g., *bat-hut, six-sit*), the child is able to tell when the words do and do not end alike.

2. Given a word pronounced by the teacher (e.g., *bat, car*), the child is able to give the letter that makes the ending sound.

b. Consonant blends

Objectives 1. When directed to listen for the first two sounds — i.e., *pl, gr, pr, cr, fl, cl, bl* — in a real or nonsense word pronounced by the teacher, the child is able to (a) identify words that begin with the same two sounds and (b) identify the two letters that make the initial sounds. ([a] From a series of three pictured objects the child selects the one(s) with the name(s) beginning with the same two sounds as the word enunciated by the teacher: *drink* (pronounced) . . . drum, table, dress (pictures). [b] From a series of four two-letter combinations, the child selects the pair that makes the initial sounds of the word enunciated by the teacher.)

2. The child is able to pronounce real and nonsense words that begin with the following blends: *pl, gr, pr, cr, fl, cl, bl, gl*. (Some examples of appropriate nonsense words: *plag, gref, prid, flin*.)

c. Rhyming elements

Objective Given a word pronounced by the teacher (e.g., *pan, ball, sat*), the child is able to give a rhyming word.

NOTE: A rhyming nonsense word should be considered an acceptable response.

d. Short vowels

Objective The child is able to give the sound and letter name of the vowel in single-syllable words with a single short vowel sound (e.g., *man, duck, doll, hop*).

e. Simple consonant digraphs

Objective The child is able to identify simple two-consonant combinations — *ch, th, sh* — that result in a single new sound. (The child is asked to identify the digraphs — i.e., two consonants with a single sound — in words enunciated by the teacher: *she, chaff, teeth, fish, beach*.)

4. Has structural analysis skills

a. Compound words

Objective The child is able to identify compound words and to specify the elements of a compound word. (The child identifies the compound word in a sentence and specifies the component words: The *football* went over the fence.)

b. Contractions

Objective The child is able to identify simple contractions (e.g., *I'm, it's, can't*) and use them correctly in sentences.

c. Base words and endings

Objective The child is able to identify the root word in known inflected words (e.g., *jump*ing, *catch*es, *run*s).

d. Plurals

Objective The child is able to tell when known words — essentially noun plus *s* forms — are singular or plural (i.e., indicate one or more than one).

e. Possessive forms

Objective The child is able to identify the possessive forms of nouns in context. (The child indicates the words in connected text that are possessive forms.)

Level C

1. Has a sight word vocabulary of 100–170 words

   Objective Given a maximum two-second exposure per word, the child is able to recognize 133 Preprimer, Primer, and First Grade words selected from the Dolch Basic Sight Vocabulary List of 220 words.

   NOTE: See the list given after Objective B.1 for the specific words. The child should be able to recognize additional sight words that occur in instructional materials to which he has been exposed.

2. Has phonic analysis skills

   a. Consonants and their variant sounds

      Objective The child recognizes the variant sounds of *s*, *c*, and *g* in words like *sit, trees, sure, picnic, circus, giant, good, drag, cage, cake, city*. (The child matches words that have similar sounds of *s*, *c*, and *g*.)

      NOTE: The following consonants have more than one sound — *c*, *g*, *s*, *q*, *d*, *x*, *t*, *z* — but variant sounds of *s*, *c*, *g* are commonest at this level.

   b. Consonant blends

      Objectives 1. When directed to listen for the first two sounds — i.e., *st, sk, sm, sp, sw, sn* — in a word pronounced by the teacher, the child is able to (a) identify words that begin with the same two sounds and (b) identify the two letters that make the initial sounds.

      2. The child is able to pronounce nonsense words that contain the following blends: *st, sk, sm, sp, sw, sn*.

   c. Vowel sounds

      1) Long vowel sounds

      Objectives 1. The child is able to pronounce real words and nonsense words with a single long vowel sound and to identify the vowel heard (e.g., *nose, brile, cheese, seat, labe*).

      2. The child is able to designate the letter that makes the single vowel sound in a word and indicate whether the sound is long or short.

      2) Vowel plus *r*

      Objectives 1. The child is able to pronounce words with *r*-controlled vowels.

      2. The child is able to name the vowel that is with *r* in nonsense words pronounced by the teacher (e.g., *darl, mur, der, forn, girt*).

      NOTE: Because *er*, *ir*, and *ur* have the same sound, *e*, *i*, or *u* is the appropriate response in *er*, *ir*, and *ur* words.

      3) *a* plus *l*

      Objectives 1. The child is able to pronounce words in which there is an *al* combination (e.g., *ball, halt*).

2. The child is able to name the vowel and the subsequent letter in *al* nonsense words pronounced by the teacher.

4) *a* plus *w*

Objectives 1. The child is able to pronounce words in which there is an *aw* combination (e.g., *draw, lawn, saw*).

2. The child is able to name the vowel and the subsequent letter in *aw* nonsense words pronounced by the teacher.

5) Diphthongs *oi, oy, ou, ow, ew*

Objectives 1. The child is able to pronounce words in which there is an *oi, oy, ou, ow, ew* combination (e.g., *house, boy, soil, cow, new*).

2. The child is able to identify the two vowels in *oi, oy, ou, ow, ew* nonsense words pronounced by the teacher. (Given an explanation that two vowels sometimes have a single sound, the child [a] indicates when words pronounced by the teacher have such a vowel team and [b] names the vowels in the team.)

NOTE: Either *oi* or *oy* and *ou* or *ow* may be an acceptable response for certain words, e.g., *soil, soy, house, cow*.

6) Long and short *oo*

Objectives 1. The child is able to pronounce words in which there is an *oo* combination (e.g., *look, book, choose*).

2. The child is able to indicate when the *oo* in key words has the long *oo* (*choose*) or the short *oo* (*book*) sound.

d. Vowel rules

1) Short vowel generalization

Objective Given a real or nonsense word in which there is a single vowel and a final consonant, the child gives the vowel its short sound (e.g., *egg, bag, is, at, gum*) except with exceptions known as sight words (e.g., *cold, bold, sight, fight*).

2) Silent *e* rule

Objective Given a real or nonsense word that has two vowels, one of which is a final *e* separated from the first vowel by a consonant, the child first attempts pronunciation by making the initial vowel long and the final vowel silent (e.g., *cake, tube, mape, jome*) except with exceptions known as sight words (e.g., *come, have, prove*).

3) Two vowels together

Objective Given a real or nonsense word that has two consecutive vowels, the child first attempts pronunciation by making the first vowel long and the second vowel silent (e.g., *boat, meet, bait, each*) except when the two vowels are known diphthongs (i.e., *oi, oy, ou, ow, ew*) or when the word is a known exception (e.g., *bread, true, August*).

4) Final vowel

Objective Given a real or nonsense word in which the only vowel is at the end, the child gives the vowel its long sound (e.g., *go, she, me, he*).

NOTE: Application of the vowel rules is best assessed individually and informally.

e. Common consonant digraphs

Objective The child is able to name the letters in the common two-consonant combinations — *ch, th, sh, wh, nk, ng* — that result in a single new sound. (The child is asked to identify the digraphs — i.e., two consonants with a single sound — in real and nonsense words enunciated by the teacher: si*nk*, fri*nk*, *wh*arl, gli*ng*, *ch*orf, *th*unk.)

3. Has structural analysis skills

a. Base words with prefixes and suffixes

Objective The child demonstrates his understanding of how base (root) words are modified by prefixes and suffixes by adding appropriate affixes to root words in context. (Given a root word, the child adds affixes to complete a sentence: An umbrella is [*use*] on a rainy day.)

b. More difficult plural forms

Objective The child is able to select singular and plural forms of words (e.g., *mice, lady, children, dresses, circus*).

4. Distinguishes among homonyms, synonyms, and antonyms

a. Homonyms

Objective The child is able to choose between homonyms, given a sentence context, e.g., Mother bought some _____ for dinner (*meet, meat*).

b. Synonyms and antonyms

Objective The child is able to tell when the words in a pair have the same, opposite, or simply different meanings.

5. Has independent and varied word attack skills

Objective In both self-directed and teacher-directed reading the child uses a variety of skills (i.e., picture clues, context clues, structural analysis, sound/symbol analysis, comparison of new to known words) in attacking unknown words. (In the oral reading of an expository passage at his instructional level of difficulty, the child uses a variety of skills to attack unknown words.) NOTE: The objective can be assessed through the administration of an informal reading inventory.

6. Chooses appropriate meaning of multiple-meaning words

Objective Given a multiple-meaning word in varied contexts, the child is able to choose the meaning appropriate to the context. (The child chooses the appropriate given definition of *spring* for each of the following contexts: The lion was about to *spring*. We had a drink at the *spring*. The violets bloom in the *spring*.)

Level D

1. Has a sight word vocabulary of 170–240 words

Objective Given a maximum one-second exposure per word, the child is able to recognize all of the words on the Dolch Basic Sight Vocabulary List of 220 words.

NOTE: See the list given after objective B.1 for the specific words. The child should be able to recognize additional sight words that occur in instructional materials to which he has been exposed.

2. Has phonic analysis skills
    a. Three-letter consonant blends

Objective The child is able to identify the common three-consonant blends — *scr, shr, spl, spr, str, thr* — in real and nonsense words pronounced by the teacher. (The child names the three letters in appropriate words pronounced by the teacher.)

    b. Simple principles of silent letters

Objectives 1. The child demonstrates his knowledge of silent letters by correctly pronouncing words like the following: *k*nife, *g*nat, *w*rite, dum*b*, dou*b*t, hig*h*, fli*gh*t, e*a*t, re*a*d, fo*u*r.

NOTE: Silent consonants commonly occur in the following combinations: $(k)n$, $(g)n$, $(w)r$, $m(b)$, $(b)t$, $i(gh)$, $(t)ch$.

2. The child is able to pick out the silent letters in words.

3. Has structural analysis skills
    a. Syllabication

Objective The child demonstrates his ability to apply syllabication generalizations by dividing given words into single vowel sound units. (The child indicates the number of parts [syllables] in a word; the child draws lines between the parts [syllables] of a word.)

NOTE: The focus should be upon pronunciation units, not formal syllabication.

    b. Accent

Objectives 1. The child is able to indicate the accented part (syllable) in known two-syllable words.

2. The child shifts the accent in words like *ad-dress'* and *ad'-dress* in view of context.

    c. The schwa

Objective The child is able to specify the syllables in known words that contain a schwa.

NOTE: The ability to identify schwa sounds has little inherent value. However, the child who is aware of the existence of the schwa sound and its applications may be more successful in sounding vowels than the child who is not. Note that although the short sound of *u* in, say, *puppy* has the sound of a schwa, it is not a schwa because it is in the accented syllable.

    d. Possessive forms

Objective The child is able to identify nouns and pronouns, in context, that denote ownership. (The child indicates the words in connected text that are possessive forms: The *boys* went to the puppet show with *their* mother.)

Level E

NOTE: Many of the skills listed at Levels A, B, C, and D need to be developed to higher degrees of sophistication at Level E. The objectives for the lower-level skills do not change at Level E, but the specifics of the evaluation change to reflect higher-level applications.

II. Comprehension

Level A

1. Develops listening skills
   a. Has attention and concentration span suitable for his age
      Objective The child is able to demonstrate active participation in class-room listening situations. (The child attends to an oral presentation and responds appropriately, i.e., follows directions, reacts with relevant questions and/or contributions.)
      NOTE: Assessment is best carried out over a span of time during which the child can be observed in a variety of situations and his behavior compared to that of his age/grade group.
   b. Is able to remember details
      Objective The child is able to remember sufficient details from an oral presentation — i.e., story, show-and-tell — to respond to specific questions, e.g., four questions regarding specific facts based upon a 100-word presentation.
2. Increases vocabulary through listening
   Objective The child begins to use new words learned in school in his own spoken language.
   NOTE: The kindergarten child is almost certain to be exposed to a number of new school-related words, e.g., *lavatory, chalkboard, custodian, recess, principal.* Such words can become the focus for informal assessment of the objective.
3. Can relate details to one another to construct a story
   Objective The child is able to relate details to one another to make a story. (The child arranges scrambled pictures to construct a story.)
4. Anticipates outcome of stories
   Objectives 1. Given a picture of an event, the child is able to select an appropriate outcome from two pictured choices.
   2. Given the facts essential for the beginning of a story line, the child is able to project relevant outcomes. (The teacher reads a story beginning:
   > It was a rainy day. Puff, the kitten, had been outside playing in the mud. She was tired when she came in and wanted a soft, warm place to sleep. She was wet and her paws were muddy. Puff walked across the kitchen floor that Mother had just washed.

   The child gives relevant responses to questions like "Where do you think Puff went?" and "How do you think Mother felt about this?")
5. Interprets pictures critically
   Objective The child is able to point out incongruities in pictures and to pick out pictures with incongruous details (e.g., a dog driving a car, a five-legged elephant).
6. Can identify main characters in a story

Objective The child is able to name and describe up to four main characters in a story told by the teacher.

NOTE: This objective can best be assessed informally.

Level B

1. Uses picture and context clues
    a. Picture clues
       Objective The child is able to use picture clues in drawing conclusions and answering questions. (The child responds to questions based on information presented in a picture.)
    b. Context clues
       Objective The child is able to use context clues in drawing conclusions and answering questions. (The child responds to riddles in which familiar animals, etc., are described.)
2. Is able to gain meaning from
    a. Words
       Objective The child demonstrates his understanding of individual words in connected text by responding correctly to specific questions with a single-word focus, e.g., questions concerned essentially with word meaning (vocabulary).
    b. Sentences
       Objective The child demonstrates his understanding of specific sentences by responding correctly to specific questions regarding the literal content of single sentences.
    c. Whole selections
       Objective The child demonstrates his understanding of a coherent passage of connected text by responding correctly to questions regarding literal meaning and appropriately to questions regarding implied meaning, i.e., inferential questions.
       NOTE: The materials used in assessing the three preceding objectives may be written at a level of difficulty appropriate for the child's (1) grade placement, (2) instructional level, or (3) independent level.
3. Uses punctuation as a guide to meaning
    Objective The child demonstrates his attention to punctuation at the ends of sentences and punctuation of dialogue through his oral reading of familiar sentences.
    NOTE: This objective is best assessed informally.

Level C

1. Is able to gain meaning from
    a. Words
       Objective The child demonstrates his understanding of individual words in connected text by responding correctly to specific questions with a single-word focus, e.g., questions concerned essentially with word meaning (vocabulary).
    b. Sentences
       Objective The child demonstrates his understanding of specific sentences

by responding correctly to specific questions regarding the literal content of single sentences.

c. Paragraphs

Objective The child demonstrates his understanding of paragraphs by responding correctly to questions regarding the literal meaning and appropriately to questions regarding the implied meaning of whole paragraphs.

d. Whole selections

Objective The child demonstrates his understanding of a coherent passage of connected text by responding correctly to questions regarding literal meaning and appropriately to questions regarding implied meaning, i.e., inferential questions.

NOTE: The materials used in assessing the four preceding objectives may be written at a level of difficulty appropriate for the child's (1) grade placement, (2) instructional level, or (3) independent level.

2. Reads in meaningful phrases

Objective In any oral reading situation, the child reads familiar material with phrasing appropriate to logical units of thought.

NOTE: This objective is best assessed informally.

Level D

1. Is able to gain meaning from

a. Words

Objective The child demonstrates his understanding of individual words in connected text by responding correctly to specific questions with a single-word focus, e.g., questions concerned essentially with word meaning (vocabulary).

b. Sentences

Objective The child demonstrates his understanding of specific sentences by responding correctly to specific questions regarding the literal content of sentences.

c. Paragraphs

1) Main idea stated

Objective The child demonstrates his understanding of paragraphs by responding correctly to questions regarding the literal meaning and appropriately to questions regarding the implied meaning of whole paragraphs.

2) Main idea implicit but not stated

Objective Given a paragraph in which a main idea is implicit but not stated, the child is able to synthesize and state an appropriate, literal main idea.

d. Whole selections

Objective The child demonstrates his understanding of a coherent passage of connected text by responding correctly to questions regarding literal meaning and appropriately to questions regarding implied meaning, i.e., inferential questions.

NOTE: The materials used in assessing the five preceding objectives are written at a level of difficulty appropriate for the child's (1) grade placement, (2) instructional level, or (3) independent level.

2. Reads for sequence of events

Objectives 1. Having read a narrative account, the child is able to recall the sequence of events in the narrative. (Having read a narrative selection of, say, 300 words, the child correctly places five selected events by occurrence in time.)

2. Given scrambled presentation of six events with an implicit narrative order, the child is able to place the events in an appropriate time sequence.

3. Gains additional skill in use of punctuation as a guide to meaning

Objective The child demonstrates his attention to punctuation — i.e., semicolon, colon, dash, varied uses of the comma — through his oral reading of familiar passages.

NOTE: This objective is best assessed informally.

Level E

1. Adjusts reading rate to
   a. Type of material
      1) Factual
      2) Fiction

      Objective Given materials written at similar difficulty levels, the child reads fiction materials at a more rapid rate (i.e., greater number of words per minute) than factual or content area material.

   b. Level of difficulty

      Objective The child adjusts his reading rate appropriately as reading materials become more or less difficult. (The child reads a given type of material — e.g., science material — written at his independent reading level of difficulty at a more rapid rate — i.e., greater number of words per minute — than similar material written at his instructional level of reading difficulty.)

   c. Purpose for reading
      1) Reading to verify or locate specific information
      2) Reading for a general overview
      3) Reading to master specific facts
      4) Reading for enjoyment

      Objective The child skims materials at a rapid rate when seeking to verify or locate specific information (i.e., a date, a name); he reads material at a lower but rapid rate when seeking an overview or general idea regarding content; he scans material at a relatively slow rate when his purpose is to master and recall factual information; and when he reads for enjoyment, he varies his rate according to his mood and interest.

   d. Familiarity with the subject

      Objective The child reads material covering subject matter with which he has general familiarity at more rapid rates than material with which he has less familiarity. (Pretested on the general content of given passages written at a standard difficulty level, the child reads the passages on which he scored high more rapidly than the passages on which he scored low.)

NOTE: The four preceding objectives are highly interrelated: Type of material, difficulty of material, purpose for reading, and familiarity with the subject should all be critical determiners of a child's reading rate and all are interrelated. Separate objectives are stated to permit the teacher to focus upon specifics in informal or semiformal reading situations. Formal assessment exercises are not likely to yield definitive information regarding the behavior described.

2. Uses punctuation and phrasing

Objective The child demonstrates his attention to punctuation and phrasing through his interpretive oral reading of familiar passages.

NOTE: This objective is best assessed informally.

3. Reads for sequence of events

Objective Having read a narrative account, the child is able to (a) recall the sequence of the specific events covered and, if appropriate, (b) place the general incident(s) covered in relation to time of occurrence of other known incidents. (Having read an account of, say, the invasion of Iwo Jima, the child is able to [a] recall the sequence of significant events in the invasion and [b] place the invasion of Iwo Jima in relation to time of occurrence of other major battles of World War II.)

4. Is able to gain meaning from

a. Words

Objective The child demonstrates his understanding of individual words in connected text by responding correctly to specific questions with a single-word focus, e.g., questions concerned essentially with word meaning (vocabulary).

b. Sentences

Objective The child demonstrates his understanding of specific sentences by responding correctly to specific questions regarding the literal content of sentences.

c. Paragraphs

1) Main idea stated

Objective The child demonstrates his understanding of paragraphs by responding correctly to questions regarding the literal meaning and appropriately to questions regarding the implied meaning of whole paragraphs.

2) Main idea implicit but not stated

Objective Given a paragraph in which a main idea is implicit but not stated, the child is able to synthesize and state an appropriate, literal main idea.

d. Whole selections

Objective The child demonstrates his understanding of a coherent passage of connected text by responding correctly to questions regarding literal meaning and appropriately to questions regarding implied meaning, i.e., inferential questions.

NOTE: The materials used in assessing the five preceding objectives are written at a level of difficulty appropriate for the child's (1) grade placement, (2) instructional level, or (3) independent level.

III. Study Skills

Level A

1. Follows simple directions

    Objective The child is able to perform the actions in simple one- and two-stage directions, e.g., "Make an X in the middle of your paper," "Draw a ball on your paper and put a dot next to it."

2. Demonstrates elementary work habits

    a. Shows independence in work

    Objective The child shows independence in his assigned work by (1) asking questions that are necessary for clarification of the task, (2) not asking attention-seeking questions once the task is clear, and (3) keeping the necessary tools — i.e., pencil, paper, crayons, scissors, etc. — at hand.

    b. Accepts responsibility for completion and quality of work

    Objective The child shows acceptance of responsibility for completion and quality of work by (1) making a reasonable effort to do neat work and (2) pacing himself to complete a task acceptably in the allotted time.

    NOTE: The two preceding objectives must be assessed by observing the child over a period of time. Special note should be made of the child who does neat work but only at the expense of extended, painstaking effort.

3. Shows development of motor coordination (eye and hand)

    Objective The child is able to make a legible copy of given manuscript writings, e.g.,

the quick brown fox

Level B

1. Follows directions

    a. Follows oral directions given to a group

    Objective The child is able to perform the actions in two-stage directions that require some judgment when the directions are administered to a group — i.e., ten or more pupils — of which he is a part.

    b. Follows oral directions given individually

    Objective The child is able to perform the actions in two-stage directions that require some judgment when the directions are given directly to him.

    NOTE: The two preceding objectives can best be assessed by observing the child's performance over a period of time, for planned situations are likely not only to have an aura of contrivance but also to be of too short duration to be very meaningful. Special note should be made of the child who responds adequately with individual attention but not in a group, or, conversely, who can take cues from the group and proceed satisfactorily but breaks down when left to himself.

c. Follows written directions

Objective The child is able to perform independently and sequentially the actions called for in a series of four to six written directions.

2. Has adequate work habits

Objective The child shows independence and acceptance of responsibility by (a) asking only the questions that are necessary for clarification of a task, (b) keeping the materials required to complete a task available and organized, (c) showing an awareness of the standards of neatness and general quality in assigned work, and (d) pacing himself to complete assigned tasks in the time allotted.

3. Recognizes organization of ideas in sequential order

Objective The child is able to recognize sequential relationships among two or three ideas.

4. Begins to make judgments and draws conclusions

Objective Given a series of four to six related facts, the child is able to respond correctly to questions requiring that he make judgments and draw conclusions on the basis of the facts presented.

5. Uses table of contents

Objective The child is able to respond to appropriate questions with information gained from the tables of contents of first-grade books.

Level C

1. Uses picture dictionaries to find new words

Objective The child is sufficiently familiar with a picture dictionary to locate newly introduced words.

NOTE: This objective is best assessed through informal observation.

2. Groups words by initial letters

Objective The child is able to put words that begin with different letters into alphabetical order.

3. Explores the library as a research center

Objective The child actively seeks out library — or learning center — resources that are appropriate for completing an assigned task.

NOTE: This objective must be assessed by observing the child's response to a number of assignments over a period of time.

4. Shows increasing independence in work

a. Reads and follows directions by himself

Objective Given a series of four to eight written directions, the child is able to read and follow the directions with no guidance from the teacher.

b. Uses table of contents without being reminded to do so

Objective The child, without teacher direction, turns to tables of contents to (1) gain general familiarity with new books, (2) look for information, and (3) find specifically assigned sections or chapters.

5. Begins to read maps

Objective Given a simple picture map, the child is able to answer questions regarding locations and relative distances.

Level D

1. Begins to use index of books

    Objective The child is able to respond to appropriate questions with information gained from the indexes of third-grade books.

2. Reads simple maps and graphs

    a. Maps

    Objective Given an appropriate map, the child is able to respond to questions regarding locations, distances — making use of a scale-of-miles — and directions.

    b. Graphs

    1) Picture graphs

    Objective Given a graph in which pictorial representations stand for multiple units, the child is able to respond to appropriate questions.

    2) Bar graphs

    Objective Given a graph in which quantity is represented by length of line, the child is able to respond to appropriate questions.

3. Realizes printed statements may be either fact or opinion

    Objective The child is able to indicate whether given statements represent fact or opinion.

4. Has beginning outlining skills

    Objective Given the major points in a formal outline, the child is able to select and fill in second-order points from well-organized paragraphs written at his instructional level of difficulty, e.g.,

    I. Birds are alike in many ways

    A.

    B.

    C.

    D.

    II. A bird's feathers are useful

    A.

    B.

    C.

5. Follows directions

    Objective The child is able to (a) remember and follow a series of directions in sequence, (b) generalize from directions for one task to a similar task, and (c) follow written directions in independent work.

6. Has adequate work habits

    Objective The child shows independence and acceptance of responsibility by (a) working independently on assigned projects, (b) making constructive use of free time, (c) adhering to standards of neatness and quality in all work, and (d) pacing himself to complete assigned tasks in the time allotted.

Level E

1. Increases and broadens dictionary skills

    a. Alphabetizes words

       Objective The child is able to alphabetize words, even when two or more of the initial letters are identical.

    b. Uses guide words as an aid in finding words

       Objective Given the guide words and page numbers from three to six dictionary pages, the child is able to specify the page on which specific words could be found.

    c. Uses diacritical markings for pronunciation aids

       Objective The child is able to pronounce unfamiliar words — e.g., *Charybdis, escutcheon, imbroglio, spiegeleisen* — by making use of diacritical markings.

2. Utilizes encyclopedia

    a. Uses guide letters to find information on a given subject

    b. Uses alphabetical arrangement to locate information

    c. Uses topical headings to locate information

       Objective Given a specific research topic to be looked up in an encyclopedia, the child is able to (1) identify an appropriate topical heading, (2) select the appropriate volume, and (3) find the topic.

       NOTE: This objective is best assessed through observation.

    d. Uses the index volume efficiently

       Objective Having identified a general topic found in the encyclopedia, the child uses the index to locate specific information on subtopics, e.g., SPACE, Space travel: development of, flight plan, history of.

3. Uses maps, tables, and graphs

    a. Gains skill in reading and interpreting political maps

    b. Reads and uses captions, keys, and legends of maps

       Objective The child is able to use the information given in maps and their captions, keys, and legends to answer questions regarding locations, distances, and directions.

    c. Selects appropriate maps to determine

       1) Direction

       2) Distance

       3) Land formation

       4) Climate

       5) Time zones

       6) Population

       Objective The child is able to locate appropriate maps and interpret them to gain information regarding direction, distance, land formation, climate, time zones, and population.

       NOTE: This objective is best assessed in naturalistic situations over an extended period of time.

    d. Answers questions requiring the interpretation of graphs

       Objective The child is able to interpret information given in graphs — i.e., circle, line, bar, and picture graphs — to answer questions regarding comparisons of quantities and related matters.

    e. Answers questions requiring the interpretation of tables

Objective The child is able to interpret information given in tables to answer appropriate questions.

4. Uses library or materials center effectively
   a. Begins to use card catalog to find information
      1) Uses author, title, and subject cards
      2) Makes use of the Dewey Decimal System of Classification to locate books on the shelf
      3) Finds fiction books as alphabetized by author's name
      4) Makes use of cross-reference cards

      Objective Given a general research topic, the child is able to utilize the card catalog in locating appropriate materials.

      NOTE: This objective is best assessed in a naturalistic situation: Given an assigned general topic, the child should (a) break it down into relevant topics to check in the card catalog, (b) check alternate (*See . . .*) and cross-references (*See also . . .*) when appropriate, (c) note the classification of relevant material, and (d) use the classification in locating materials on the shelf.
   b. Uses other reference materials
      1) Atlases
      2) Almanacs
      3) Pamphlet file, picture file, etc.
      4) Magazines and subject index to children's magazines
      5) Newspapers

      Objective Given a need for specific information, the child makes use of appropriate references.

      NOTE: This objective is best assessed in naturalistic situations over an extended period of time. The assessment must be made in view of materials available.
   c. Locates and uses audio-visual materials

      Objective The child is able to locate and utilize available tape recorders, filmstrips, tachistoscopic and controlled presentation devices — e.g., Controlled Reader, Tach-X, Shadowscope — when appropriate.

      NOTE: Observations must be the basis for assessment of this skill: The child should know (1) when and where to use audio-visual materials, (2) the software that is appropriate for use with the hardware, and (3) the accepted procedures for operating the equipment he chooses.
   d. Knows procedure for checking books and materials in and out

      Objective The child knows and follows the established procedure for checking books and materials in and out of the library or materials center.
5. Recognizes and uses the various parts of texts and supplementary books and materials

   Objective The child can locate and use when appropriate (a) tables of contents, (b) lists of figures, (c) glossaries, (d) indexes, and (e) bibliographies and lists of sources.

6. Organizes information
   a. Gains skill in note-taking
      1) Begins to take notes in own words
      2) Keeps notes brief
      3) Learns to take notes selectively
         a) Selects main idea
         b) Selects supporting details
      4) Arranges ideas in sequence
      5) Identifies source of materials by use of
         a) Bibliography
         b) Footnotes

      Objective   The child is able to take notes from varied sources in a form that is useful to him, i.e., permits him to retrieve information as needed.

   b. Uses outlining skills
      1) Knows correct outline form
         a) Selects main points
         b) Selects and orders details

      Objective   Given selections of three or more paragraphs written at his instructional level of difficulty, the child is able to select and order main points and details up to third order — i.e., I.A.1 — in third grade and up to fourth and fifth order in sixth grade — i.e., I.A.1.a.1).

      2) Outlines materials when appropriate

      Objective   The child uses his outlining skill to organize the concepts and details he derives from reading materials.

      NOTE: Assessment of this objective must be done informally over an extended period of time: The child should use his outlining skill spontaneously when his purpose for reading is to identify and recall concepts and supporting details.

      3) Organizes own thoughts by outlining

      Objective   Given an oral or written assignment, when appropriate the child organizes his thoughts by developing an outline.

      NOTE: Assessment of this objective must be done informally over an extended period of time.

   c. Summarizes material
      1) Writes brief summaries of stories and expository material

      Objective   The child is able to write concise, two- to five-sentence summaries of stories and expository materials of five or more paragraphs (1,000 words or more).

      2) States important points expressed in discussion

      Objective   Having listened to or participated in a discussion, the child is able to identify the major issue and objectively specify the main points of view expressed.

7. Evaluates information
   a. Realizes printed statements may be either fact or opinion

      Objective   Given statements in or out of context, the child is able to make valid judgments as to whether the statements represent fact or opinion. (Given a passage like the following, the child indicates statements that represent opinion:

> Television is used as a means of education. Telecasts from the United Nations and news about important issues make many people aware of what's going on in the world. Many children watch special TV programs in school.)

b. Checks statements with those in other sources to evaluate validity

Objective When confronted with questionable statements and/or controversial points of view, the child seeks further information from varied sources in order to check their validity.

NOTE: Assessment of this objective is most realistically based upon observations over a period of time. Recognition of questionable or controversial statements is implicit in the objective, and this recognition proceeds from the child's ability to see statements as fact or opinion, which is the focus of the preceding objective.

c. Evaluates information in terms of his own experience

Objective The child relates new information to his personal experiences and evaluates both the new information and the past experiences in terms of the relationship.

NOTE: Assessment of this objective is most realistically based on observations over a period of time. One basis for assessment would be observations of reactions to commercial advertisements of products with which the child has had experience: The child should be able not only to criticize in terms of his personal experience but also to reevaluate his past observations in light of new information, e.g., note when a product had been inappropriately used, recognize unrealistic expectations.

d. Evaluates relevance of materials to topics

Objective Given an assigned list of topics, the child is able to choose from among available sources those that are likely to include relevant information on specific topics.

e. Compares various viewpoints on the same topic

Objective Given expository selections written from two or more points of view but regarding a single topic, the child is able to (1) detect inconsistencies and (2) recognize probable sources of bias in each selection.

f. Identifies propaganda

Objective The child is able to recognize the classic propaganda techniques — i.e., testimonial, bandwagon, plain folks, card stacking, transfer — when they are used in persuasive writing.

8. Follows directions

Objective The child is able to (a) remember and follow a series of directions in sequence, (b) generalize from directions for one task to a similar task, and (c) follow written directions in independent work. NOTE: The objective is the same as at Level D. The complexity of directions would, of course, increase from level to level.

IV. Self-Directed Reading

Level A
1. Cares for books properly
2. Is aware of sequential order of books
3. Begins to show initiative in selecting picture books

Level B
1. Begins to apply independent word study skills
2. Is able to find answers to questions independently
3. Begins to do recreational reading
4. Begins to select suitable reading materials independently

Level C
1. Broadens skills listed at Levels A and B
2. Develops increasing fluency

Level D
1. Develops varied purposes for selecting material
2. Begins to do independent research assignments
3. Is able to locate sources of information
4. Applies reading skills to subject matter areas

Level E
1. Conducts research independently
   a. Applies work study skills to independent work
   b. Uses bibliography as guide to materials
   c. Makes own list of sources in research work
2. Reads independently
   a. Enjoys reading and reads widely
      1) Cherishes and rereads favorite books and stories
      2) Shows interest in building a personal library
      3) Uses reading increasingly as a leisure-time activity
   b. Keeps a brief record of library book reading
   c. Enjoys sharing reading experiences with others

V. Interpretive Skills

Level A
1. Reacts to pictures and relates to own experiences
2. Shows interest in stories read
3. Begins to react to mood of poems and stories

Level B
1. Sees humor in situations
2. Reads with expression
3. Has empathy with characters

Level C
1. Recognizes implied ideas
2. Identifies character traits
3. Begins to make judgments

4. Begins to draw conclusions

Level D

1. Recognizes reactions and motives of characters
2. Has ability to relate to stories set in backgrounds different from his own
3. Makes simple inferences about characters and story outcomes

Level E

1. Reaches conclusions on the basis of stated facts
2. Relates isolated incidents to the central idea of a story
3. Understands character roles
4. Recognizes and analyzes subtle emotional reactions and motives of characters
5. Handles implied ideas
6. Recognizes story or plot structure
7. Gains skill in interpreting and appreciating types of language (figurative, idiomatic, picturesque, dialectal)
8. Senses subtle humor and pathos
9. Reacts to writer as well as writing
   a. Begins to identify elements of style
   b. Begins to identify the author's purpose in writing
   c. Begins to evaluate and react to ideas in light of author's purpose
10. Forms and reacts to sensory images
11. Perceives influence of different elements within selection
    a. Notes impact of time and place
    b. Follows sequence of events
    c. Understands cause-effect relationship
12. Identifies and reacts to tone and mood

VI. Creative Skills

Level A

1. Engages in creative dramatic play based on stories read by teacher
2. Reflects mood in use of voice

Level B

1. Has ability to enjoy rhythm in words
2. Has ability to see and hear rhyming words
3. Can interpret ideas and stories through discussions, dramatizations, drawings, etc.
4. Has ability to do cooperative planning
5. Participates in development of experience charts
6. Tells original stories

Level C

1. Shows initiative in large-group activities
2. Uses voice intonation creatively
3. Writes original stories

Level D

1. Shares in creative dramatics

      a. Acts out stories read

      b. Creates own plays

  2. Identifies with people and situations encountered in stories

Level E

1. Participates in choral speaking
2. Memorizes poems
3. Tells stories to the group
4. Plans dramatizations of stories and poems
5. Shares books with others
6. Composes original stories and poems
7. In artistic media expresses ideas gained from reading

References

Atkin, J. M. "Behavioral Objectives in Curriculum Design: A Cautionary Note." *Science Teacher,* 1968, 35, 27–30.

Eisner, E .W. "Educational Objectives—Help or Hindrance?" *School Review,* 1967, 75, 250–260, and "A Response to My Critics," 277–282.

Eisner, E. W. "Instructional and Expressive Educational Objectives: Their Formulation and Use in Curriculum." Paper presented at the annual meeting of the American Educational Research Association, Los Angeles, February, 1969.

Kliebard, H. M. "Curricular Objectives and Evaluation: A Reassessment." *High School Journal,* 1968, 51, 241–247.

Krathwohl, D. R. "Stating Objectives Appropriately for Program, for Curriculum, and for Instructional Materials Development." *Journal of Teacher Education,* 1965, 16, 83–92.

Madison Public Schools. *Guide to Teaching Reading and Literature.* Madison, Wis.: Madison Public Schools, Curriculum Department, 1964.

Maguire, T. O. "Value Components of Teachers' Judgments of Educational Objectives." *AV Communications Review,* 1968, 16, 63–86.

Otto, W. *Overview of the Wisconsin Prototypic System of Reading Instruction in the Elementary School.* Practical Paper No. 5. Madison: Wisconsin Research and Development Center for Cognitive Learning, 1968.

Otto, W., and Peterson, J. *A Statement of Skills and Objectives for the Wisconsin Prototypic System of Reading Skill Development.* Working Paper No. 23. Madison: Wisconsin Research and Development Center for Cognitive Learning, 1969.

Otto, W., Ruth Seaman, Camille Houston, Betty McMahon, and Pat Wojtal. *Prototypic Guide to Reading Skill Development in the Elementary School.* Working Paper No. 7. Madison: Wisconsin Research and Development Center for Cognitive Learning, 1967.

CHAPTER 3

Developing Reading Maturity

In Chapter 2 the basic skills that need to be developed in a school reading program were outlined. As these skills are being learned, it is important for the reader to have cognitive and affective experiences with reading that go beyond the point generally regarded as constituting mastery of basic reading skills. The ability to use reading to experience higher-level cognitive and affective experiences indicates a condition of reading maturity. The mature reader, then, is able to use the basic reading skills he has mastered for a lifetime of personal growth.

The ultimate test of a school reading program is the effect reading has on the behavior of students. Jennings (1965, p. 142) describes some possible effects of a reading experience on a person's behavior as follows: "The one aspect of mature reading that appears most obvious and immediate is the difference we feel within ourselves as a consequence of this reading. This may be as trivial as the matter of having read one more book or as great as a turn-about in political belief or religious conviction." No standardized test has as yet been constructed to measure the kind of impact Jennings refers to. Consequently, any school which has the development of "mature" readers as one of its instructional objectives must look to more than standardized test results to ascertain whether or not it is realizing this objective.

Educators have reported some disturbing observations regarding the reading maturity of many supposedly good readers. Osenburg (1962) examined the assumption that students who are identified by objective tests as superior readers must also be in possession of the other mental powers for comprehending and explaining what they have read. His subjects, high school seniors enrolled in the accelerated English programs of four high schools, had been rated by nationally used standardized objective reading tests in the top fifteen percentiles. These students were asked to name the subject of a poem and explain their answers. Since the subject was not named in the poem, the problem was to keep all the facts presented in mind and select a subject to which all the author's descriptions and not just some would apply. Forty-six per cent of the students identified the subject incorrectly. Osenburg describes the students' responses as follows: ". . . most incorrect answers resulted from careless reading or from an inability to draw logical inferences or from both. Some students jumped to their conclusions apparently after having read only a part of the poem, either skimming over the remainder or ignoring it entirely." From this study and a second related one which measured the difference between the ability to recognize a correct answer and to recall it, Osenburg concluded that "superior" readers are superior only in the ability to recognize a correct answer on an objective test, and that the higher-level reading skills are not necessarily developed in them. Hafter and Douglas (1958) devoted eight years of study to college students failing because of reading disability and concluded that the chief difficulty is not in the basic skills of word recognition and comprehension but in the thinking skills involved in most reading activities. They estimate that two-thirds of the students entering college have this difficulty. Adler (1940, p. 38) writes of his experiences with the immature reading of college juniors and seniors and their consequent inability to obtain full value from reading a literary selection. Sheldon (1955) found that literate persons in general tend to be immature readers. Clearly no school may assume that it is developing mature readers because its students score high on objective reading tests or go on to college. In 1940 Adler (p. 69) described the situation as follows: ". . . the defect which the [reading] tests discover is in the easier type of reading — reading for information. For the most part, the tests do not even measure the ability to read for understanding. If they did, the results would cause a riot." Unfortunately, Adler's assessment is still valid today.

What Is Reading Maturity?

Reading maturity is a condition of readiness limited only by the reader's total personal growth. The mature reader is ready to react to an author's ideas with a variety of cognitive and affective behaviors. The following model illustrates the range of cognitive and affective behaviors available to the mature reader. The cognitive behaviors are arranged according to the hierarchical classification of Bloom *et al.* (1956); the affective behaviors are arranged according to the hierarchical classification of Krathwohl *et al.* (1964). Complete discussions of these classifications and the distinguishing characteristics of each category are provided by these authors.

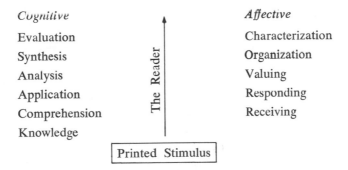

Cognitive		*Affective*
Evaluation		Characterization
Synthesis		Organization
Analysis	The Reader	Valuing
Application		Responding
Comprehension		Receiving
Knowledge		

Printed Stimulus

Maturity in reading is a condition that can be present in beginning readers as well as in experienced readers. It is not an absolute in that a person either has it or doesn't have it. It is rather a condition that exists commensurate to a person's related capabilities. Certainly a bright, emotionally secure child with a rich experiential background is likely to attain a higher level of reading maturity than one with less ability and fewer advantages. And certainly the level of reading maturity is likely to be greater for the older student with more education than for the younger student. But younger students and disadvantaged students may become mature readers also.

The student who brings the full range of his thinking and feeling powers to a reading act is a mature reader. He comprehends not only the stated but also the implied meanings of the author. He recognizes and responds to nuances of language and subtleties of meaning. As he reads, he learns, applies, analyzes, synthesizes, and evaluates. He is satisfied, frustrated, delighted, disquieted. He is personally changed by a reading experience, and the change is reflected in his behavior.

Obviously, not every person is able to do all of these things, and not everyone will do these things to the same degree or in the same way. Therefore, a properly functioning reading program introduces the beginning reader to the many potentialities that reading offers him and cultivates his ability to experience these potentialities in accordance with his individual total personal growth.

The School Program

A school system with a reading program committed to the development of mature readers needs to have its teaching staff at all academic levels aware of this goal. It is not uncommon to find teachers stressing the mechanics or basic skills of reading and only incidentally or never using reading to stimulate higher-level cognitive and affective behaviors in students. Unfortunately, the inadequacies of this kind of teaching may not be disclosed by an evaluation program that relies on standardized test results. In fact, teachers who emphasize decoding and literal comprehension to the near or total exclusion of developing maturity in and through reading may produce students who fare well on standardized reading tests. Therefore, schools need to employ measures that test the effectiveness of their reading programs beyond the limits of most standardized reading tests. Measures should be employed to determine whether or not each teacher's concept of reading and each teacher's instructional practices are conducive to developing the condition of reading maturity in students. These measures will be discussed in some detail later in this chapter.

It might be helpful to the development of specific classroom strategies to conceptualize the reading program as consisting of three rather distinct phases: (1) developmental reading, (2) functional reading, and (3) recreational reading. In a good reading program the phases are interdependent and mutually reinforcing, as the accompanying figure illustrates.

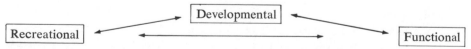

Perhaps the best way to show the uniqueness of each phase is to do so in terms of (1) the immediate objectives of each, (2) the motivation of the student in each, and (3) the materials used in each. The following scheme illustrates these different aspects:

	Developmental	Functional	Recreational
Immediate objectives	Development of reading skills, attitudes, and habits	Learning specific content through reading	Deriving personal satisfaction from reading
Student motivation	Extrinsic motivation (teacher assigns tasks and gives or withholds grades and/or other rewards)	Extrinsic motivation (teacher assigns tasks and gives or withholds grades and/or other rewards)	Intrinsic motivation (student selects his reading activities and is rewarded by personal satisfaction derived from reading)
Materials	Basal series, workbooks, kits, programmed learning, etc.	Materials used in the content areas of the curriculum	Storybooks, biographies, magazines, newspapers, etc.

According to this conceptual model, remedial, adapted, and corrective instruction as generally provided would be part of the developmental phase because all three types emphasize attitudinal and skill development. Enrichment or accelerated programs could fit into any of the three phases depending upon the kind of enrichment or acceleration being emphasized. It should be kept in mind that the ideal is to have the objectives, motivations, and materials of each phase blend with those of the others, so that the distinctions exist primarily for determining emphases for the different phases of the reading program. For example, students would, it is hoped, derive satisfaction from the developmental exercises they engage in and would be intrinsically motivated to read history, science, or other content area materials. The reading of self-selected materials and materials assigned in the content areas would presumably increase vocabulary and comprehension skills as well as develop positive attitudes toward reading. The ultimate objective, then, is the development of mature readers in and through all of these reading activities. Different aspects of this development are emphasized in different phases of the total reading program.

An evaluation of the developmental, functional, and recreational phases of a school's reading program by an administrator and his staff could be a valuable undertaking. Discussions of specific instructional strategies for each phase plus strategies for effecting transfer among the phases could result in some useful curriculum guides for teachers.

If the developmental, functional, and recreational phases of a reading program are working well so that each one reinforces the others, certain student behaviors should be occurring in all three. These behaviors may be specified and looked upon as the behavioral objectives of a reading program. At the same time they may be looked upon as the characteristics that distinguish the mature reader from the immature reader. Once again, it should be pointed out that reading maturity does not manifest itself in the same way or to the same degree in all individuals.

However, people for whom reading seems to be a vehicle for personal growth and development do perform differently with a reading selection from the way people who are not so positively affected by reading perform.

Characteristics of the Mature Reader

This section discusses five characteristics that distinguish the mature from the immature reader. The five are interrelated and together enable the reader to experience a variety of cognitive and affective reactions to a printed stimulus. Nevertheless, they can be looked at separately and described to suggest ways for teachers to develop them in students. Since this is not primarily a "how to do it" chapter, the emphasis will not be upon specific instructional practices or materials for fostering these characteristics in students. However, some illustrative teaching practices and evaluation measures pertinent to each characteristic have been included and may help a staff begin a program to improve reading instruction. Certainly, classroom teachers with some motivation and representative samples will be able to suggest many more instructional practices and evaluation measures than are given here. A teaching staff so engaged may wish to regard each characteristic as a behavioral objective. Again it is advocated that standardized reading tests not be relied upon to determine whether or not such objectives are being attained. Some different measures are recommended for use in determining whether each objective is being realized.

Reading for Purpose

The mature reader reads for specific purposes. He may set these purposes himself, or they may be set for him by someone else. The object is for him to become increasingly self-reliant in determining reading purpose.

Reading for purpose can be as simple as scanning a chapter to find a name or a date, or as sophisticated as becoming thoroughly familiar with a character to portray him in a play. The mature reader recognizes the wide range of possible reasons for reading, selects one or more reasons prior to each reading act, and proceeds with his purpose in mind. His reasons may vary from the need to escape from a busy day to the desire to master the concept behind a mathematical formula. In any case, he knows what he wants to get from his reading.

Because he has an objective, the mature reader emerges from his reading experience with a distinct communication that is valuable to him. The results of his reading are quite different from those reached by the nondirected reader, who often emerges with only some general notions of the content he has passed through. The mature reader has what he wants; the immature reader often doesn't know what he has when he finishes reading — and if he does know, he is frequently at a loss for what to do with it.

The mature reader is always ready to change his purpose or add purposes as he reads. He may start a chapter in a history book to learn the effects of a particular legislative decision on the economy of a state. Shortly he may decide to find out the political motivations of the legislators who made the decision. His focus changes, but he is always in purposeful pursuit. The beginning reader may read to discover what Father has in the box and then to discover what the family will do with Father's surprise. He is not just reading; he is reading to find things out. The mature reader who meets two different characters in a novel may wonder how they will solve the conflict that is certain to arise in an anticipated meeting. He may search for clues to a character's feelings or words that describe a scientist's frustration. The immature reader does not read with this kind of inquiring mind.

One of the writers is reminded of the many times he taught Jack London's *Call of the Wild* to average-ability tenth-grade English classes. For each assignment of one or more chapters the classic purpose "Read it carefully so that we can discuss it tomorrow" was given. Sometimes a little motivation was added: "This is an exciting chapter. You'll enjoy it." The discussion the following day was almost always extremely one-sided. It proceeded something like this:

"Well, do you agree with me that this is an exciting chapter?" Some affirmative nods, some shoulder shrugging, some heads turning toward the window. "Obviously some of you enjoyed it. Can you tell us what you liked about this particular chapter?" Pause. "Anyone?" Pause. "Sally?"

"It was exciting and interesting."

"Jack?"

"I agree. It was interesting and good adventure. And exciting."

"Did anyone notice the way the author used words that gave the reader a vivid picture of the action taking place and almost made him feel as if he were there?" Evidently no one did. "Open your books to the first page in the chapter. Listen to this sentence and notice the descriptiveness of the verbs as well as the adjectives. 'He was *crying* with *sheer* rage and eagerness as he *circled* back and forth for a chance to *spring* in.' Close your eyes for a moment. Try to picture that. Imagine yourself sneaking up to take movies of that moment before open conflict." Heads turning back from the windows. Some straightening up in the seats. Some looks of concentration. Some looks of satisfaction in discovery. "Let's consider another aspect of this chapter. What did London seem to be saying in this chapter about the relationship between the civilized and the primitive?" Attentive silence. "Are you sure we read the same chapter?" Some smiles, some more shrugs. "All right, listen and I'll tell you what this chapter is all about." Through his years of teaching tenth-grade English, the teacher became the best teller of *The Call of the Wild* certainly in the school and perhaps in the entire state. The pessimists in the class must have felt very stupid and convinced that they would never learn to read properly, and the optimists must have felt very fortunate to have such a smart teacher. And one day it occurred to the teacher that if the students were told to watch for some of these things as they read and given some strategies for involving themselves in certain ways at certain places in the chapter they could discover *The Call of the Wild* themselves.

Teaching Students to Read for Purpose. What, then, does the teacher do to teach students to read for purpose and ultimately to cause them to develop the ability to set their own reading purposes?

First of all, students at all academic levels need to know that any given reading selection is written for a particular purpose or for particular purposes. An author decides what responses he wants from a reader. He writes to inform, to give pleasure through carefully selected words, to persuade, etc. Students must also know that what they receive from a reading selection may go beyond the author's intended communication. Russell (1961, p. 454) reports that a fourth-grader once remarked, "I like stories that mean more than they mean." This student responded not only in terms of the author's purpose but also in terms of some the author never intended.

To teach these concepts, teachers need to acquaint students with materials written for different purposes and show how personal purposes not perhaps intended by the author may be realized from given selections. Students might be asked to discuss the purposes of the authors of selections supplied by the teacher. They might be encouraged to ask questions of selections before they read them. Another good teaching procedure would be to have students list purposes for which they might read and then match their lists with selections likely to satisfy those purposes.

Probably the best way to teach students to read for purpose is by assigning, prior to reading, questions or other tasks that can be satisfied through the assigned selection. Guilford (1960) recommends skillful questioning as a means of stimulating different kinds of thinking. Writing tasks, specified prior to reading but to be completed after reading, are effective in giving students experiences in reading for purpose. The key word is *preparation*. The reader who is prepared by another or who prepares himself to gain certain ideas or feelings from a selection is more likely to have a personally productive reading experience than the reader who is not reading for clearly defined purposes.

Teachers at all academic levels and in all content areas should teach reading for purpose. The elementary teacher must begin a child's development in this regard in keeping with the child's total personal development and the reading materials suitable for him. As the child grows and his reading materials become more sophisticated, his purposes for reading and ability to achieve those purposes should grow accordingly. Each content area and each sequential stage of the curriculum present different opportunities for expanding a student's ability to read for purpose.

Evaluating Ability to Read for Purpose. How can a teacher evaluate a student's ability to read for teacher-prescribed purposes and to set his own purposes?

The only way to test a student's ability to read for teacher-prescribed purposes is to examine the product of his reading in terms of what he was asked to produce. Did he answer the question he was asked? Does his written product satisfy the requirements of the task he was given? Does his discussion indicate a synthesis of this reading experience with previous experiences? If the practice he has in reading for prescribed purposes is effective in increasing his ability in this regard, he should be able to master increasingly sophisticated tasks with harder and harder material.

Two factors are involved in the student's ability to set his own purposes: (1) his ability to judge the content of a selection on the basis of a rapid survey and (2) his ability to raise questions or formulate other meaningful tasks relative to a reading selection. One way of testing the first of these is to ask the student to predict the content, organization, and author's purpose in various selections on the basis of a rapid survey. A student who becomes increasingly efficient and accurate with this kind of exercise is obviously learning how to set his own reading purposes. In regard to the second factor, Eisner's (1965) comment is pertinent: ". . . it seems that rather than to rely upon examinations which deal only with assessing the student's ability to provide answers, it might be well for teachers to construct examinations which tap the student's ability to raise significant questions." Students who are able to raise significant questions and set meaningful tasks relative to reading selections with more and more discrimination and insight are necessarily improving in their ability to set reading purposes for themselves.

Reading Organization

The mature reader organizes his reading. Most writing is a highly organized process. Authors usually structure their ideas according to an organizational pattern. A selection may have a temporal organization, a most-important-to-least-important organization, a least-important-to-most-important organization, a building-to-a-climax organization, a cause-effect organization, etc. Some writers use a pattern that has one main or topic idea in each paragraph; others choose to let more than one paragraph support or build to a summary idea. It is not desirable that all writing follow the same organizational plan. It is desirable that most written products have a discernible organizational plan.

Reading comprehension and retention of what is read are both enhanced by organized reading. Ideas in a reading selection need to be connected and weighted in the mind of the reader. Comprehension is more than coming to grips with ideas in isolation. It is a careful encountering, relating, and sorting of ideas into an existing cognitive structure. Ausubel (1964, p. 234) comments pertinently:

> Since potentially meaningful material is always learned in relation to an existing background of relevant concepts, principles, and information, which provide a framework for its reception and make possible the emergence of new meanings, it is evident that the stability, clarity, and organizational properties of this background crucially affect both the accuracy and the clarity of these emerging new meanings and their immediate and long-term retrievability. If cognitive structure is stable, clear, and suitably organized, accurate and unambiguous meanings emerge and tend to retain their dissociability strength or availability. If, on the other hand, cognitive structure is unstable, ambiguous, disorganized, or chaotically organized, it tends to inhibit meaningful learning and retention. Hence, it is largely by strengthening relevant aspects of cognitive structure that new learning and retention can be facilitated.

The mature reader knows that authors use different organizational patterns. He also knows that it is important for him to learn the organizational pattern of a reading selection as early as possible in his reading of that selection. Having found a particular pattern, he follows it, always alert to any changes that might occur as the content or purpose of the communication causes the author to change the pattern.

Organizing one's reading means more than outlining. Some materials do lend themselves to the kind of outline in which main ideas are identified and supporting or less important but closely related ideas are recognized as belonging with a particular main idea. Other materials may require a sequential kind of organization in which one thing happens after another and so on until a process is completed. Still another organizational pattern may be of a cause-and-effect nature.

Thorndike (1917), after studying mistakes made in reading paragraphs, commented as follows:

> Understanding a paragraph is like solving a problem in mathematics. It consists in selecting the right elements of the situation and putting them together in the right relations, and also with the right amount of weight or influence or force for each. The mind is assailed as it were by every word in the paragraph. It must select, repress, soften, emphasize, correlate and organize, all under the influence of the right mental set or purpose or demand.

It is these reactions or responses to a selection that result in good comprehension and retention for the mature reader and poor comprehension and retention for the immature reader.

Teaching Reading Organization.   To be able to teach students to organize their reading, teachers must be thoroughly familiar with the materials they assign to be read. They must understand the structure of the material and why it is structured as it is. Without this knowledge it is impossible for them to help students prepare themselves for the particular structures they will encounter.

Students at all academic levels need assistance in organizing their reading. Much about reading organization may be learned incidentally, but most students profit from specific instruction in this regard. Just as setting purpose for reading becomes a more sophisticated process as more sophisticated materials are introduced into the curriculum, so does the process of reading organization. Secondary school teachers are in a particularly good position to teach reading organization because they are thoroughly trained in certain subject matter areas and consequently know the structures of their contents well. Therefore, mature readers begin to develop the ability to organize their reading in the primary grades and continue to do so through their entire school careers. Immature readers are often applying to complex materials an ability that is suitable only for simple materials.

To teach reading organization teachers need to make students aware that (1) most writing is organized, (2) different materials are organized differently, and (3) the reader must know the particular organizational pattern of a selection and actively pursue the writer's message according to that pattern.

Sometimes overhead projections are used to teach students how to organize their reading. Transparencies showing clear-cut organizational patterns may be projected for student viewing and discussion. Excerpts from different kinds of materials (i.e., a story with a surprise ending, a social studies article, a science text) can illustrate clearly how a reader needs to set his thinking in a certain way to get the most from each organizational pattern.

Having students outline selections in writing is good teaching procedure. How-ever, it should be used only with relatively short selections. Outlining can be a deadly affair, likely to teach a student nothing more than how to tolerate boredom, unless it is used sparingly and meaningfully.

Summarizing is another way students can learn to organize their reading. Some teachers have found it beneficial for students to explain the mental processes they used to arrive at their particular summary statements. Often, in retracing their steps to a summary statement, students develop a keen awareness of (1) the author's organization and (2) the importance of organizing reading for compre-hension.

Evaluating Reading Organization. How does a teacher know that students are organizing their reading? The effects should be reflected in better comprehension and better retention. Students who organize their reading respond differently to questions about their reading from the way students who do not organize respond. The mature reader organizes his reading and can almost always answer questions like the following: What is the main idea in this selection? What did the author do to heighten reader interest, support his position, or clarify a point of view? What were the highlights of this story in the order they happened? What caused a particular thing to happen? Students should be able to answer these questions not only immediately after reading but weeks and months after reading, depending upon the significance of the selection, the importance given to it in class, and the academic level of the students. Obviously, the questions themselves and how they are asked will be different for different age groups. However, reading organization is desirable and can be evaluated for students from the primary grades on.

The student who completes a reading experience but is unable to communicate what he has read in an orderly fashion is an immature reader and easily evaluated by the teacher who asks the kinds of questions or assigns the kinds of tasks that require reading organization. This student knows he has been somewhere, but he cannot retrace his steps. If prompted, he can recall bits and pieces of a reading selection and often gives the impression of having rather good comprehension abilities, especially on objective tests. The mature reader, by way of comparison, is able to recall his reading and communicate about it in an orderly fashion and with a minimum of prompting. The teacher who listens carefully to a student tell about what he has read or who reads carefully what a student writes about what he has read will be able to tell whether or not the student is organizing his reading.

Reading to Enlarge Vocabulary

The mature reader uses reading experiences to enlarge his vocabulary. Wide reading is recognized as a good way to enlarge vocabulary. However, wide read-ing does not guarantee vocabulary development; there must be a conscious attempt on the part of the reader to improve his vocabulary. In this regard, the immature reader is not characterized by his failure to read but by his failure to take advan-tage of the opportunities for vocabulary development that reading offers.

The kind of vocabulary development referred to here is not only the addition of previously unencountered words to a student's reading vocabulary but the utilization of words from his reading vocabulary in his speaking, writing, and listening vocabularies. It is, further, the kind of development that causes the student to respond differently to shades of meaning in the same word used in different contexts and in words which are nearly, but not quite, synonymous.

Speculating about the number of words and word meanings in the English language, Laird (1957, p. 53) says,

> Three quarters of a million? That would seem conservative, and we still have to define "a word." Some of these so-called "words," forms which have come to us with some continuity, have many uses. If one thinks of these words as the carriers of units of meaning, then many of the words single in form become multiple in use and meaning. Many words have dozens of meanings. . . . A rough check of random sections in various dictionaries suggests that we may safely say there are more than twice as many named meanings in English as there are recognized words. How many named meanings does a writer of English have before him, then, when he tries to compose a sentence? Two million? Certainly there are many times what any human being could ever learn, or learn to use. And yet we are constantly obtaining new words.

Since English writers have myriads of words and meanings at their disposal, it follows that readers of English must be skillful interpreters of words. They must know that a word has meaning in a particular context; and they must respond to words not as fixed but as changing entities. The mature reader recognizes this phenomenon and learns new meanings for words as he encounters them in different contexts.

The mature reader is also aware that words have an aesthetic value for man. Langer (1966, p. 65) says,

> The process of transforming all direct experience into imagery or into that supreme mode of symbolic expression, language, has so completely taken possession of the human mind that it is not only a special talent but a dominant, organic need. All our sense impressions leave their traces in our memory not only as signs disposing our practical reactions in the future but also as symbols, images representing our "ideas" of things; and the tendency to manipulate ideas, to combine and abstract, mix and extend them by playing with symbols, is man's outstanding characteristic.

From his experiences with enjoyable reading matter the mature reader develops an openness to obtaining satisfaction from his responses to words in print.

Another aspect of the mature reader's contact with words in print is that he increases his ability to react to words used to stimulate emotional as well as ideational behavior. He is alert, that is, to words used for propaganda purposes or other objectives that may be attained by eliciting an emotional arousal from a reader. He knows when to be wary of words chosen to involve him emotionally rather than rationally and when to put down his defenses and permit himself to react emotionally to poetic, descriptive, or other emotionally stimulating words. From his cumulative reading experiences he becomes better able to judge the intent of emotionally charged words and more discriminating in his willingness to respond to those words.

The mature reader has a variety of means at his disposal for making words unfamiliar at sight familiar. He does not rely on one method alone for analyzing words. He knows that the other words which surround an unknown word may define the latter for him. Therefore, he searches the context for clues to its meaning. He also knows that analyzing the structure of a word may disclose its meaning. The mature reader finds roots, prefixes, and suffixes to aid him in obtaining word meaning. He may put his phonic skills to work to move a word from his sight word vocabulary to his listening vocabulary, which may contain the word giving him trouble. If all these strategies fail, the mature reader has well-developed dictionary skills to rely on and a positive attitude toward using the dictionary.

A necessary characteristic for someone who uses reading experiences to enlarge his vocabulary is curiosity about words. He wants to know where they come from, what they mean, how they change their meanings, how people react to them, etc. He wonders why an author used a particular word, and he respects the choice of a highly communicative word. He incorporates in his reading a search for new words and the answers to the many questions prompted by his interest in words.

Teaching Students to Enlarge Their Vocabularies Through Reading. Teachers at all academic levels are in an excellent position to help students use their reading experiences to enlarge their vocabularies. Besides teaching them the various word analysis skills, they can teach them about the nature, history, and power of words and give them reading materials that stimulate interest in and respect for words. Poetry, carefully selected to match the interests, maturity, and reading ability of students, is often used successfully to foster a fondness for words. Discussions of words used in advertising communications awaken students to the persuasive power of words. Alerting students to key, descriptive, or unusual words in a selection they are about to read is good procedure. There are informative, humorous, and profound writings about words that may give students new insights and increased sensitivity to words. For example, Hayakawa (1949) writes about "snarl-words" and "purr-words," and Carl Sandburg (1922) cautions readers to beware of using "proud" words. Children in the primary grades can supply words to describe pictures and be involved in other pleasant and meaningful activities productive of vocabulary growth through reading. There is no scarcity of things to do to enlarge vocabulary through reading with students of all ages. The need is to take the time to construct lessons and motivate students to (1) develop the concept of vocabulary development through reading, (2) make vocabulary development a part of their reading experiences, and (3) use newly acquired words in meaningful speaking and writing activities. Students must have opportunities to use their increasing vocabularies in speech and writing. Words learned through reading will soon be forgotten if they are not practiced. When students do use newly learned words, it is important that the teacher acknowledge this manifested growth and provide suitable rewards.

Evaluating Vocabulary Growth Through Reading. There are many ways to evaluate students' vocabulary growth through reading. One way is to discuss in class new words encountered while reading or familiar words found used in an unusual way or in an especially effective way. If students know that this activity is a regular part of the curriculum, they will learn to be prepared. It might be pointed out that this is a good evaluation activity for all content area classes in the secondary school, especially where supplementary reading is liberally assigned or strongly encouraged. Asking students to define or substitute words used in their writing is a way to determine whether or not they understand the words they are using. Careful listening to student reports and discussions and careful reading of writing submitted by students will also permit evaluation of the transfer of words met in reading to speech and writing. Some teachers have required students to keep notebooks or periodically submit short reports of their observations of words while reading. If called for sparingly and in a spirit of genuine sharing, these can be effective evaluative exercises as well as good instructional procedures.

Getting Meaning from Sentences

The mature reader uses his knowledge of the meaning-bearing elements in English sentences to interpret the meaning of each sentence. The English sentence is a dynamic, versatile entity with definite meaning-bearing elements that can be observed and classified. Lefevre (1964) maintains that English sentences use four "signaling" systems: (1) word-form changes, (2) structure words, (3) syntactical-function order in sentence patterns, and (4) intonation.

A major characteristic of the evolution of the English language has been retention of some inflectional word-form changes, some prefixes, and some suffixes but increasing reliance upon structure words (a, the, is, up, because, how, etc.) and syntactical-function order to convey meaning. Intonation has always been and remains vital to communicate the meaning of sentences. Therefore, a reader of English must learn to respond correctly to sentence patterns, structure words, and word forms and to supply intonations as he reads. If he fails to do any one of the four, he is not making use of the signals within sentences and is in danger of misinterpreting their messages.

The difference between mature and immature readers in this area of concern is chiefly one of degree. The mature reader is more alert to the signals as he reads sentences and more aware of how each signal is directing him to respond. As he encounters increasingly sophisticated sentences in his academic progress, he increases his ability to respond to their signals accordingly. This is, then, a developmental process beginning with a student's first experience with reading sentences and ending only when the most difficult sentences he will need to interpret have been mastered.

Although word-form changes are not so prevalent in the English language as they once were, they do exist and need to be correctly interpreted. Inflections still signal time (ed), number (s), possession ('s), objects (me), person (she, her), comparison (warmer, warmest), and subjunctive mood (were); and prefixes and suffixes are frequently used. It is obvious that students who miss these signals may get the general drift of a reading selection, but they will certainly miss the specifics or fine points of the selection and hence cannot be considered mature readers. As a matter of fact, if some of the signals are not noticed or not interpreted correctly, it is possible for a reader to misinterpret a message completely.

Structure words have become important in the English language. They have relatively little meaning by themselves, but they do serve various functions necessary to comprehending sentence meanings. Lefevre (1964) presents a treatment of structure words for the reader who desires more information than is given here. Suffice it to say that structure words (1) introduce phrases (*in, up, with*), (2) introduce clauses (*since, because, if*), (3) help verbs (*am, is, have*), (4) introduce questions (*who, how, why*), (5) introduce nouns (*a, some, any*), and (6) connect (*and, but, or*). Structure words perform other functions, but these are perhaps the ones most easily recognized. The mature reader knows the importance of structure words in gaining the precise meaning intended by an author and pays careful attention to the signals they give him.

Getting meaning from syntactical-function order in sentence patterns requires readers to respond appropriately to words or word groups that perform definite functions within sentences. Although English sentences may take many different forms, a rather rigid grammatical system dictates their word order. For example, a mature reader of English, by assigning the proper relationships to the various word groups, will receive a clear message from the following sentence: *Grinning broadly, the small boy reached for his prize while the big boy scowled in defeat.* No one could get much meaning from the following construction even though all of the words and punctuation marks are there: *Scowled in defeat for his prize the grinning broadly reached, small boy while the boy big.* The mature reader recognizes noun, verb, adjective, and adverb functions of words and word groups according to their relative positions in a sentence. The immature reader may become consciously or unconsciously confused and assign adjectival functions to noun groups or make other errors likely to result in misinterpretation. What is needed is a sentence "sense" that rests upon the student's experiences with oral communication.

Intonation is essential to getting meaning from English sentences. Anyone who has compared a seasoned user of profanity with a neophyte cusser knows that cuss words demand a certain "music" to be truly effective. Intonation might be considered the "music" of the language. Variations in rate, pitch, and volume are necessary for conveying ideas in sentences. For example, note the different meanings communicated when the following different variations are applied:

```
        not
I am       go/ing        (my mind is made up)

I
    am not go/ing         (someone else, perhaps, but not I)

            go/ing
I am not                  (I thought I was)
```

Mature readers apply the knowledge they have about intonations in spoken communication to written communication. In simple terms, they read silently, as well as orally, with expression. Immature readers may miss much meaning from a sentence because they do not bring intonation variations to the words and word groups as they read them. This does not mean that the mature reader vocalizes excessively, although some passages seem to require a certain degree of subvocalization at least. It does mean that the mature reader recognizes that the printed language represents oral language and, in effect, tunes in on sentences. He brings a background of listening experience to his reading.

Teaching Students to Get Meaning from Sentences. To teach students to be alert to word-form changes, structure words, syntactical-function order, and intonation teachers must thoroughly understand the nature of these four elements. They will find many ways of imparting it to students so that their reading is improved.

Reading to children is excellent at all ages if the reader is articulate and reads with expression. Having children read orally to entertain or inform an audience is good practice. There seems little doubt that teaching children the different functions of words and word groups in English sentences is beneficial to their reading comprehension. Studies have indicated that knowledge of the structure of language is an important factor in reading comprehension. This does not mean that studying traditional grammar will improve reading comprehension. It means that letting students arrive inductively at understandings about the systematic nature of English grammar and the different functions performed by words and word groups in certain positions in sentences is likely to aid reading comprehension. Having students write sentences that "say something" may teach students to recognize word-form changes, syntactical-function order, structure words, and intonation. The importance of paying careful attention to structure words may be taught by showing how difficult it is to get precise meaning from a sentence with nonsense words substituted for structure words (*Ega men walked kerna degen him direl Paul biggle complaining.* [*The men walked away from him because Paul was complaining.*])

Certainly, there are many more good instructional practices for teaching students the meaning-producing elements in English sentences. Perhaps a useful inservice project for an administrator and his staff or some selected members of his staff would be to study and develop a list of activities for teaching these elements.

Evaluating Students' Ability to Get Meaning from Sentences. Teachers will recognize growing ability to get meaning from sentence elements by the students' written and oral comments about reading passages. Comprehension questions that require precise reading to be answered correctly may be constructed and asked of students either before or after they read. Responses to these questions will help the teacher evaluate whether the students are alert to prefixes and suffixes, modifying phrases and clauses, structure word signals, etc. Oral reading by students will help the teacher evaluate their ability to get meaning from intonation. One of the best ways to appraise progress in this regard is to discuss certain passages with the students, asking them to explain their statements by referring to particular sentences in the passage.

Varying Rate and Style of Reading

The mature reader varies his rate and style of reading according to the material he is reading and his purpose for reading it. The mature reader does not read everything the same way; the immature reader often does. For the immature reader, reading is a definite, set process which he employs with all reading materials. For the mature reader, reading is a flexible process which he changes as his reading materials and purposes for reading change.

Fast readers do not necessarily comprehend better than slow readers, nor do slow readers necessarily comprehend better than fast readers. There are both fast and slow readers who have good comprehension. Therefore, the problem is not only one of improving comprehension. Efficiency and the degree of pleasure desired from reading are also involved in the matter of varying one's reading rate and style.

Reading rate is a misleading term; *rate of comprehension* is more descriptive. Since comprehension is the object of the reading process, moving the eyes rapidly across lines of type is not in itself reading. Consequently, a reading rate score is meaningless without an accompanying comprehension score. Furthermore, reading rate and comprehension scores mean little unless one knows the kind of material from which the scores were obtained and why the reader was reading it. In regard to reading rate, then, it might be said that the mature reader lets his rate be governed by the material he is reading and his purpose for reading it. He has many different reading needs and is able to move from one speed to another to enhance his comprehension and pleasure.

The mature reader also varies his reading style according to the material he is reading and his purpose for reading it. He may change his style of attack from selection to selection or within a selection. For example, he knows that the best way to read a novel to get the most it has to offer is to begin on the first page and proceed to the last. He also knows that a chapter in a textbook may be read best by surveying the entire chapter quickly, noting what seem to be key sentences, before actually beginning a page-by-page reading. Within a selection, the mature reader may move quickly through several paragraphs and then read a particular sentence slowly and carefully. He may halt his reading completely at times to savor the visual imagery produced by a vivid description or to ponder an intriguing idea. He employs more subvocalization with a poem and may even read it aloud. A mathematics problem may also require considerable vocalization to be understood. The context surrounding an unfamiliar word may need to be searched to find the meaning of the word, or an account of a sequential scientific process may need to be retraced to insure comprehension and retention. The mature reader shifts gears, as it were, as he moves through written communication.

The ability to vary reading rate and style is lacking in beginning readers. It needs to be developed carefully and precisely from the time the child starts to master the most basic reading skills, and development needs to be continued as the child progresses to more and more sophisticated materials. In the initial stages of reading instruction the child is too concerned with decoding and meaning-getting processes to be trained in reading flexibility. Therefore, it is wise to postpone such training until he has indicated his relative mastery of basic decoding and comprehension skills. However, with these skills finally in hand, he is ready to be taught how to vary his rate and style. Some children learn to be flexible readers without specific teaching, but most require the help of a teacher to attain this important characteristic of reading maturity.

Teaching Students to Vary Their Rate and Style of Reading. The teacher must first of all teach the child that the world is full of many different kinds of reading materials which generate different ideas and feelings. It is important to ask different kinds of questions about varying materials and assign the kinds of tasks relative to different reading experiences. Students at all academic levels should have opportunities to discuss why they select certain materials to read, what different materials offer readers, and what specific reading selections have done for them. Discussing "how" they read particular selections also illuminates the concept of flexibility. Specific directions for reading a certain selection are often helpful. For example, students may be told to scan the entire selection before reading, to pause and reflect at designated words or passages, and to read other designated passages rapidly. In this way they get the "feel" of reading flexibility.

It is better not to emphasize reading rate with students who do not have good word recognition skills. However, students who have good word recognition skills can rather easily be taught to read faster with no loss in comprehension. Timed exercises with reading selections at a difficult level appropriate for the student's vocabulary and comprehension achievement will increase reading rate. Three kinds of mechanical devices purport to be helpful: tachistoscopic devices, film projection devices, and pacer or accelerator devices. There are numerous claims of success from teachers who have used these devices to increase students' reading rate, but their value is seriously questioned by many educators. The problem of transfer from the machine to the book cannot be denied, and the criticism that good readers don't read in the mechanical fashion prescribed by the particular setting of the machine seems valid. Since regressions are frequently the cause of slow reading, placing an index card over each line of print as it is read may serve to break the habit of regressing and thereby improve reading rate. Two things should be kept in mind: (1) Exercises to increase rate should always include comprehension checks at the level of comprehension desired, and (2) students must be taught the desirability of slow reading for some materials and/or some purposes.

Evaluating Students' Ability to Vary Their Rate and Style of Reading. Teachers may use a number of measures to discover whether students are varying their rate and style of reading according to material and purpose. Checking the time students take to read different kinds of reading materials is one evaluation technique. Asking them to retrace their progress through a selection or through two different selections telling how they varied their reading attack within the selection or between the selections sometimes demonstrates development in reading flexibility. Asking them to locate the answer to a particular question within a specified period of time is revealing. Giving them a limited amount of time to read and summarize a selection is also a good test. Obviously, the selections used for these evaluations need to be carefully chosen, the tasks assigned carefully constructed, and a reasonable number of minutes provided to complete the tasks.

Evaluating the Present Program

The preceding discussions of the five characteristics that may be used to distinguish the mature reader from the immature reader are meant to serve schools desirous of improving their reading programs in several ways. As mentioned earlier, they may be used as objectives toward which an entire staff might work. They may be used as guidelines for evaluating the present reading program of a school that wishes to look beyond the limits of most standardized testing programs. They may also be used as guidelines for the development of a scope and sequence chart for reading. A staff might profitably spend some time adding specific instructional activities to those mentioned here for each of the characteristics. Adding other characteristics to the five just discussed would be a worthwhile project for a staff and perfectly appropriate since these five are not intended to be the only marks that differentiate mature from immature readers.

Developing reading maturity is the ultimate goal of the developmental reading program. This chapter is meant to help an administrator and his staff achieve that goal. There is always the danger that a staff will fall short of this objective because the objective is not clearly defined for them or because they don't apply suitable evaluation measures. Reading maturity is like any other educational objective. It needs a clear definition, specific teaching, and precise evaluation. Its attainment cannot be assumed to be a by-product or a spontaneous outgrowth of a student's mastery of the basic reading skills discussed in Chapter 2 of this book.

The following questions may be used by administrators and teachers to help them evaluate certain key elements in their reading programs. The responses given should allow a staff to determine whether their school's reading program is providing students with the kind of program they need to become mature readers. The questions and the short discussions included with each one are meant to provoke thought and further discussion. Perhaps they will also provoke additional questions to evaluate instructional programs committed to developing mature readers.

1. *What is the teacher's concept of reading?* Roma Gans (1967) says, "When I go into a group, I realize first of all that I carry something in. I reflect what I think reading means." Teachers who look upon reading as a decoding process employed solely to get information from print are unlikely to communicate to their students that reading can be a total personal involvement with the ideas and feelings of another human being.

One of the big problems here is that too many teachers are not themselves mature readers. Johnson (1956, p. 123) says, "Reading is something we do, not so much with our eyes, as such, as with our knowledge and interests and enthusiasm, our hatreds and fondnesses and fears, our evaluations in all their forms and aspects. Because this is so, a fondness for reading is something that a child acquires in much the same way as he catches a cold — by being effectively exposed to someone who already has it."

It is deplorable that many American teachers, especially elementary school teachers, are not reading enthusiasts. From the results of a study that investigated the reading habits of college students, most of whom were planning to be elementary school teachers, Odland and Ilstrup (1963) drew the following implications:

> Among a group of individuals who will be elementary classroom teachers there were many who seemed to possess an interest in reading and who had developed a power of selection which would guide their reading toward worthwhile literature. It cannot be ignored, however, that there were many individuals who read very little either in books or in magazines. There is also cause for concern when one observes the popular choices of the students in books and magazines. In fact, there would seem to be basis for asking if the adults who accept the responsibility of teaching young children the values of reading really consider reading a valuable medium of communication.

It is interesting to speculate about the amount and kind of reading that these prospective teachers engage in after they assume teaching positions. We have talked with many classroom teachers at academic levels from kindergarten to Grade 12 about their personal reading habits. The majority report that they do not read as much as they would like to or feel they should because of lack of time. To expect them to read less on the job than when they were students seems plausible because of the many demands placed on the classroom teacher in and out of school.

Teachers need time to read — time not only to read curriculum guides and professional journals and newsletters and bulletins but also to read essays and biographies and novels and things that inspire and excite them. Reading programs would probably be more effective in developing mature student readers if teachers spent more time reading. It is unfortunate that being well read and having a fondness for reading are not necessary qualifications for a teacher. A school system would be wise to seek out teachers with these qualifications. And when they are found, they should be given released time to enable them to spend a specified period of time each day reading.

2. *Is the teacher's knowledge of the vocabulary, language structure, and organizational patterns of assigned reading used to help students comprehend and utilize what they read?* Writing is a highly selective process. Authors choose their vocabulary, language patterns, and organization according to the nature of their content, what they want to stress, the mood they wish to convey, etc. The mature reader is alert to these elements in a selection and reads with awareness of the author's intentions and techniques. Teachers who have studied carefully the materials they assign are able to chart a course for their students to follow while reading. This is not to say that students should be led by the hand through reading matter. It is rather suggested that they be alerted before they read to specialized vocabulary, unusual sentence structure, and organizational patterns which may make comprehension difficult. Perhaps the adage "Forewarned is forearmed" states the case.

3. *What kinds of questions are students asked about their reading?* Lorge

(1960) says about questioning, "The art of questioning can be directed toward seeing similarities or differences (concept formations), or seeing common elements among concepts (generalization), or recognizing the limitations or advantages (evaluation). Questions can be formulated toward seeing sequences (structure and restructure), toward evidence and proof (verification)." Evaluating the questions teachers ask students about their reading is one way of measuring the effectiveness of the reading program in mature readers. It is not enough that teachers ask "some" students higher-level questions "sometimes." All students, regardless of their mastery of basic skills, need frequent opportunities to answer higher-level questions about their reading. If they do not have these opportunities, they will not develop the degree of maturity in reading that the ability they do have permits them.

Many administrators and teachers are finding Sanders' *Classroom Questions: What Kinds?* (1966) helpful in evaluating the kinds of questions being asked in their classrooms. This paperback book provides guidelines for constructing questions at the cognitive levels of Memory, Translation, Interpretation, Application, Analysis, Synthesis, and Evaluation. It is relatively easy to prepare evaluation sheets for an observer to use in assessing the current cognitive levels of questions being asked in a classroom or throughout a school. Such an assessment might well be the basis for an in-service program devoted to constructing better questions for student readers. Sanders' guidelines would be extremely helpful to this kind of in-service focus.

4. *Are students being taught to discriminate between material that warrants careful, thoughtful reading and material that does not?* Not all material warrants or permits involvement of the higher-level cognitive and affective behaviors. The student who reads every assignment the same way because he has been told explicitly or implicitly that "You may be tested on this" is not developing an important characteristic of the mature reader: variation of reading style. Teachers often communicate the idea that everything we do in the class is important and then reward students for factual recall on tests. Consequently, students learn to read for short-term factual recall above all else.

5. *Are students given time to read deserving materials thoughtfully and with feeling?* Time is a precious commodity in an ever expanding curriculum, and there is often a tendency to "cover the course" regardless of the effect the curriculum is having on the student. Mature reading is time-consuming because it requires recall, contemplation, evaluation, synthesis, etc. It can involve decision making, attitude changing, or basking in the positive reinforcement of a pet idea. These behaviors are not experienced hurriedly or in a state of anxiety over finishing the assignment. There must be time for reflection and rewards for reflecting if students are to become mature readers. In reference to the superior student, Sheldon (1955) says, "Because of the premium placed on speed, he often does not have the opportunity of reflecting on what he has read and making the higher level inferences that he can do with time and direction. He is often found reading on a level much lower than that of which he is capable." The same is true of the average and below average student.

6. *Is the reading of nonassigned materials encouraged and rewarded?* Most

people feel more comfortable in clothes they select themselves. The same is true of reading matter. A carefully selected book or magazine is likely to command the reader's attention. Most teachers provide for students' self-selection of reading matter but often do not give the reading of self-selected materials the same status as the reading of assigned materials. Teachers evidence great concern for what a student learns from assigned reading; he is seldom permitted to make much of his free reading. And when tests are given and grades assigned or groups formed, the energy he puts into his free reading doesn't seem to count very much. Interest in a selection is a major factor in reading comprehension. Bernstein (1955) found that ninth-grade boys and girls who read two stories with equal readability difficulty but different interest levels read the more interesting story with superior comprehension. It would seem reasonable to expect similar results at all academic levels and with all kinds of reading materials. Students should be given opportunities to select and read materials that interest them. School programs which encourage pupils to read in the areas of their interests create situations conducive to effective reading.

7. *What kinds of activities are students involved in relative to their reading?* Speaking and writing are natural activities to precede or follow a reading experience. Talking about ideas and feelings heightens students' awareness of them, and writing makes students think. Using Sanders' guidelines, teachers can construct speaking and writing tasks that stimulate students to think about their reading at various cognitive levels and thereby experience a variety of affective responses to a reading selection. Group discussions about selections often result in attitude changes or the formation of new values. Oral reading to entertain or inform listeners who are without access to the selection often brings heightened understanding and appreciation of certain materials and the words and language patterns of the English language. Debates about ideas encountered in print force students to read critically, support assumptions with facts, and reason logically. Artistic illustrating of characters, ideas, or plot development stimulates total personal involvement in reading. Creative dramatics or modern dance permits student readers to express themselves about a reading selection. These and many other reading-related activities develop mature reading skills and habits in students at all academic levels.

Studies and observations of classroom interaction point up the absence of these kinds of activities in schools. Aschner (1963) studied verbal interaction in classrooms and reported that most interaction involved routine and cognitive memory. Next came convergent thinking, then evaluative thinking, and finally, least often, divergent thinking. Reading programs lacking reading-related activities that stimulate students to respond to their reading above the level of literal comprehension and to gain satisfaction from those responses are unlikely to produce mature readers. These activities should not be reserved for the "better" readers. All readers need them. Nor should they become Friday afternoon or the day before Christmas vacation or ". . . if we get time" activities. They must be taught regularly and precisely with the ultimate objective of the reading curriculum, utilization of reading for personal growth, clearly in sight.

The seven questions posed above might be used by administrators in their supervisory work with individual teachers, or to guide an entire staff concerned with the development of reading maturity. Although teachers generally acknowledge reading maturity for students as the ultimate objective of the reading program, they may find it difficult to change their behavior in the classroom so that this objective receives immediate attention. Too often, the kind of development in reading that is being discussed here is reserved for a future time that never arrives. Perhaps some teachers rely too heavily on the assumption that maturity in reading develops without special instruction when students become proficient in decoding the language and in literal comprehension. This assumption is undoubtedly true for some students. Unfortunately, the evidence cited earlier in this chapter suggests that for most students it is false. Administrators would be wise to convince their teachers that most students need to be taught to read maturely. Together, a teaching staff might arrive at a list of instructional practices likely to help students attain the desired level of reading ability.

References

Adler, Mortimer J. *How to Read a Book*. New York: Simon & Schuster, 1940.

Aschner, Mary Jane McCue. "An Analysis of Verbal Interaction in the Classroom." In *Theory and Research in Teaching*. New York: Bureau of Publications, Teachers College, Columbia University, 1963.

Ausubel, David P. "Some Psychological Aspects of the Structure of Knowledge." In Stanley Elan (Ed.), *Education and the Structure of Knowledge*. Chicago: Rand McNally, 1964.

Bernstein, Margery R. "Relationship Between Interest and Reading Comprehension." *Journal of Educational Research*, 1955, 49, 283–288.

Bloom, Benjamin S., *et al*. *Taxonomy of Educational Objectives. Handbook I: Cognitive Domain*. New York: McKay, 1956.

Eisner, Elliot. "Creativity and Psychological Health During Adolescence." *High School Journal*, 1965, 48, 465–473.

Gans, Roma. "Meeting the Challenge of the Middle Grades." In *What Is Reading Doing to the Child?* Highlights from the Sixteenth Annual Reading Conference of Lehigh University. Danville, Ill.: Interstate Printers and Publishers, 1967.

Guilford, J. P. "Frontiers in Thinking That Teachers Should Know About." *Reading Teacher*, 1960, 13, 176–182.

Hafter, Irma T., and Douglas, Frances M. "Inadequate College Readers." *Journal of Developmental Reading*, 1958, 1, 42–53.

Hayakawa, S. I. *Language in Thought and Action*. New York: Harcourt, Brace & World, 1949.

Jennings, Frank. *This Is Reading*. New York: Bureau of Publications, Teachers College, Columbia University, 1965.

Johnson, Wendell. *Your Most Enchanted Listener*. New York: Harper & Row, 1956.

Krathwohl, David R., *et al*. *Taxonomy of Educational Objectives. Handbook II: Affective Domain*. New York: McKay, 1964.

Laird, Charlton. *The Miracle of Language*. New York: Fawcett World Library, 1957.

Langer, Susanne K. "The Lord of Creation." In *The Borzoi College Reader*. New York: Knopf, 1966.

Lefevre, Carl A. *Linguistics and the Teaching of Reading.* New York: McGraw-Hill, 1964.

Lorge, Irving. "The Teacher's Task in the Development of Thinking." *Reading Teacher,* 1960, 13, 170–175.

Odland, Norine, and Therese Ilstrup. "Will Reading Teachers Read?" *Reading Teacher,* 1963, 17, 83–87.

Osenburg, F. C. "Concerning Objective Reading Tests: A Minority Opinion." *Journal of Developmental Reading,* 1962, 5, 275–279.

Russell, David H. *Children Learn to Read.* Boston: Ginn, 1961.

Sandburg, Carl. "Primer Lesson." In *Slabs of the Sunburnt West.* New York: Harcourt, Brace & World, 1922.

Sanders, Norris M. *Classroom Questions: What Kinds?* New York: Harper & Row, 1966.

Sheldon, William D. "Reading, a Facet of the Literate Person." *Journal of Education,* 1955, 138, 14–18.

Thorndike, Edward L. "Reading as Reasoning: A Study of Mistakes in Paragraph Reading." *Journal of Educational Psychology,* 1917, 8, 323–332.

CHAPTER 4

Reading and the Other Language Arts

Unlike the "cheese" in the children's singing game, reading does not stand alone. Reading is a language process and as such it is properly placed within the total language arts curriculum with writing, speaking, and listening.

Reading shares many characteristics with writing, speaking, and listening. Wheeler and Wheeler (1955) looked for similarities and differences among the language arts and reported finding the seventeen similarities that follow:

Thinking is carried on in terms of linguistic symbolism.

They are influenced by experiential background.

Progress checks are needed at all grade levels.

They are of important value to an individual's intellectual growth — building new concepts, new relationships, etc.

They need systematic instruction and opportunities for practice at all grade levels including pre-school through college.

Over-emphasis on technicalities such as grammar, spelling, pronunciation, etc., tends to impede general progress and efficiency.

Development depends upon associative learning powers.

Development is affected by maturity, or readiness.

Development depends upon opportunities for growth.

Development depends upon ability to synthesize these elements into total linguistic thought-patterns.

Development is affected by motivation — purpose, rapport, attitudes, environmental atmosphere, and general conditions of learning.

Development depends upon capacities for mental imagery — oral, aural, visual, kinaesthetic and tactile. In other words, development depends upon *memory* of word forms, meanings, and all other language elements.

They are affected by familiarity with the subject.

They are affected by vocabulary development.

They are affected by feelings, tensions, and other forms of emotions.

They are affected by ability to see relationships and organize ideas.

They are affected by personal tastes, interests, and levels of appreciation.

Wheeler and Wheeler concluded that

Certain of these [language skills] may become helpful to more than one of the arts "when transference is definitely taught," as in the process of seeing relationships, organizing thought units, critical evaluation, creative thinking, or punctuating according to thought units rather than blindly following rules.

In this chapter we shall discuss reading as a language process and show that growth in reading is one facet of a child's total language growth. A child's development in speaking, listening, and writing skills has a direct bearing on his reading ability. It follows that instruction in one of the language arts is beneficial to the other arts as well. It also follows that reading may be retarded by lack of development in the other arts. Loban (1963), for example, reported the results of the first seven years of a longitudinal study planned to follow 338 kindergarten children through Grade 12. He found that those children who were high in general language ability, as measured by vocabulary scores at the kindergarten level and language ratings by teachers, were also high in reading ability. His data also showed that the gap between students high in language ability and students low in language ability widens from year to year.

Reading and Language

Carroll (1964, p. 338) conceptualizes reading as a two-stage process of translation and comprehension. He describes the translation stage as being, "on the basis of the written message, the construction or reconstruction of a spoken message or some internal representation of it. . . ." Translation, then, is a matter of establishing the appropriate grapheme-phoneme relationships so that what began as meaningful sounds in the mind of the author is transmitted to a reader by graphemes representing those sounds. The reader associates the same sounds with the graphemes as the author did and in effect translates the printed symbols. The author encodes the message, and the reader decodes it.

Carroll (p. 344) also describes the comprehension stage in the reading process:

Comprehension, whether of speech or writing, is a process not completely understood and difficult to describe briefly, in any case. It can be described linguistically as a process of comprehending morphemes (minimal meaning units) and the grammatical constructions in which they occur. The lexical meaning of morphemes can be stated in terms of objective referents and their attributes and relationships; the meaning of grammatical constructions can be described in terms of structural relationships among persons, things and/or events in spatial and temporal configurations. The native speaker of a language normally acquires a wide range of both lexical and grammatical meanings without their having been explained to him. Problems of reading comprehension appear to arise mainly when texts contain lexical, grammatical, or ideational materials which happen to be outside the reader's repertoire.

Carroll equates reading with listening when he says, ". . . reading is a process of apprehending thought. This can also be well said of listening; there is no difference in principle between speech and writing with respect to the intellectual demands they make" (p. 345).

Lefevre (1964) contends that misapprehending the relationships between spoken and written language patterns is the most decisive element in reading failure. He regards the sentence, not the word, as the minimal meaning-producing element in the English language and discusses four meaning-bearing elements in English sentences: (1) word-form changes (*boy — boys — boy's; cold — colder — coldest; mention — mentionable — unmentionable*), (2) structure words (*in, because, and*), (3) syntactical-function order (*The doctor examined the lawyer. The lawyer examined the doctor*), and (4) intonation (**I** *don't like him. I don't like* **him.**) These four meaning-bearing elements were discussed in Chapter 3 and will be taken up again later in this chapter. Suffice it to say here that Lefevre and other linguists have provided evidence that although the English language has obvious irregularities it is basically highly systematic. For the teaching of reading, this systematic nature of English has implications at both the decoding stage and the comprehension stage; and the same implications hold for the teaching of writing, speaking, and listening. It is possible to state generalizations about decoding and comprehending English that are applicable to all of the language arts.

Both Carroll and Lefevre describe reading as a linguistic process that cannot be considered apart from speaking, listening, and writing. It is unfortunate that in school the language arts are often taught separately, thereby preventing the benefits that might come from a simultaneous development. We maintain that at all stages of reading development carefully coordinated listening, writing, and speaking activities will bring enhanced growth in reading. We do not claim that one may learn to read by being taught to listen, to write, or to speak. We do maintain that a person's reading ability is one part of his total language development and that the best results will be realized if the teaching of all four language arts is integrated. The remainder of this chapter is concerned with the contributions each of the other three language arts can make to growth in reading.

Reading and Listening

Horrworth (1967) defines listening as "the process of directing attention to and thereby becoming aware of sound sequences." To the term *auding* she gives a more precise definition: "the gross process of listening to, recognizing, and interpreting spoken symbols." From her interpretation of the research on listening she draws the following paradigm: "Auding = Hearing + Listening + Cognizing." While we recognize the need for a distinction between *listening* and *auding* for research purposes, we feel that it is appropriate to use the term *listening* to include hearing and cognizing for general discussion purposes.

Reading and listening are both receptor skills and involve essentially the same mental processes. The mental process in reading is triggered and maintained by visual stimuli, and the mental process in listening is triggered and maintained by auditory stimuli. With both, the ability to attend to the stimuli being transmitted according to the intent of the transmitter determines the productiveness of the activity. Thorndike's (1917, p. 326) description of correct reading seems equally applicable to listening:

In correct reading (1) each word produces a correct meaning, (2) each such element of meaning is given a correct weight in comparison with the others, and

(3) the resulting ideas are examined and validated to make sure that they satisfy the mental set or adjustment or purpose for whose sake the reading was done. Reading may be wrong or inadequate (1) because of wrong connections with the words singly, (2) because of over-potency or under-potency of elements, or (3) because of failure to treat the ideas produced by the reading as provisional, and so to inspect and welcome or reject them as they appear.

Empirical investigations have supported the hypothesis that listening and reading achievement are positively correlated. Cleland and Toussaint (1962) found that the STEP Listening Test showed a high positive correlation (.6679) with the Gates Reading Survey — Form II and with the Durrell-Sullivan Reading Capacity Test (.7030). There seems to be little doubt that training in listening can do more for reading growth than improve auditory discrimination and enlarge the hearing vocabulary. However, if training in listening is to affect reading ability, it seems important that such training be directed toward specific skills that are common to both listening and reading. For the majority of his subjects, Reddin (1968) found no significant effect of listening instruction on reading to identify main idea, on reading to note details, and on ability to read critically. However, the instruction he provided consisted of a series of eighteen lessons which utilized a variety of approaches and materials. The amount of direct instruction in the skills measured may have been considerably less than was needed. Kelty (1954) found that fourth-grade students who were given practice in listening to note details improved significantly in their ability to read for purpose. She also found that training in listening to find the main idea and to draw conclusions resulted in positive, but not significant, changes in her subjects' abilities to read for those purposes.

Although the evidence available is not completely clear-cut regarding the direct effect of listening instruction on reading ability, we believe that listening skills can be taught so that they transfer to reading experiences. The transfer may not be immediate and direct, but ultimately, over a period of time, concepts such as listening for purpose, organizing ideas while listening, and making inferences while listening will be attained and applied to reading by most students. Therefore, systematic teaching of listening skills that are applicable to reading experiences is likely to improve reading performance.

For most people, listening is the major avenue for learning. Numerous studies of classroom interaction have shown an inordinate amount of teacher talk and pupil listening. Anderson (1965, p. 80) comments,

No one questions the importance of listening as a means of learning for boys and girls. Paul Rankin's pioneering study showed that high school students in Detroit spent 30 per cent of the time they devote to language each day in speaking, 16 per cent in reading, 9 per cent in writing and 45 per cent in listening. Dr. Miriam Wilt more recently found that elementary school children spent about 2½ hours of the five-hour school day in listening.

Rankin's study was reported in 1928 and Wilt's in 1950. With the increased use of audio aids such as tape recordings, phonograph records, films, and television, listening skills are becoming more and more important.

The need for listening instruction is apparent. In addition to being a major learning tool, listening contributes to reading ability. However, of all the language arts, it probably receives the least systematic, precise, regular instruction. After a review of the literature relative to the attention given listening in the school curriculum, Dixon (1964) concludes,

> From the appearance of the first research on listening in 1917 to the present, the record of the place of listening among the language arts is a chronicle of neglect. Overlooking listening is accentuated by its preeminence as a phase of communication. The momentous impact of listening competence in the lives of children and adults — and especially in contemporary international affairs — demands that it be raised from its low estate to a place of prominence in educational research and in the curriculum.

As listening instruction comes to play a larger role in the language arts curriculum and as better instruments and methods are developed for researching its effects on reading achievement, the relationship between listening instruction and reading ability will probably become more clear-cut. At the present time there is enough subjective and objective evidence that listening instruction affects reading ability in a positive way to warrant suggesting some specific instructional practices designed to improve listening ability and enhance growth in reading. To our knowledge, none of the suggestions that follow has been subjected to controlled research. All are drawn from the teaching experience of the writers, classroom observations, and dialogue with teachers judged to be exemplary language arts teachers. They are meant to illustrate practices that cause skills common to both listening and reading to transfer from listening to reading experiences. Essentially, we are suggesting ways to integrate listening and reading activities so that development in both listening and reading skills is served. Creative teachers and administrators will be able to add other proposals, perhaps from their own experiences. Three things should be noted about the suggestions presented here: (1) Each lesson is directed to a single listening skill that is also a reading skill, (2) the selection and task used to teach a particular listening skill are similar to the selection and task to which transfer is desired, and (3) with some modifications, the suggestions may be employed in either elementary or secondary schools.

Listening for the Main Idea

Both listening and reading require the student to identify main ideas and hold them apart from supporting information. This process of organization aids comprehension and recall. A major objective of listening and reading instruction is to teach students to identify main ideas as they are presented within a communication.

One teacher arranged a fifteen-minute tape-recorded conversation with the school principal. The principal's hometown, his education, his motives for becoming an administrator, his philosophy of education, and other things were discussed. When the tape was played to the teacher's sixth-grade students, they were asked to listen carefully and note the major topics. At the conclusion of the interview they were asked to write a headline for each major topic discussed as if the topic were to be developed as a human interest story in a newspaper. Headlines such as the following were produced.

School Principal Formerly Math Teacher
Present Educational System Not Meeting Needs of Creative Students
Small Schools Better for Meeting Student Needs

After this listening experience the students read a short biography and discussed orally and in writing the main events in the life of the subject and his attitudes toward various social issues. The teacher felt that the students' ability to select the most significant elements in the biography was improved by the listening experience that preceded the reading.

Listening for Cause-Effect Relationships

The ability to note cause-effect relationships while listening and reading is a necessary study skill in all content areas of the curriculum.

Before his students read a chapter in their social studies textbook dealing with legislation passed during the progressive era, one teacher provided a listening experience designed to alert them to cause-effect relationships in their reading. In a series of tape-recorded interviews with local aldermen he asked the aldermen to discuss the reasons they had voted as they had on certain issues. As they listened, the students noted the specific factors which had influenced the way the men voted. The students then read the assigned chapter in their text, presumably with more skill in noting the causes for enacting specific legislation during the progressive era.

Listening for Purpose

In general, students who know something about what they are going to listen to or read and who know what they want to get from their listening or reading are likely to be more successful with these activities than students who do not. Many teachers at various academic levels teach the formula for productive listening that appears in materials published by Science Research Associates, Inc., Chicago, Illinois, in much the same way they teach the formula for productive reading, also included with SRA materials. The similarities between the two formulas are obvious, and it is apparent that they may be used to reinforce each other:

For Listening	*For Reading*
T (Tune in)	S (Survey)
Q (Question)	Q (Question)
L (Listen)	R (Read)
R (Review)	R (Recite)
	R (Review)

Listening for Facts

Getting the facts is important in most listening and reading experiences, especially those that are school related. Practice in listening for facts may help students read for facts. For example, a science teacher might tape-record a number of detailed descriptions of products or processes without directly naming them, and ask students to identify the products or processes. If these listening exercises were presented with some regularity, they would provide excellent opportunities for improving the ability to listen for factual details. It would be a simple matter for the teacher to show the similarity between the details presented orally and those presented in reading assignments. In this way students would be kept aware of the need to pay close attention to factual detail in scientific reading matter and would have regular practice in doing so.

Reacting to Intonation

A major meaning-bearing element in English sentences is intonation. Much of the meaning people get from listening to spoken English is derived from the speaker's intonations, which Lefevre (1964) refers to as the "melody" of the language. The English writing system, except for a few punctuation marks, does not provide the reader with directions for supplying intonations. To obtain meaning from written English, he must supply the appropriate intonations from his knowledge of English language intonation patterns. He must recognize, then, that the language he reads is the same language he listens to and that supplying intonation is necessary to reading comprehension.

The market is rich with phonograph records and tape recordings of short selections and entire books. These recordings are sometimes effective in helping students establish the proper relationship between spoken and written language. Teachers may improve their students' reading performance with a given selection by having them listen to the recorded version of the selection before they read or by having them silently read along with the recording.

Just a few instructional practices have been presented to show the possibilities open to creative teachers who wish to integrate listening and reading for the benefit of both arts. The sound tracks of movies, records of Broadway musicals, audio recordings of television shows, and sound effects records are some other media available to most classroom teachers.

Reading and Writing

Whether instruction in writing will improve students' reading ability is determined essentially by the quality of that instruction. O'Donnell (1963) questioned whether there is a higher correlation between reading comprehension and awareness of structural relationships of words and sentences than between reading comprehension and the ability to verbalize grammatical rules and terminology. His subjects were given the Cooperative Test of Reading Comprehension, the Iowa Grammar Information Test, and a Test of Recognition of Structural Relationships in English constructed by the author. A higher correlation (.75) was found between the test of sentence structure and the Iowa Grammar Test than between reading comprehension and knowledge of sentence structure (.44). O'Donnell concluded that the relationship between the tests was not sufficiently high to support a conclusion that teaching linguistic structure would develop reading comprehension, nor was it conclusively shown that such teaching would not. In another study O'Donnell (1962) prepared a test to measure awareness of sentence structure and studied the performance of 101 high school seniors upon this test and upon the Cooperative Test of Reading Comprehension and the Iowa Grammar Information Test. Moderate correlations were found to exist between reading comprehension and awareness of sentence structure (.44) and grammar (.46) and between vocabulary and awareness of structure (.46). A correlation of .90 was found between vocabulary and awareness of grammar. O'Donnell concluded that the good reader must be consciously or unconsciously aware of the basic structural relationships of words in sentences.

Gibbons (1941) studied the relationship between third-grade children's ability to understand the structure of sentences and their reading achievement. She found a correlation of .89 between the ability to see the relationship between parts of a sentence and the ability to understand the sentence. A correlation of .72 was found between ability to see the relationship between sentence parts and total achievement in reading. Gibbons' study corroborates Thorndike's (1917) study cited earlier in this chapter and in Chapter 3. The ability to respond correctly to relationships within and between sentences is all-important to good reading comprehension. Squire (1965) points out that consciousness of form in reading any literary work is vital. He says, "Research suggests that those who are able to observe form in their own writing are best able to perceive it in the writing of others." He also says, "Awareness of the form of English sentences is thus increasingly seen as a foundation for effective communication, but awareness of sentence form, not an awareness of grammatical generalizations." If by teaching writing we mean teaching students to recognize the parts of speech and different sentence patterns, it seems safe to predict that the instruction will have little if any positive effect on their reading. On the other hand, if we teach writing as a thinking process emphasizing logic and rhetoric and providing ample opportunity for constructing communicative sentences and paragraphs, reading ability will probably be improved. Strang (1967, p. 151) says, "Practice in constructing clear paragraphs is a good prelude to improving paragraph comprehension."

Reading, Writing, Thinking

Adler (1940, p. 111) comments, "Thinking usually tends to express itself overtly in language. One tends to verbalize ideas, questions, difficulties, judgments that occur in the course of thinking. If you have been reading, you must have been thinking; you have something you can express in words." The point to be made here is that expressing in writing ideas that are relevant to a reading selection will sharpen a reader's interpretation of the selection and heighten his awareness of the relationship between language structure, vocabulary, and reading comprehension. It will also give him practice in the basic ingredient in reading comprehension: thinking. Burack (1965) says, "We ask our students to write because writing makes them think. . . . Writing is ultimately an exercise in logic. . . . For some of our students writing will mean the freeing of the intellect. For some it will be the disciplining of that intellect." In a discussion of the "superior" reader, Sheldon (1955) deplores the fact that teachers settle for too little from students who have had a reading experience:

> In the area of perceptual and conceptual development, the teacher can aid this child in a refinement of his concepts and percepts rather than adding continuously to unrefined percepts and concepts. This individual has a need to clarify in a precise fashion the concepts which he adds to his understanding. He also needs to spend more time in considering the classification and application of what he has read to what he is going to do. This is the individual who needs to develop the art of summarization. He also needs to be taught how to gather material relative to a topic while weeding out material which is not relevant. He then needs to be taught to write this material in a precise and clear manner.

No one would dispute the position that the reading process is ultimately the thinking process, and there seems to be widespread agreement that writing is a means of improving thinking.

Writing has been used successfully to stimulate thinking about a reading selection at desired cognitive levels. Smith (1968) found that one kind of writing task could be constructed to elicit Interpretation-level thinking and another to elicit Synthesis-level thinking about the same short story. Smith and Barter (1968) found the same to be true of a social studies article. The writing tasks were based on the selections, studied by the students before they read the selection and completed by them after the reading. The written products manifested thinking about the reading selection at the cognitive levels desired. The studies by Smith and by Smith and Barter show that a carefully constructed writing task may be used to affect significantly a student's reading experience with a particular selection.

Neither the instructional practices that were suggested relative to development in listening and reading nor those proposed here for effecting transfer between development in writing and development in reading have been validated by research. They are based on the teaching experience of the writers, observations of good teachers at work, and dialogue with teachers. The recommended practices are directed at using writing activities to help the student (1) understand that there is unity and logic in writing and (2) respond more accurately to the following meaning-bearing elements in English sentences: word-form changes, syntactical-function order, structure words, and intonation. The four elements are those identified by Lefevre (1964) (see the discussion in Chapter 3). Undoubtedly, writing instruction can be helpful in developing reading ability in more ways than are indicated here. It is to be hoped that the following practices will be used by teachers not only as described but also with modifications to fit different materials and to satisfy different objectives. Again, several things should be noted about them: (1) Each writing activity is closely associated with a particular reading activity (Pooley [1961, p. 48] says of this practice, "So far as possible, artificial barriers between the two types of activities should be removed, allowing the child to advance and mature in the conviction that what is written is meant to be read and what is read becomes the substance or the point of departure for writing"); (2) each writing activity emphasizes one element that is common to both writing and reading (i.e., properly relating words and word groups, following a logical sequence, manifesting an awareness of changes in meaning produced by changes in word forms, etc.); and (3) with modifications, most of the suggested instructional practices are applicable at different academic levels.

Writing with Unity and Logic

A senior high school English teacher asked his students to complete a sentence beginning with "I believe modern science. . . ." When they had done that, he asked them to write several more sentences, each of which offered a supporting reason for their specific beliefs. When they had completed their writing, they read Philip Wylie's short essay "Science Has Spoiled My Supper," in which he argues that today's scientifically processed and packaged foods are poor substitutes for yesterday's garden-to-table or oven-to-table victuals. The teacher felt that his students were more alert to the paragraph-by-paragraph development of Wylie's thesis because of their own recently written statement and support of thesis.

Writing and Word-Form Changes

Word-form changes are not plentiful in the English language, but they are exceedingly important to accurate interpretation. Whether Mary was happy or *un*happy with her new teacher would be crucial to anticipating her behavior in the rest of a story. Word-form changes which signal possession (*'s*), plurality (*s*), past time (*ed*), superlative (*est*), etc., are vital to meaning.

Lack of attention to word-form changes and incorrect interpretation of word-form changes are common among low-ability readers, as their oral reading gives frequent evidence. Preliminary to a reading lesson with students having difficulty noting and responding correctly to word-form changes, a teacher might identify the changes likely to give trouble in the lesson to be read and prepare students for them. A list of sentences such as the following could be presented prior to the reading. Writing the correct word in each space would help alert the students for encountering similar word-form changes in their reading.

John is _____ than Bill.

(whose) _____ dog bit the mailman.

Three _____ raced around the track.

Of all the bicycles hers was the _____ .

Mary was as happy as Sue was (prefix) _____ .

Writing and Syntactical-Function Order

English is a word-order language. Depending upon their placement in a sentence, words and word groups give rise to certain images. For example, the difference between "His dog bit Henry" and "Henry bit his dog" is considerable. A more sophisticated example of the necessity for observing the rules of syntax is the following: "Walking into the dentist's office, his heart pounded wildly." Consider the likelihood of misinterpretation on the part of a reader not keenly aware of the syntactical signals in this excerpt from a magazine article:

It was an ungainly bird with long, droopy wings, but it could fly incredibly high, cruising at more than 50,000 feet as a matter of routine and even reaching 70,000 feet. The United States dubbed it the U-2 — the "U" stood for "utility" — and said it was a weather-research plane. Actually, the high-flying machine was designed as a "sky-spy," and assigned to carry out high-altitude reconnaissance missions over the Soviet Union and other Communist countries for the Central Intelligence Agency. Built in an incredible 80 days by Lockheed Aircraft's Clarence (Kelly) Johnson at the company's super-secret "Skunk Works," the plane flew unmolested over Russian territory from 1956 to 1960 gathering information on Soviet radar and missile installations.[1]

The reader of English must respond to many different syntactical patterns. His awareness of the need to have a variety of responses and his accuracy in responding can be increased through writing exercises that allow him to manipulate words and word groups. From his comparisons of the language used by elementary school children low in general language proficiency and elementary school children high in general language proficiency Loban (1963, p. 88) concluded,

Not basic sentence pattern but what is done to achieve flexibility within pattern proves to be a measure of proficiency with language at this level. Since formal instruction in grammar — whether linguistic or traditional — seems to be an ineffective method of improving expression at this level of development, one can conclude that elementary pupils need many opportunities to grapple with their own thought in situations where they have someone to whom they wish to communicate successfully. Instruction can best aid the pupils' expression when individuals or small groups with similar problems are helped to see how their own expression can be improved. This instruction would take the form of identifying elements which strengthen or weaken communication, increase or lower precision of thought, clarify or blur meanings.

For this instruction to be of maximum benefit the student must (1) know the purpose of the exercises and (2) have opportunities to discuss the different interpretations that may be given to the sentences he constructs when he puts words in different positions.

An exercise used by many teachers is the one in which students are asked to write the word *only* in different places in the sentence *I love you*. Another simple

[1] *Newsweek,* February 17, 1969, p. 20.

practice is to have students write a sentence using a word such as *stone*. Sentences like the following are almost always produced:

Stone the criminal.
They built a *stone* wall.
The *stone* was heavy.
He tripped over the *stone*.

It is, then, relatively easy to help students learn inductively that where a word is positioned in a sentence is a major factor in how the word functions.

More mature students may be asked to write two sentences with different meanings using only the following words and word groups:

the men   running   moved   before them   into the battle
  the horses   like the wind

The resulting sentences may communicate quite different ideas:

Like the wind the running horses moved the men into the battle before them.
Running like the wind the men moved the horses before them into the battle.

Enterprising teachers will be able to supply many more writing exercises of this type.

Writing and Structure Words

Although structure words have been called "empty" words because they have no content, they carry the burden of meaning in English sentences. They signal the all-important relationships among words and word groups. As words in the English language continue to lose their meaning-bearing inflections, structure words become increasingly important.

Typically, teachers do less teaching about structure words than about other words. Teachers spend considerable time discussing and building experiential backgrounds for words such as *supermarket, elephant,* and *train*. Much less emphasis is given to *because, when between,* etc. Consequently, readers may interpret individual content words correctly but fail to put them together correctly to produce the meaning intended by an author.

One teacher uses short writing exercises to help students understand the important functions performed by structure words and to get them to pay close attention to structure words encountered in their reading. Periodically, before a reading assignment, this teacher dictates a statement to his students — for example, "Pete was angry. . . ." Then he asks the students to complete the sentence by answering why Pete was angry — Pete was angry *because* Bill stole his girl. Or he may ask them to add something equally important to his statement — Pete was angry, *and* the chairman was asking for a motion to adjourn. Or he may ask what happened because of it — Pete was angry; *therefore,* the party was a flop. Obviously, this kind of activity can be varied by using different statements and having students complete them or introduce them in different ways. The activity may be carried on in a light, humorous atmosphere, with students sharing their additions to the teacher's statements with each other, or it may be conducted in a serious vein, with each student's additions kept to himself. It may also be modified to meet the needs of students at various academic levels and to be pertinent to specific subjects in content area classes.

Writing and Intonation

Rate, pitch, and stress are important elements in the communication of ideas. With the exception of a few punctuation marks, the English writing system does not provide the reader with intonation marks. He must understand that the language he sees is the same language he hears and supply the appropriate intonations from his knowledge of the melodies of different sentence patterns. One characteristic of poor readers is the lack of appropriate expression in their oral reading. It may be assumed that this is typical of their silent reading as well. Writing may be used to help students understand the relationship between spoken and written language and read both orally and silently with meaningful expression.

Having students write short papers to be read orally is one way to help readers with limited expression become more aware of the relationship between the spoken language and the written language. These writing tasks should concern themselves with matters which the student feels strongly about. A younger student may be encouraged to write about his recent birthday party, how he felt when he had the mumps, or a scary walk home from an evening movie. Older students may write position papers such as "In Protest of the Present Grading System," "The Inconsiderate Adult," and "In Defense of Nonconformity." It is relatively easy for teachers to collect similar selections written by other authors for the students to read silently after they have read their own products orally.

Writing editorials and letters to the editor for magazines and newspapers is good practice for developing expressive reading. Students may be told to think, write, and then read what they have written to themselves. Students following this procedure have been observed making appropriate facial expressions and hand gestures as they read their editorials and letters to themselves.

Writing scripts to be read for a live audience or into a tape recorder is helpful in developing expressive readers. Students working in groups of three or four may profit from writing dialogue and rehearsing their parts with one another. The advantage of having dialogue written by a student to be read by himself is that the dialogue fits his own personality.

Reading and Speaking

There is substantial evidence that oral language development is the base upon which development in reading is built. The child who is unable to articulate the sounds of his language and orally express his ideas in the sentence patterns of his language is not a good candidate for reading instruction. Strickland (1963) says,

Oral language, speech, holds the primary position in any consideration of language. Psychologists have shown that when one writes or reads something an act of inner speech takes place but is inhibited at the level of muscular performance. Writing is simply a way of representing speech and our systems of orthography are always incomplete and inaccurate in their representation of spoken language. We write using letters which represent sounds. The act of reading involves recognizing the sounds which the letters represent, putting meaning into them, and reacting to that meaning. It is a matter of using the stimulus of the marks on the page to recreate speech.

Students are unable to re-create speech they don't have in their oral vocabulary. The base for reading, then, is speech. We agree with those who would postpone reading instruction until the child's oral language is reasonably well developed. For some students this may mean extended readiness activities; for others it may mean specialized instruction by speech teachers rather than reading instruction.

From his study of children ranking extremely high in language proficiency and children ranking extremely low in language proficiency Loban (1963, p. 88) concluded,

> . . . the superiority of the high group in handling oral signals effectively — their skill at using pitch, stress, and pause — combined with their relative freedom from using partial structural patterns is impressive. It would be difficult not to conclude that instruction can yet do more than it has with oral language. Many pupils who lack skill in using speech will have difficulty in mastering written tradition. Competence in spoken language appears to be a necessary base for competence in writing and reading.

Strickland (1963) did a three-year study of the informal speech of elementary school children, concluding that children will profit from manipulating words and sentences. She says,

> The run-on sentences characteristic of many young children and the choppy or incomplete sentences of others are evidence of need for help in putting ideas together into well-knit and logical sentence schemes. A teacher might pick up from time to time a sentence or some ideas used by a child and encourage the group to find ways to express those ideas in better form. Children might write the kernel sentences on slips of paper, write their individual responses to such questions as what, when, why, where, or how, attach them to the kernel in a variety of ways and read their sentences aloud for the reaction of the group. The tests for a good sentence would be, "Does it make sense?" "Does it say what you mean?" "Does it sound right?" . . . Consider also the improvement in oral reading which might result from experience with manipulating pitch and stress in sentences of the children's own devising. Children whose oral reading is poor show little skill in turning the stimulus of the printed words into meaningful speech. Children are intrigued to discover how one changes meaning by the way in which he handles pitch and stress in such a question as, "Are you going tonight?" Such understanding would almost inevitably improve comprehension in silent reading as well.

Some specific instructional practices proposed by Strickland have been briefly described. Others are suggested here to serve as illustrations to help teachers devise some of their own. Like those recommended previously, they derive from our classroom experience, observations of good teachers at work, and dialogue with teachers. Obviously, some oral language activities that affect reading ability, such as responding with the correct phonemes to presented graphemes, are appropriate only to beginning readers. We are not concerned with them at this point. Nor are we concerned with specialized instruction for students with speech defects or for students who are learning English as a second language. The suggested practices are designed to improve the oral language of students for whom more practice and more precision with speech is likely to result in more accurate reading. With some modifications, these practices may be used with students at various academic levels.

The Language Experience Approach

This method of teaching reading uses speaking in close association with reading and may be modified to fit the needs of students at different academic levels. In beginning reading it requires the teacher to stimulate children to talk about an experience they have shared. As they talk, the teacher writes their sentences on a chalkboard or a chart. The children then read what they have spoken and heard. Wilt (1968) says of this method,

> In the transitional stage between speaking and listening the encoding of the child's own ideas and thoughts into visual symbols that he as well as others can see and understand is probably one of the most significant discoveries the child will ever make. Say it, see it, read it. A cycle that ties experience into the very core of the child's being helps him to bridge the gap from talking to written-down speech.

Teachers at academic levels through the senior high school may use the language experience approach to strengthen both speaking and reading skills. One senior high school English teacher divides her class into groups of four or five students. A "recorder" is appointed by the teacher for each group — the only one in the group permitted to write. Each group is given the task of producing a logical paragraph. Sometimes the assignment is to produce a paragraph that takes issue with an existing school policy. Sometimes it is to describe a picture, describe a common experience, or narrate an amusing happening. The recorder writes down the sentences exactly as the students speak them. Later each group's paragraph is read orally by a member of the group other than the recorder. With practice, the students become quite skillful at producing coherent sentences in logical sequence.

Developing Intonation Awareness

That misapprehending the relationships between written and spoken language is the *most* decisive element in reading failure, as Lefevre (1964) contends, is debatable. However, certainly many poor readers lack a "feel" for the language, manifested by their inability to read orally with expression and proper phrasing.

One teacher has her students vary their intonations to have a single sentence communicate different ideas. For example, depending upon the speaker's rate, pitch, and stress, the horse in the following sentence could be either a winner or a loser:

He was a real sight coming down the stretch — what a horse!

It is not difficult for teachers to construct other sentences that may be used for the same purpose. After they attain the concept, students enjoy making up their own sentences and having other students read them according to their individual interpretations. Discussions of the context surrounding a particular interpretation are worthwhile additions to this activity.

Play Reading

Reading through plays orally is a speech activity that is likely to improve silent reading as well as oral reading. Some teachers maintain classroom collections of plays and periodically give groups of students opportunities to read through a scene, an act, or an entire play for the other members of the class. Since a variety of plays is readily available, it is often possible to find a play with a "just right" part for a student who needs a particular kind of reading experience. It is important for the students who read the play to have opportunities for silent reading and rehearsals before reading to an audience. Students should not be asked to read for an audience without preparation. Nor should the audience "follow along" in books or duplicated scripts while the players read. The responsibility for communicating the playwright's message should rest entirely with the oral readers. Obviously, they must understand the author's intent and how each speech contributes to the total development of the play.

There is also merit in having students read short plays or episodes they write themselves. Certainly, this is more time-consuming and requires additional instruction. Perhaps writing and reading their own plays is more beneficial for younger students and for those with retarded reading ability than for older students and for good readers. It is sometimes difficult to find published plays that younger students and poor readers can read successfully. Therefore, they perform better and achieve better results when they write and read their own. Older students and good readers, on the other hand, encounter little difficulty with a play written by a professional author; and they enjoy the overall quality of a published play.

Other Oral Reading

The role of oral reading in the language arts program has been a controversial subject. Some educators recommend frequent oral reading as an instructional practice to improve both oral and silent reading. Others recommend oral reading only for diagnostic purposes and audience situations. The latter are in vogue at present although there are signs that using oral reading to develop silent reading skills is making a comeback. Like most controversies, the truth probably lies somewhere in between. We believe that oral reading does promote good silent reading and recommend it be used for that purpose more frequently than we typically observe its use in the classrooms we visit. We hastily add a note of censure to the "round robin" procedure in which students take turns reading orally while other students follow along with their copies of the selection. Oral reading for diagnostic purposes should be a relatively private affair, and oral reading to entertain or inform should be prepared ahead of time and presented to an audience that is listening, not following along. With those conditions in mind we reiterate our recommendation for increased opportunities for students to read orally at all academic levels.

Most authorities agree that oral reading is essential in beginning reading in-struction. The child needs to learn the relationship between the spoken language and the written language, and the teacher needs to be keenly aware of the child's thought processes as he reads and of his reading skills development. The necessity for oral reading experiences decreases as the child becomes an inde-pendent reader. He no longer has to respond to the printed symbols vocally, and the teacher can measure his progress in ways other than listening to him read. However, he can continue to benefit from oral reading even though oral reading should take proportionately less of the time devoted to reading instruction than it did in the beginning stages.

Short selections, ranging from several sentences to several paragraphs, are probably better than long ones for oral reading: They can be prepared in less time, and most students are unable to sustain a fluent performance beyond a few paragraphs. It is important to the objectives of reading improvement that the oral reading be done well.

Teachers at all academic levels and in all content areas might clip short selections from newspapers, magazines, old textbooks, and other sources. The entire passage need not be read orally. The teacher might tell the content of the selection to the concluding paragraph or paragraphs and have a prepared student read the rest to the class.

Teachers might also maintain collections of short selections or excerpts from selections that treat a particular topic. Several students might be given different selections to prepare and read to the class, thereby providing oral reading experi-ences of short duration and at the same time covering a topic in some depth.

Somehow, teachers have come to believe that if anything important needs to be read to the class, they and not their students should read it. Students soon learn that what they are given to read orally will probably not be "in the test." Consequently, they do not view oral reading done by students as being of much worth. The result is shoddy oral reading and inattentive listening. Teachers can change this attitude by giving students proof that what the latter read orally is of major import to the goals of the class.

Attitudes Toward Reading

The importance of developing positive attitudes toward reading cannot be over-emphasized: Skills are learned better when attitudes toward learning them are positive, and they are utilized better when attitudes toward reading are positive. The National Council of Teachers of English (1956, p. 129) is explicit in asserting that "If the study of literature does not provide enjoyment, the teaching has been a failure." This assertion might be applied to the entire reading program. If students do not develop positive attitudes toward reading while they are learning to read, the teaching is a failure.

We believe that integrating the teaching of reading, writing, speaking, and listening is conducive to the development of positive attitudes toward using the language arts for functional and recreational purposes. With an integrated approach it is possible to use writing, speaking, and listening not only to reinforce reading skills but also to provide enjoyable reading-related experiences.

An attitude has been defined by Allport (1964) as a "set" or "readiness" to respond to a particular object with positive or negative behavior. Since attitudes have intensity as well as direction, a child may choose to read for enjoyment, but only, say, when the television set is broken. It is true that attitudes are predispositions to behave in particular ways, but they do not necessitate behavior. A student, for example, may have a positive attitude toward reading poetry but not read it because of his fear of being teased by his peers or by an older sibling.

The behavior being sought by teachers who strive to develop positive attitudes toward reading has been categorized by Krathwohl et al. (1964) as "Willingness to Respond." Many familiar educational objectives fall within this category:

Voluntarily reads magazines and newspapers. (Chooses to read when options for using leisure time are presented.)
Voluntarily uses reading to find information about his environment.

When students develop positive attitudes toward reading, it is up to the teacher to maintain them. Since we tend to repeat experiences which have given us pleasure and avoid experiences which have been unpleasant, the teacher's task is to help the student obtain a personal fulfillment or satisfaction from his reading. Krathwohl et al. categorize this behavior as "Satisfaction in Response." Familiar educational objectives that fall within this category are the following:

Finds pleasure in reading for recreation.
Enjoys reading books on a variety of themes.
Appreciates good literature.

Regarding attitude development, then, the teacher's task is twofold: (1) She must motivate students to read and (2) she must help students obtain satisfaction from their reading. The other language arts may be used to help the teacher reach this twofold goal.

Before reading a particular selection, students can be involved in writing, speaking, and listening activities that motivate them to read with purpose and interest. After the selection has been read, other writing, speaking, and listening activities may be used to help them utilize their reading in enjoyable ways. Activities presented before reading should arouse interest and stimulate purposeful reading; those presented after reading should provide enjoyable reading-related tasks. Activities which do not meet these requirements are likely to cause students to develop negative rather than positive attitudes toward reading. Teachers who use the other language arts to build positive attitudes toward reading, therefore, must know their students' interests and abilities well, assign reading selections that match them, and construct reading-related activities accordingly.

Writing Tasks

Writing tasks may be used effectively to motivate students to read a particular selection. The tasks may be assigned and completed before reading or assigned before reading to be completed afterward. An example of the former is the following:

Write a short paragraph telling what you would do if a boy new to your school tried to take over. Would you tell the "big shot" off, avoid him, poke him in the nose, or what? What should happen to a fellow who won't stop showing off? When you have finished your paragraph, read "Rah Rah Roger."

An example of a writing task assigned before reading to be completed after reading is the following:

In the story "Rah Rah Roger" a boy who transfers to a new school makes a fool of himself. After you finish reading the story, write a statement that you feel would have put Roger in his place had it been said to him by a fellow student at some point during the story. Be ready to read your statement and tell at what point in the story it would have been most effective.

It is possible that writing tasks relative to a reading selection that are assigned after reading may cause students to develop positive attitudes toward the selection. However, our experience suggests that tasks assigned prior to reading are more productive of positive attitudes toward a selection than those assigned later. This is an area that is in need of much research.

Listening and Speaking Experiences

One of the present writers conducted a highly successful reading-related listening and speaking activity with high-ability ninth-grade English students. The literary selection to be read was Edgar Allan Poe's "The Fall of the House of Usher." Because of Poe's style students frequently find reading him a chore rather than a pleasure. The class period preceding the reading of the story was spent listening to music and discussing the visual imagery it evoked. Parts of the *Peer Gynt Suite, Sonata Pathetique, Grand Canyon Suite,* and other musical selections likely to invoke a response similar to the desired response to Poe's story were played and discussed by the students, who were then asked to read the story and note where certain music seemed to "fit." After reading, volunteers prepared taped readings of sections of the story with fitting background music. Most of the students genuinely enjoyed "The Fall of the House of Usher" and asked to read other stories by Poe.

Teachers at all academic levels should be encouraged to construct interesting reading-related language arts activities. The development of positive attitudes toward reading must be an educational objective vigorously pursued by all teachers. Our schools are producing too many students who are skillful readers but who never choose to read for pleasure.

References

Adler, Mortimer J. *How to Read a Book*. New York: Simon & Schuster, 1940.

Allport, Gordon W. *Pattern and Growth in Personality*. New York: Holt, Rinehart & Winston, 1964.

Anderson, Paul L. *Language Skills in Elementary Education*. New York: Macmillan, 1965.

Burack, Boris. "Composition: Why? What? How?" *English Journal*, 1965, 54, 504–506.

Carroll, John B. "The Analysis of Reading Instruction: Perspectives from Psychology and Linguistics." In *Theories of Learning and Instruction*. The Sixty-Third Yearbook of the National Society for the Study of Education. Chicago: University of Chicago Press, 1964.

Cleland, Donald L., and Isabella H. Toussaint. "The Interrelationships of Reading, Listening, Arithmetic, Computation and Intelligence." *Reading Teacher*, 1962, 15, 228–231.

Commission of the English Curriculum of the National Council of Teachers of English. *The English Language Arts in the Secondary School*. New York: Appleton-Century-Crofts, 1956.

Dixon, Norman R. "Listening: Most Neglected of the Language Arts." *Elementary English*, 1964, 41, 285–288.

Gibbons, Helen D. "Reading and Sentence Elements." *Elementary English Review*, 1941, 18, 42–46.

Horrworth, Gloria L. "Listening: A Facet of Oral Language." In *Research in Oral Language*. Champaign, Ill.: National Council of Teachers of English, 1967, pp. 40–49.

Kelty, Annette P. "An Experimental Study to Determine the Effect of Listening for Certain Purposes upon Achievement in Reading for These Purposes." *Abstracts of Field Studies for the Degree of Doctor of Education*. Greeley: Colorado State College of Education, 1954, vol. 15.

Krathwohl, David R., *et al. Taxonomy of Educational Objectives. Handbook II: Affective Domain*. New York: McKay, 1964.

Lefevre, Carl A. *Linguistics and the Teaching of Reading*. New York: McGraw-Hill, 1964.

Loban, Walter D. *The Language of Elementary School Children*. Champaign, Ill.: National Council of Teachers of English, 1963.

O'Donnell, Roy. "Awareness of Grammatical Structure and Reading Comprehension." *High School Journal*, 1962, 45, 184–188.

O'Donnell, Roy C. "A Study of the Correlation Between Awareness of Structural Relationships in English and Ability in Reading Comprehension." *Journal of Experimental Education*, 1963, 31, 313–316.

Pooley, Robert C. "Reading and the Language Arts." In *Development in and Through Reading*. Chicago: University of Chicago Press, 1961.

Reddin, Estoy. "Listening Instruction, Reading and Critical Thinking." *Reading Teacher*, 1968, 21, 645–658.

Sheldon, William D. "Reading, a Facet of the Literate Person." *Journal of Education*, 1955, 138, 14–18.

Smith, Richard J. "The Effect of Reading for a Creative Purpose on Student Attitudes Toward a Short Story." *Research in the Teaching of English*, 1968, 2, 142–151.

Smith, Richard J., and Clinton R. Barter. "The Effects of Reading for Two Particular Purposes." *Journal of Reading*, 1968, 12, 134–138.

Squire, James R. "Form Consciousness, an Important Variable in Teaching Language, Literature and Composition." *Elementary English*, 1965, 42, 379–389.

Strang, Ruth. "Teaching Reading to the Culturally Disadvantaged in Secondary Schools." In *Developing High School Reading Programs*. Newark, Del.: International Reading Association, 1967.

Strickland, Ruth G. "Implication of Research in Linguistics for Elementary Teaching." *Elementary English*, 1963, 40, 168–171.

Thorndike, Edward L. "Reading as Reasoning: A Study of Mistakes in Paragraph Reading." *Journal of Educational Psychology*, 1917, 8, 323.

Wheeler, Lester R. and Viola D. "Some Characteristic Differences and Similarities among the Language Arts." *Journal of Education*, 1955, 138, 2–8.

Wilt, Miriam. "Talk-talk-talk." *Reading Teacher*, 1968, 21, 611–617.

Movement Toward Improvement

Part Two of this book discusses aspects of a school program that need consideration if improved reading instruction is desired. The general theme is that improvement is achieved only when there is administrative commitment to change and action to improve. We believe that school administrators perceive their primary role to be one of instructional leadership. We also believe that they are capable of leading their teachers and communities in continuous program improvement. Therefore, each chapter is optimistic as well as informative.

Chapter 5 reviews some of the basic concepts presented in Part One, then discusses such practical concerns as time schedule, materials, and evaluation. Finally, we suggest professional books and periodicals on the process of reading instruction for administrators and teachers to consult.

Chapter 6 stresses the importance of gaining community support for reading program improvement. Specific ways to disseminate information to the public are given, and illustrative answers are suggested for questions about reading instruction that are frequently asked by parents.

In Chapter 7 the need for specialized reading personnel is explained, and their identification, training, and utilization are discussed. Model job descriptions for specialized reading personnel are offered as guides for administrators who wish to construct new job descriptions or change existing ones.

Chapter 8 presents underlying conditions and guidelines for effective in-service reading programs. Specific suggestions are offered for selecting resource people, involving teachers, setting objectives, and other procedures. The importance of administrative commitment to changing teachers' classroom behavior and of positive teacher attitudes toward in-service education is emphasized.

Chapter 9 describes seventeen in-service programs that were successful in improving teachers' instructional practices. These are models to be adapted to individual school resources and needs. They range in scope from the primary grades through senior high school in academic levels served and from 1 to 700 in number of teachers involved.

Part Two, then, is both descriptive and prescriptive in its emphasis on improving the reading program through administrative commitment that initiates action.

CHAPTER 5

Steps in the Right Direction

Adequate reading programs are not purchased neatly packaged or "turned on" when an enthusiastic administrator or reading specialist decides, or is delegated, to flick the switch. A thoughtfully conceived, well-organized reading program is the product of the coordinated efforts of many people over a period of time. Likewise, efforts to improve existing programs, no matter how sound and sincerely motivated, must proceed with the understanding and support of many people both within the school staff and in the community. All of Part Two of this book is devoted to the consideration of approaches to the development, improvement, and maintenance of adequate reading programs: Public relations, the procurement and training of specialized personnel, and in-service education are discussed in detail. First, however, we shall examine what we feel are the bases for further development. While there is no inherent sequence, when school personnel begin seriously to consider these bases they are taking significant steps toward improving the reading program.

Some Basic Concepts

Movement toward improving a school's reading program can logically begin with the consideration and acceptance of the basic concepts that will guide further developments. Both philosophical and pragmatic concerns will, of course, shape the conceptual statements that finally represent consensus at the individual school or district level. Here we shall only suggest a starting point by reviewing the six key themes from Part One of this book. Together they provide a conceptual base for program improvement.

1. *The person is the focal point in the reading program.* Unless and until developing the reading skills of the person is considered more important than covering material, it is not likely that any significant progress will be made toward better reading instruction. Everyone who has ever attempted to introduce practices designed to implement individualized assessment/instruction in reading has heard some of these reactions from certain teachers: "That sounds like a fine idea, but if I took time to do all those things my class would never finish the book and be ready for the next grade." (This despite the fact that the instruction is already beyond the grasp of a third or more of the pupils in the class.) "We can't take the time. Our principal [or some other villain, usually from the central office] expects us to cover the material in the curriculum guide." (This despite three facts: [a] Nobody has seen the curriculum guide since it was printed, [b] nobody has ever heard an administrator actually state such an expectation, and [c] a third or more of the pupils in the class are already hopelessly behind the cur-

riculum guide — which was finally located under a pile of papers in the teachers' lounge.) "Well, I'd just as soon do it, but then what happens when they get to junior high?" (This one is deceptive because the illogic has a veneer of apparent concern for the person. The reasoning seems to be that somehow children will benefit from being dragged through material, regardless of whether they can grasp it or not, and that once this has been done they will be ready for whatever comes next.) And so on.

Once the decision is made to give the person — not the material — prime concern, the way is clear for changes that will have a real impact upon what goes on in the classroom. Stopping short of such a decision will probably lead only to a reshuffling of groups or grouping practices, a new testing program, some new classifications for pupils with problems, and a renewed quest for the ultimate method for teaching reading to everybody in the same way.

2. *The purpose of the reading program is to help each pupil to read as nearly as possible at his capacity level.* An all-school reading program may include a number of component programs, e.g., the developmental, corrective, adapted, accelerated, and remedial programs discussed in Chapter 1. They serve specific purposes, but they share the same goal. Only if this goal is kept clearly in mind will the efforts expended in each context be likely to attain the coordination necessary to permit movement within the total program. Perhaps the most important aspect of the purpose stated is the focus upon capacity rather than grade level. The program must be so structured as to help each person to read as well as his capacity permits, not as well as his grade level indicates.

As we have said, the components of the total reading program that we have discussed are intended mainly to demonstrate the need for a variety of instructional approaches. In a local situation the components can be combined and defined to conform to reality. The ideas presented should be adapted, not adopted.

3. *"Reading" amounts to more than the simple decoding of printed symbols.* "Reading" is variously defined. Some writers, particularly those with a strong behavioristic orientation, seem to be satisfied with an extremely narrow definition, one that limits "reading" to the largely mechanical act of transforming visual symbols into verbalizations. Others go to the opposite extreme, insisting that "reading" includes the understanding and interpretation of not only printed symbols but also signs and symbols in general. We feel that reading must go beyond simple decoding at least to the point of including the grasp of literal meaning. (See also the discussion of the fifth theme, which has to do with reading and the other language arts.)

Chapter 2 outlined six areas of reading skills: word attack, comprehension, study skills, self-directed reading, interpretive reading, and creative reading. Taken together, they represent an operational definition of "reading" that is broad based yet not unrealistic in terms of what we feel can and should be covered by a well-conceived reading program. The concept of reading broadly defined is, in fact, probably a necessary basis for the development of a dynamic reading program. One of the first steps toward program development, then, is to work toward staff acceptance of a definition of reading that will not prove to be delimiting. The outline in Chapter 2 provides a framework within which such a definition can be worked out.

4. *A statement of the scope and sequence of reading skill development can serve as a framework for the instructional program in reading.* The outline of reading skills in Chapter 2 provides a model for such a scope and sequence statement as well as for a broad definition of "reading." Again, the outline need not be adopted as is; it should be adapted and, if necessary, extended in order to be in tune with the local philosophy and with local instructional practices. The scope and sequence statement finally adopted should represent consensus, and it should, of course, undergo constant change as new ideas are put into practice. Our knowledge is not yet so advanced that we can expect a scope and sequence statement to be a permanent thing.

Essentially, a consensual scope and sequence statement so well worked out that it is familiar and useful to teachers can permit flexibility in the instructional program in reading. Apparently one of the major reasons for a lock-step approach to reading instruction is that many teachers are genuinely afraid not to follow rigidly a particular set of materials lest there be gaps in the skill development of their pupils. Unfortunately, their perception embodies a good deal of truth, for the coverage and pacing in different materials tend to vary significantly. With an acceptable skill development framework, however, teachers have the option of checking systematically to see that the essential skills are in fact being covered when a variety of materials is used. Such checking also yields information about the appropriateness of the instructional pacing for each pupil, and adjustments can be made whenever and wherever skill development begins to lag. Of course the existence of the consensual framework also expedites communication among teachers, so a pupil's transition from one teacher to another can be more efficiently accomplished.

5. *Reading is but one of the language arts.* To isolate reading from the other language arts is to fractionate the language development process. As we have pointed out in Chapter 4, many of the skill development activities in the several areas of reading, writing, speaking, and listening are mutually reinforcing. Teachers need only to be consciously aware of the overlaps to begin to maximize the efficiency of their teaching by insuring that their pupils, too, develop such an awareness. Many of us have too long tended to think in terms of rather discrete lists of skills for each area, while in fact all the lists turn out to look remarkably alike.

Moffett (1968, pp. 16–24) recently pointed out what he calls a "major misconception of the language arts concerning reading." A series of quotations may come closer to a fair representation of his point of view — which is shared by others and is relevant here because the issues raised must be confronted before critical decisions regarding development of the reading program can be made — than a summary in our words.

A long list of mental activities that any psychologist would consider general properties of thinking that occur in many different areas of human experience have somehow or other been tucked under the skirts of reading. "Recalling," "comprehending," "relating facts," "making inferences," "drawing conclusions," "interpreting," and "predicting outcomes" are all mental operations that go on in the head of a non-literate aborigine navigating his outrigger according to cues from weather, sea life, currents, and the positions of heavenly bodies. Not only do these kinds of thinking have no necessary connection with reading, but they have no necessary connection with language whatever. [p. 16]

The prevailing assumption in education . . . is that failing to comprehend a text is something more than just a literacy problem and yet still a *reading* problem. This is impossible. If a reader can translate print into speech — read it aloud as sentences with normal intonation patterns — and still fails to grasp the idea or relate facts or infer or draw conclusions, then he has no *reading* problem; he has a *thinking* problem, traceable to many possible sources, none of them concerning printed words. [p. 16]

Reading has been so broadly construed that his [the reading specialist's] job is in some ways an impossible one. He is made responsible for general mental activities like recalling, inferring, and concluding that belong no more to reading than to any other intellectual activity. Vocabulary building and concept formation are placed in his domain, even though neither of these has any necessary connection with reading. Subject-matter reading, as in science and social studies, is supposed to require additional "skills" that also fall under his charge, when in fact what is difficult for the young reader are the vocabulary, the concepts and the knowledge context, all of which can be learned without ever opening a book. There are educators who would have us recognize dozens of different reading skills; some even count a couple of hundred. [p. 17]

Let me make it clear that I would not for one moment de-emphasize reading, if by that one means reducing the amount of reading or neglecting comprehension. On the contrary, if we dispense with the notion of reading skills and with the practices based on it, it will be possible to let children do more reading of an authentic sort and at the same time to help them develop the faculties necessary to read for meaning. [p. 18]

We find ourselves with a paradoxical impulse to say that this point of view represents at the same time an oversimplification and an overcomplication. The statement that the traditional reading skills are not reading skills at all and that the reading specialist need no longer concern himself with such matters is a reckless oversimplification. To say that a responsibility is someone else's is to say nothing unless that "someone else" is both willing and able to do something about it. We see no one eagerly waiting to take up the torch. Yet the statement that in certain instances and in certain forms many of the so-called *reading* skills are in fact *thinking* skills is a nit-picking overcomplication. Of course, the statement is true, and every reading teacher who has ever given even superficial thought to the matter is aware of it. In fact, it is this very awareness that has caused reading teachers to seek more and more to go beyond reading classes and reading texts to see that the skills — call them what you will — receive the attention they require.

But to heap countercharge upon charge is to evade the essential issue. As we see it, the issue is whether "reading" is something more than translating printed symbols into spoken sounds. We think it is. But we will concede that perhaps reading people have been so zealous in their work that they have tended to neglect closely related areas and certain applications. To put reading back among the language arts is to take one step in the right direction. It may even have been presumptuous of reading people to claim certain skills as *reading* skills. Nevertheless, we have always found reading people to be perfectly willing — nay, *eager* — to share them.

6. *The ultimate product of a successful reading program is the mature reader.* If intelligent decisions regarding the structure and operation of the reading program are to be made, the product — the mature reader — must be clearly conceived. Once the characteristics of reading maturity have been agreed upon, the procedures for working toward that goal can be worked out in a reasonably straightforward manner. Therefore, the nature of the end product should be considered carefully and, it is to be hoped, agreed upon by a school staff very early in the sequence of events aimed at the improvement of the reading program.

In Chapter 4 we discussed five characteristics of the mature reader:

The mature reader . . .

. . . reads for a purpose. He knows why he is reading and he adapts his approach to his purpose.

. . . organizes his reading. He sorts new ideas encountered in reading and relates them to his existing background of knowledge and experience.

. . . enlarges his vocabulary through reading. He attends to and masters new words encountered in his reading, uses them in his speech and writing, and expands his understanding of the multiple meanings and shades of meaning attached to certain words.

. . . uses his knowledge of meaning-bearing elements of sentences to interpret sentence meaning. He responds to the signaling systems inherent in written English sentences — word-form changes, structure words, syntactical-function order — and supplies intonation patterns as needed in order to interpret the messages in sentences.

. . . varies his rate and style of reading according to the material being read. He adapts his approach to the demands of the reading task.

These five characteristics may provide the focus for local discussions of what constitutes maturity in reading, the end product of the reading program. They can also supply a continuity of focus for reading development beyond the explicit skill development focus of the elementary school.

Again, we feel that the six key themes from Part One provide a conceptual base for improving the reading program. Given a sound base, the following deserve explicit attention early in the improvement process: consideration of a realistic time schedule, construction of local norms, examination of the readability of materials and the reading abilities of individuals with a view toward matching the person and the material, consideration of approaches to evaluation of the program and materials used in instruction, and development of a professional library.

Realistic Time Schedules

Attempts to improve reading programs are often begun with no realistic notion of how long it will take to reach either short- or long-term goals. More often than not the implicit expectation seems to be that even complex actions will be completed or in operation almost immediately. Actually, of course, many of the actions that we have discussed will require considerable time for consummation. In devising an acceptable scope and sequence statement, for example, time will be needed for laying the groundwork with the staff and for the actual preparation of the statement; and, if the statement is to serve as a guide to the individualization of instruction, working out the details of assessment and instruction will take still more time.

Two dangers arise when time schedules are not worked out in advance. First, evaluations of new procedures are likely to be premature and therefore to yield negative or not very impressive results. We are concerned because we have seen too many promising innovations aborted when positive feedback from premature attempts at evaluation was not forthcoming. Second, initial enthusiasm is likely to flag after a while even under optimum conditions, and when there is no realistic time schedule there is no provision for interim checking and pacing. A project with a long-term time schedule — anything longer than, say, one year — should subsume a series of specific short-term goals. These can help sustain interest over the longer haul.

Any attempt here to provide model time schedules for selected types of projects would probably be more misleading than informative, so we shall proceed with extreme caution. Local conditions vary greatly, and the speed with which activities can proceed depends upon such factors as the quality of the existing reading program, the background and experience of the staff, and the resources available. One generalization that seems safe is this: The better the reading program is to begin with, the more readily and rapidly innovations and improvements can be implemented. The best estimates regarding time schedules can be worked out, after a frank appraisal of the existing program and local conditions, by the responsible administrators in consultation with the entire staff that is to be involved. A final word of caution: To establish a firm base for future development takes time — much more time than to adopt flashy innovations that tend to dazzle temporarily but burn out quickly.

Local Norms

In the present discussion *local norms* means any set of norms developed for a specific test by a test user; *national norms* means those developed and made available by the test publisher.

Publishers' norms typically are based upon the performance of samples of pupils from supposedly representative areas of the nation. They permit comparisons of local students' scores with those of broadly based samples of students. Such comparisons, probably best limited to group performance, provide one means for checking on the results of local efforts. But, as we have pointed out, national norms may reflect performance that is grossly different from what should be expected in view of local conditions. Furthermore, the performance of individuals is most usefully compared with that of other individuals with similar educational backgrounds with whom they are actually competing in school.

Local norms can be established as data from sufficient numbers of students become available. We feel they are worth establishing for two main reasons. First, they do permit comparisons of individuals with other local students. Of course, the establishment of local norms does not eliminate most of the standardized test limitations that we have discussed in detail, so caution must still be exercised when comparisons are made. Second, once sufficient data have been gathered to justify confidence in local norms, there can be reasonable assurance that realistic comparisons are being made. For example, in a community populated mainly by upper-middle-class professional people not only group reading achievement but also group IQ scores are likely, for the usual well-known reasons, to exceed national norms. In such a situation, satisfaction with reading achievement that exceeds national norms is not justified. In general, local norms will provide a more useful base for comparisons than national norms. Specifically, the results of efforts to improve a local reading program are best examined in terms of comparisons of subsequent samples of performance with established local norms.

There is, perhaps, a third reason for the establishment of local norms: The decision to go ahead with the construction of local norms is tangible evidence of concern for a realistic base for examining the local reading program. Such tangible demonstrations of commitment are extremely important in the early stages of getting efforts to improve the reading program under way.

In addition to supplying national norms, some publishers provide directions for developing local norms in their test manuals. Clearly stated directions for preparing local norms are given in the *Manual for Interpreting Scores* of the *Cooperative English Tests,* published by the Educational Testing Service. We can briefly summarize the procedure suggested for setting up percentile norms for one particular grade level.

First, prepare a *score distribution* for the scores from students tested at the same point in their academic careers. (The suggestion is that data from at least 200 students be considered. Percentile ranks can be computed for smaller numbers, but the larger the sample, the more stable the norms.)
a. Find the lowest and highest scores in the sample.
b. Set up two-score intervals running from highest to lowest, e.g., 170–171, 168–169, 166–167, etc.
c. Tally the number of scores falling in each two-score interval.
Second, determine *percentile rankings.*
a. Find the *cumulative frequency* for each two-score interval: Add the frequencies in the score distribution *from the bottom up,* so that the number

opposite each two-score interval equals the sum of the frequencies for that interval plus all the intervals below it.

b. Compute the percentile rank for each two-score interval by (1) finding one-half of the *frequency* for that interval, (2) adding the result to the *cumulative frequency* for the interval just below the interval being considered, (3) dividing the result by the total number of students in the norms group (rounding to the nearest hundredth), and (4) multiplying that result by 100.

A sample work sheet for computing percentile norms is given in Figure 4. The procedure would simply be repeated with appropriate sets of data to establish norms for other grade levels and for other tests. Note the "Percentile Band" column in the Score Distribution Sheet. Percentile rankings for any particular score are given in the publisher's norms in terms of a band (e.g., 30–59) rather than a specific number (e.g., 44) in order to reflect the fact that an individual's performance is not entirely stable; thus, it is more appropriate to say that his score falls in the 30–59 range than to say it falls precisely at 44. The publisher's manual includes the necessary information for computing percentile bands for local norms for the test in the example. When information for computing percentile bands is not readily available, additional care must be taken in interpreting scores and score conversions, particularly when judgments are to be made regarding "differences" between percentile rankings.

As a final word regarding local norms, one point that we have already made bears repeating: The development of local norms deals with but one of the limitations of standardized tests. The simple fact of their existence should not become cause for a false sense of security regarding concern for the individual person.

Readability and Reading Ability

Much has been said about the readability of various materials and the relationship of readability to reading ability and to the development and improvement of reading ability. Materials, even those designated for a particular grade level, vary greatly in difficulty: Content area texts, for example, have repeatedly been rated two or more "grade levels" more difficult than reading texts ostensibly for the same grade level; but even more troublesome, reading texts have been shown to vary sharply — and not necessarily in an increasing difficulty progression — in difficulty within a given book. Unfortunately, though, the standardization of readability ratings offers no easy salvation, for readability ratings (Dale and Chall, 1948; Lorge, 1944; Spache, 1953; Yoakam, 1951) typically are based upon mechanical factors like average sentence length and frequency of "difficult" words and prepositional phrases, while important but less readily quantifiable factors like concept load, style, and reader's interest are ignored. And there is no denying the variability in reading ability, interest, background, and intellect to be found among the pupils in any classroom. The task of matching reader and reading material is no easy one. Yet in order to develop fluency in reading, as well as the other characteristics of reading maturity, a student must have oppor-

School and College Ability Tests

Sequential Tests of Educational Progress

SCAT-STEP
Score Distribution Sheet

Name of Test _Cooperative English Expression - Form 2A_   Time of Testing _Spring 1962_ Fall or Spring

School, College, or Group _Newport City Schools_   Grade or Class _11_

Other Characteristics of Local Norms Group _139 boys and 161 girls)_

Score Group	Tally	Frequency	Cumulative Frequency	Percentile Rank	Percentile Band
170 - 171	I	1	300	99	99 - 100
168 - 169		0	299	99	99 - 100
166 - 167	I	1	299	99	98 - 99
164 - 165	II	2	298	99	97 - 99
162 - 163	III	3	296	98	95 - 99
160 - 161	₩	5	293	97	91 - 99
158 - 159	₩ III	8	288	95	86 - 98
156 - 157	₩ ₩ III	13	280	91	81 - 97
154 - 155	₩ ₩ ₩ I	16	267	86	74 - 95
152 - 153	₩ ₩ ₩ IIII	19	251	81	67 - 91
150 - 151	₩ ₩ ₩ ₩ I	21	232	74	59 - 86
148 - 149	₩ ₩ ₩ ₩ II	22	211	67	52 - 81
146 - 147	₩ ₩ ₩ ₩ III	23	189	59	44 - 74
144 - 145	₩ ₩ ₩ ₩ III	23	166	52	37 - 67
142 - 143	₩ ₩ ₩ ₩ II	22	143	44	30 - 59
140 - 141	₩ ₩ ₩ ₩ I	21	121	37	24 - 52
138 - 139	₩ ₩ ₩ IIII	19	100	30	18 - 44
136 - 137	₩ ₩ ₩ III	18	81	24	13 - 37
134 - 135	₩ ₩ ₩ I	16	63	18	9 - 30
132 - 133	₩ ₩ IIII	14	47	13	5 - 24
130 - 131	₩ ₩ II	12	33	9	3 - 18
128 - 129	₩ ₩	10	21	5	1 - 13
126 - 127	₩ II	7	11	3	1 - 9
124 - 125	III	3	4	1	0 - 5
122 - 123	I	1	1	1	0 - 3
-					-
-					-
-					-
-					-
-					-
-					-
-					-
-					-
-					-
-					-
-					-
-					-
-					-
-					-
-					-

Total Number of Students . . . . _300_

This form is a worksheet for preparing local norms. Directions for recording information and computations are given in the SCAT or STEP MANUAL FOR INTERPRETING SCORES for the test used.

Published 1957 · Cooperative Test Division Educational Testing Service · Princeton, New Jersey · Los Angeles 27, California

D88R50X

FIGURE 4: Example of Local Norms Computation

tunities to read widely from materials that, to him, are easy to read — materials he is able to handle comfortably in terms of both the mechanics (vocabulary, sentence structure, decoding demands) and the conceptual load of the content. And in order to begin to cope with materials of ever increasing difficulty he must be exposed to ever more challenging *but not frustratingly difficult* materials.

Even with the best of intentions, it is hard to match reader and material; but all too often, particularly at the upper grade levels, teachers make no real attempts to do so, essentially because they are at a loss as to how to proceed. It is imperative, therefore, that very early in a program improvement sequence some explicit attention be paid to the matter of matching readers and materials. Teachers who see the need and have some notion of what to do about it will be ready and able to pay attention to the person in the reading program.

Simplified Versions of Written Material

A number of researchers have reported that content area materials can be rewritten so that students can read them with less difficulty in terms of word attack and with greater comprehension. Much more could be done to simplify the reading task without sacrificing any of the content in many presentations. Usually the most straightforward way to say anything is the best way to say it, and skillful teachers can use a rewriting technique to improve both comprehension and writing skill. Publishers ought to encourage their writers to strive for clarity, for at present the rewriting of more than a tiny sampling of content area materials is beyond the scope of activities in which classroom teachers can realistically engage. For the most part, teachers must make use of the materials that are available; equally important, in terms of learning to cope with the world as it is, pupils must learn to deal with the kinds of materials that will confront them outside of the classroom. And, of course, outside the content areas the straightforward presentation of facts is not always the goal. Critics of attempts to simplify the literary classics have said all that needs to be said regarding the rewriting of literature; perhaps many of their arguments could be applied equally well to rewriting in any area.

The conclusion we have reached is that, for practical purposes, the rewriting of materials for greater readability amounts to only a token approach to the matching of reader and reading material. We have no desire to become involved in debates regarding the desirability of such projects. The simple fact is that with few exceptions teachers and pupils will have to continue to cope with materials as they are.

Informal Reading Inventories

We feel that the task of matching reader and materials is most realistically tackled through the use of informal reading inventories or, at least, through applications of the informal inventory idea.

Betts (1946, Chap. XXI) was one of the first writers to describe in detail the construction and function of informal reading inventories. In the time since he made his statement many other writers have advocated the use of the informal inventory as a means of learning about reading levels; and, of course, adaptations and extensions — some of them sensible and some not so sensible — have been suggested. Whatever the adaptations, we feel that the informality of the informal inventory is its major strength and the one characteristic that must not be tampered with if it is to serve its unique purpose. Yet, if informal inventories are to have a vital role in a given situation, there must be some agreement as to their makeup. It is for this reason — and not to formalize the informal — that we deal with the informal inventory in some detail. (While we generally agree with Betts's suggestions, differences result from a distillation of other writers' suggestions and our own observations.)

Informal reading inventories are constructed from materials in use in the classroom. An accepted procedure is to select from a series of basal readers, beginning at the preprimer level and continuing for each subsequent difficulty level, passages to be read and responded to in terms of comprehension questions. (Some suggestions for achieving greater versatility are made later, but for the moment we shall stay with the basal reader example.) From the preprimer through first-grade materials the passages are 100 words in length, followed by five comprehension questions; from the 2^1-to 3^2-level materials the passages are 150 words long, followed by six questions; and from materials at the 4^1 level and above the passages are 150 words long, followed by eight questions. The total number of words in each passage is, of course, an approximation, for complete sentences must be included. The comprehension questions are devised by the teacher and should have to do with (1) the literal meaning of the entire passage or its parts, (2) meanings that are not explicitly stated but can be inferred from what is given, and (3) the meaning of individual words (vocabulary), when appropriate. The tendency, in our experience, is to ask questions only regarding specific facts presented; this, we feel, is not likely to reveal comprehension of the passage.

The inventory is administered by having the child begin at the level where he can comfortably handle both the word attack and comprehension tasks and continue to read through more difficult levels until he can no longer do so. He may be asked to read passages of comparable difficulty silently and orally. With the oral reading, which should be unrehearsed, the focus is upon his word attack skills; with the silent reading the focus is upon his comprehension. In oral reading, the following are noted as "errors":

Omissions. Technically, all words left out are "omissions," but a word inadvertently skipped probably does not reflect the same sort of problem as a word refused. We are inclined to encourage teachers to use their judgment and to record an error only when they feel a child has omitted a word because he doesn't know how to tackle it.

Substitutions. Again we are inclined to be less concerned about substitutions that make sense in context than about *confabulations,* or obvious guessing.

Mispronunciations. These are "miscalls" and evidence of inability to attack new words.

Insertions. These are words that are interjected as the passage is read.

Repetitions. There is little agreement as to *whether* or *when* repetitions should be counted as errors. A child may repeat a word or phrase simply to stall for time to analyze a troublesome word. On the other hand, persistent, habitual repetitions may be evidence of a serious problem. Again, teacher judgment is probably a better guide than any arbitrary criterion regarding when to count an error.

Some writers feel that there should be a third passage at each level of difficulty to be read to the pupil in order to establish the highest level at which he can respond to questions unhampered by his own ability to cope with the reading task.

The following levels can be established through use of the inventory:

Independent Reading Level. The pupil reads with about 99 per cent accuracy in word attack and about 90 per cent comprehension. This is the level at which he could reasonably be expected to read with virtually no help from anyone else.

Instructional Reading Level. The pupil reads with about 95 per cent accuracy and a minimum comprehension of about 70 per cent. At this level he can read and comprehend with some teacher supervision and assistance.

Frustration Level. The pupil reads with less than 90 per cent word attack accuracy and less than 50 per cent comprehension. At this level he can no longer function adequately. Johnson and Kress (1964) have, however, made a worthwhile point regarding the frustration level: "If the child is ready for instruction at one level and completely frustrated at the next, there is clear cut evidence that he has many problems to be overcome through instruction at the appropriate level. . . . If there is considerable spread between the instructional and frustration levels, there is a better chance for fairly rapid progress. There is evidence that he can continue to use his reading abilities with fair effectiveness when he meets more difficult material than that truly appropriate for instruction."

Hearing Capacity Level. This is the highest level at which the pupil can comprehend at least 70 per cent of material read to him. Theoretically, it is the level at which he *could* read if he had no problems with the mechanics of reading. In fact, as often as not, the task simply reflects the pupil's effectiveness as a listener, so the hearing capacity level may turn out to be *below* his instructional level in reading. Caution should, therefore, be used in interpreting the meaning of an individual's hearing capacity level.

Informal reading inventories need not, of course, be constructed only within the context of a basal reader series. Although the gradation of the basals provides a useful format for identifying more than one level of ability, more often than not a teacher's main interest will be in finding out whether a particular person can read a specific book. In such cases the informal inventory procedure can be adapted to a single book in the following way: Select a passage of 100–150 words, formulate appropriate comprehension questions, then administer by having the pupil read the passage orally and respond to the questions; an estimate of whether the book is at his independent, instructional, or frustration level can readily be made. Such an approach, combined with judgments based upon other knowledge of individuals — i.e., interests, background, prior instruction — can help to insure not only proper matching of books and readers but also adequate comprehension of essential content.

A self-administering informal inventory can also be useful, especially at the upper elementary and secondary levels. Passages of 150 words can be marked off in any text or library book and comprehension questions provided — either inserted in the book or kept in a file. Students who know the criteria for establishing independent, instructional, and frustration levels can then determine for themselves the suitability of any book for their particular ability and purpose. If this approach to book selection can be established, there is likely to be much less frustrated plodding through too difficult or too easy materials and much more rewarding, self-motivating reading.

Readability: A Personal Matter

In the informal inventory approach there are no assumptions regarding theoretical *grade levels* of performance or *readability levels* of materials. Instead, the idea is to examine the response of an individual person to a given book in order to decide on the suitability of the material for him. With our present knowledge there is no effective substitute: Readability formulas are, as we have pointed out, hung up on the mechanical aspects of the reading task, and the reading capabilities of the person are determined as much by his response to specific content as by his general skill in the mechanics of reading.

An essential first step toward the improvement of reading instruction involves a careful examination of the concept of *readability*. We believe that whatever a person can read is, to him, readable. The most straightforward approach, then, is to devise means for examining readability in terms of the match between person and materials. The informal inventory approach offers such a means. Time spent in coming to agreements on the details of the approach is, in our opinion, likely to be more productive in terms of improved instruction than time spent in rehashing and applying the readability formulas and otherwise overcomplicating the problem.

Approaches to Evaluation

Very early in the sequence of program improvement some decisions must be made regarding evaluation of (1) materials used in the program and (2) the program itself.

Evaluation of Materials

The fact that extensive, well-supported research has not led to the discovery of a best method or set of materials for teaching reading was pointed out in Chapter 1. Indeed, such a discovery is unlikely. But the fact remains that in certain situations, with certain pupils and certain teachers, some materials will produce satisfactory results and some will not; some will be received enthusiastically by pupils and teachers and some will not; some will be worth the money they cost and others will not. There is, of course, no formula for evaluating materials for good and all: Criteria will differ, depending on expectations and local applications and on the resources available to local schools. Serious thought should be given to the evaluation of materials, however, because almost invariably attempts at program improvement are accompanied by tryouts of new materials and the mechanical devices that often go with them.

Perhaps the main point to be made here amounts to a word of caution: The sales representatives of producers of materials and devices should not become, by default, the final arbiters in materials selection at the local level. We all know of school administrators who have made ill-considered purchases, often solely on the advice of salesmen, that are used reluctantly or not at all by teachers in the classroom. It is probably no exaggeration to say that one of the residual benefits of the influx of federal money through various programs is storerooms filled with materials and devices that never should have been bought. We all know, too, of reading consultants who have stocked up on their favorites, much to the chagrin of their successors and the teachers who are obliged to use them. The best way to avoid such problems is, obviously, to pre-evaluate. Decisions to purchase should never be made by a single individual. Tentative decisions should be reached by a group that includes representatives who know (1) what the local resources are, (2) what alternatives are available, and (3) the opinions and preferences of the potential users. Final decisions should come only after tryouts on a limited scale.

Evaluation of materials begins, then, with pre-evaluation. There is no point in trying out materials that are unrealistically expensive, that are known to be second rate, or that are fundamentally unsound. While to say this may be to state the obvious, we have seen too many tryouts of the outrageous, the ridiculous, and the bizarre — usually in the name of "innovation," for too long now education's sacred cow — to be unconcerned. Once well-considered decisions to try out certain materials on a limited basis have been made, systematic feedback must be sought and digested.

Positive feedback may come in the form of increased pupil achievement, improved attitudes of teachers and/or pupils, savings of time and/or money, or in more nebulous ways, like testimonials from parents, pupils, or teachers. This is not the place to suggest the many shapes feedback may take or to speculate about what may be most appropriate for a given product in a given situation. But some notion of what is to be accepted as positive feedback should be established in advance and the amount of time to be allowed for the tryout specified so that decisions can be made as to whether to continue, to expand, or to abandon. Again, both administrators and potential users should participate in the decisions.

A word of caution: Be sure that materials are evaluated according to the purpose for which they were intended. Some materials, for example, are intended for use in developing the reading skills; others, mainly for recreational or for functional reading situations. Skill development materials, then, should be judged in terms of their usefulness for skill development, not necessarily — or not primarily — for their information content or their appeal to independent reading interests. Some materials that are extremely useful for teaching specific skills would have little appeal in a free reading situation. Be sure, too, that the pupils are consulted when appropriate — particularly regarding materials for recreational reading.

Evaluation of the Program

An earlier section pointed out the need to establish realistic time schedules for program change. The point bears repeating here, for premature attempts at evaluation are not likely to yield positive results.

Ultimately, an improved reading program should lead to improved achievement in reading, but significant changes in group achievement test scores may be slow in coming. Such changes are likely to appear only after other kinds of changes — changes in instructional procedures, in teachers' attitudes, in children's attitudes, in the administrative setup, in services offered, in parental involvement, and many more — have had sufficient time to occur and have an impact. When action is instigated to bring about these interim changes, plans should be made to examine the results.

At all times the key to program evaluation is a single question: Is every reasonable attempt being made to focus upon the person in the reading program? The question can be rephrased for Timmy, who is in the first grade; for Susan, who is a slow learner; for Max, who is having some difficulties in junior high; for Julie, who is a college-bound senior. If the answer is always an unqualified *Yes*, the elusive goal has been reached. If it is only sometimes *Yes*, sometimes a qualified *Yes*, sometimes an outright *No*, what remains to be done can be determined through analysis of the causes for the negative statements. Elaborate checklists can tell us no more.

A Professional Library

Although much remains to be discovered about the teaching and learning of reading skills, a great deal has already been said. Anyone with even a casual interest in reading — from either the teacher's or learner's viewpoint — must be impressed by the amount of material available; and the more serious scholar, once he has had a chance to do a bit of probing, must be absolutely awed by the numbers of research reports, discussions, conference reports, methods texts, and instructional materials that exist. Each year several books and hundreds of research reports and discussion-type articles are added to the literature. Obviously in so vast a body of work there is much that is highly technical and intended only for readers within specialized interest areas; there is also much that is passé, redundant, and just plain trashy; but there is a great deal of the gutsy, practical stuff that good instructional programs are made of.

Much dissipation of effort can be avoided if, from the very beginning, steps toward improving the reading program are guided by what is already known — or at least by what has already been tried.

A faculty group that sets out to improve reading instruction should have an inquiring attitude. There should be an interest in what has succeeded and what has failed in the past and in what is current. In our experience, an inquiring attitude is nurtured in the most tangible way by making professional books and journals readily available. A substantial step in the right direction, then, is taken by getting together a good professional library.

The pages that follow list professional books and journals that might be included in such a library. Each entry on the book list is briefly annotated; we have attempted to identify the major theme of the book and have not hesitated to interject our biases. The journals are divided into three categories: those that are devoted wholly to reading, those that regularly carry reading-related articles, and those that occasionally carry reading-related articles. For each journal listed the address to which inquiries regarding subscriptions may be directed is given; we decided not to cite subscription rates because they tend to change frequently and there may be different rates for individuals, for members of the sponsoring organizations, and for libraries. Neither list is meant to be exhaustive; the books and journals are those that we have found to be particularly useful and/or provocative.

Professional Books

Anderson, I. H., and W. F. Dearborn. *The Psychology of Teaching Reading.* New York: Ronald Press, 1952. Although the book is now almost two decades old, it remains a standard reference. Chap. 5, "The Psychology of Word Perception," is a fine review of early work in the area, and portions of the chapter have been widely cited.

Austin, Mary C., C. L. Bush, and Mildred Huebner. *Reading Evaluation.* New York: Ronald Press, 1961. The authors present an overview of approaches to evaluation in reading. Coverage ranges from informal inventories and checklists to the all-school testing program. A standard reference.

Austin, Mary C., and C. Morrison. *The First R: The Harvard Report on Reading in the Elementary Schools.* New York: Macmillan, 1963. The results of an exhaustive survey of in-service training of reading teachers, methods and techniques for teaching reading, the role of administrators in the reading program, and related topics are reported, and forty-five recommendations for the improvement of reading instruction are made.

Bamman, H., Ursula Hogan, and C. Greene. *Reading Instruction in the Secondary School.* New York: Longmans, Green, 1961. The discussion of reading in the content areas in the secondary school is worthwhile. A list of reading skills for the secondary school is given.

Barbe, W. B. *Educator's Guide to Personalized Reading Instruction.* Englewood Cliffs, N.J.: Prentice-Hall, 1961. The focus is upon the individualization of instruction in reading. Barbe's graded lists of elementary level reading skills have been used extensively by teachers and reading consultants.

Barbe, W. B. *Teaching Reading: Selected Materials.* New York: Oxford University Press, 1965. A book of selected readings in the general area of reading.

Bereiter, C., and S. Engleman. *Teaching Disadvantaged Children in the Pre-school.* Englewood Cliffs, N.J.: Prentice-Hall, 1966. While they have not written a book on reading instruction per se, the authors have something to say about the preschool training of disadvantaged children that is relevant to the concerns of reading teachers.

Bloomfield, L., and C. Barnhart. *Let's Read: A Linguistic Approach.* Detroit: Wayne State University Press, 1961. This book is an overview of the Bloomfield-Barnhart approach to teaching reading by a linguistic approach as they see it. Barnhart's basal series, *Let's Read*, is built solidly on the foundation presented here. *Let's Read* is the prime example of what has been dubbed a "micro-linguistic" approach to teaching reading: *The fat cat sat on a mat.*

Bond, G., and M. Tinker. *Reading Difficulties, Their Diagnosis and Correction.* New York: Appleton-Century-Crofts, 1957. A methods text for remedial reading.

Bond, G., and Eva Wagner. *Teaching the Child to Read* (4th ed.). New York: Macmillan, 1966. That this book on general developmental reading is in its fourth edition speaks for itself.

Brueckner, L., and G. Bond. *The Diagnosis and Treatment of Learning Difficulties.* New York: Appleton-Century-Crofts, 1955. The authors deal with learning problems in the several basic skill areas, including reading.

Buros, O. K. (Ed.). *The Sixth Mental Measurements Yearbook.* Highland Park, N.J.: Gryphon Press, 1965. The standard reference on tests in general and reading tests in particular. Specific tests are described and reviewed, and information regarding availability, cost, etc., is given.

Carter, H. J., and D. J. McGinnis. *Teaching Individuals to Read.* Boston: Heath, 1962. A methods text for elementary reading.

Chall, J. S. *Learning to Read: The Great Debate.* New York: McGraw-Hill, 1967. A potboiler that has been aggressively publicized and acclaimed by some as the reading teacher's key to salvation. For another point of view, see the review by George Spache in the Winter, 1969, issue of the *Journal of Reading Behavior.*

Cohn, S. M., and J. Cohn. *Teaching the Retarded Reader.* New York: Odyssey Press, 1967. A paperback guidebook for teaching disabled readers.

Cruickshank, W. M., *et al. A Teaching Method for Brain Injured and Hyperactive Children.* Syracuse: Syracuse University Press, 1961. The title accurately describes the contents. Particular attention is paid to reading and writing.

Dawson, M. A. (Ed.). *Developing High School Reading Programs.* Newark, Del.: International Reading Association, 1967. A well-edited collection of articles in which the focus is upon the development of a high school reading program and its various components.

DeBoer, J. L., and Martha Dallman. *The Teaching of Reading* (rev. ed.). New York: Holt, Rinehart & Winston, 1964. A methods text for elementary reading.

Dechant, E. V. *Improving the Teaching of Reading.* Englewood Cliffs, N. J.: Prentice-Hall, 1964. A methods text for elementary reading.

deHirsch, K., J. J. Jansky, and W. S. Langford. *Predicting Reading Failure.* New York: Harper & Row, 1966. The report of a research project designed to identify a battery of tests to be used at the kindergarten level to pre-identify reading failures. The review of the literature and the approach are worth examining, but the publication of tentative results in book form appears to have been grossly premature.

Della-Piana, G. M. *Reading Diagnosis and Prescription.* New York: Holt, Rinehart & Winston, 1968. A useful handbook for developmental as well as remedial reading teachers. Includes an interesting discussion of individually prescribed instruction and many other perceptively presented summaries, suggestions, and points of view.

Diack, H. *Reading and the Psychology of Perception.* New York: Philosophical Library, 1960. The author maintains that letters have meaning and that the principles of Gestalt psychology could be the ruination of reading instruction. A well-written, provocative book by one of the authors of the *Royal Road Readers*, a basal series published in England.

Durkin, Dolores. *Phonics and the Teaching of Reading.* New York: Bureau of Publications, Teachers College, Columbia University, 1962. A paperback guide to the use of phonics in the teaching of reading. A useful reference for the teacher who wants to "brush up" on phonics.

Durkin, Dolores. *Children Who Read Early.* New York: Teachers College Press, 1966. Report of careful research designed to examine the characteristics of children who learn to read before they enter school.

Durr, W. K. (Ed.). *Reading Instruction: Dimensions and Issues.* Boston: Houghton Mifflin, 1967. A book of selected readings in which the focus is upon the methods, materials, and organization of reading instruction.

Fernald, Grace M. *Remedial Techniques in Basic School Subjects.* New York: McGraw-Hill, 1943. This is the book in which Fernald herself describes the Fernald tactile-kinesthetic approach to teaching severely disabled readers. Modifications and adaptations of the prototype are now commonplace; a look at the original could be enlightening.

Fries, C. G. *Linguistics and Reading.* New York: Holt, Rinehart & Winston, 1963. The book embodies a prominent linguist's notion of how reading should be taught. An excellent review of the history of reading instruction in the United States is given in the first chapter.

Frost, J. L. *Issues and Innovations in the Teaching of Reading.* Glenview, Ill.: Scott, Foresman, 1967. A book of selected readings well chosen to expose the reader to a variety of viewpoints and issues in the area of reading instruction.

Gray, W. S. *On Their Own in Reading* (rev. ed.). Glenview, Ill.: Scott, Foresman, 1960. The book presents an overview of the scope and sequence of a balanced approach to the development of word attack skills.

Harris, A. J. *How to Increase Reading Ability* (4th ed.). New York: Longmans, Green, 1961. In our opinion, the classic remedial reading methods text.

The popularity of the book — the fifth edition is in preparation — is well deserved. The presentation is straightforward enough for the beginning student, but the coverage is comprehensive enough for the advanced student.

Harris, A. J. *Effective Teaching of Reading.* New York: McKay, 1962. A methods text for elementary reading.

Heilman, A. W. *Principles and Practices of Teaching Reading* (2nd ed.). Columbus, Ohio: Merrill, 1967. An extremely popular methods text for elementary reading. The chapters on phonics and on sex differences in reading achievement have been given particular, and deserved, attention.

Karlin, R. *Teaching Reading in High School.* Indianapolis: Bobbs-Merrill, 1964. A methods text for teaching reading in the secondary school.

King, M. L., B. D. Ellinger, and W. Wolf (Eds.). *Critical Reading.* Philadelphia: Lippincott, 1967. A book of selected readings on the development of critical reading skills.

Kirk, S. *Teaching Reading to Slow-Learning Children.* Boston: Houghton Mifflin, 1940. This book has probably attained the status of classic as a description of an approach to teaching reading to mentally retarded children.

Kottmeyer, W. *Teacher's Guide for Remedial Reading.* Manchester, Mo.: Webster, 1959. A handbook filled with many practical suggestions for the teacher of corrective as well as remedial reading.

Lee, Dorris M., and R. V. Allen. *Learning to Read Through Experience* (2nd ed.). New York: Appleton-Century-Crofts, 1963. The authors present their approach to teaching reading as an integral part of the communication skills.

Lefevre, G. A. *Linguistics and the Teaching of Reading.* New York: McGraw-Hill, 1964. The essential message is that the sentence, not the word, is the main meaning-bearing element in the English language. The writer advocates an experience approach to the teaching of reading.

McKee, P., and W. K. Durr. *Reading: A Program of Instruction for the Elementary School.* Boston: Houghton Mifflin, 1966. A methods text for elementary reading.

Malmquist, E. *Factors Related to Reading Disabilities in the First Grade of Elementary School.* Stockholm: Almquist & Wiksell, 1958. The book is a report of a large-scale study of factors related to reading achievement in the first grade. Although the study was done in Sweden — and more than a decade ago — the review of the literature and the omnibus approach of the study are worth careful examination.

Money, J. (Ed.). *Reading Disability: Progress and Research Needs in Dyslexia.* Baltimore: Johns Hopkins Press, 1962.

Money, J. (Ed.). *The Disabled Reader.* Baltimore: Johns Hopkins Press, 1966. The two books edited by Money are both "collected papers" from conferences at Johns Hopkins University. The papers represent varied orientations and points of view regarding reading disability and its treatment.

Taken together, the books offer the serious reader an excellent overview of thinking and action in the area of reading disability.

Otto, W., and D. Ford. *Teaching Adults to Read.* Boston: Houghton Mifflin, 1967. The focus is upon helping illiterate adults through the primary stages of learning to read. A review of materials for teaching basic reading skills to adults is given in Chap. 4.

Otto, W., and K. Koenke. *Remedial Teaching: Research and Comment.* Boston: Houghton Mifflin, 1969. A book of selected readings that parallels *Corrective and Remedial Teaching* (see below) in its coverage. Suggestions for making personal evaluations of journal articles — both research and discussion-type articles — are given in the introductory chapter.

Otto, W., and R. McMenemy. *Corrective and Remedial Teaching.* Boston: Houghton Mifflin, 1966. The book covers learning disabilities in handwriting, spelling, oral and written expression, and arithmetic, as well as reading.

Robinson, Helen M. *Why Pupils Fail in Reading.* Chicago: University of Chicago Press, 1946. This book is frequently cited. It was one of the early attempts to examine multiple causal factors in reading disability.

Rogers, C. R. *Client-Centered Therapy.* Boston: Houghton Mifflin, 1951. Rogers' book on client-centered therapy remains a good reference for the reading teacher who is concerned about the person in the program. The chapter on student-centered teaching merits careful consideration.

Russell, D. H. *Children Learn to Read* (rev. ed.). Boston: Ginn, 1961. A methods text for elementary reading.

Russell, D. H., Etta E. Karp, and E. I. Kelley. *Reading Aids Through the Grades* (rev. ed.). New York: Bureau of Publications, Teachers College, Columbia University, 1951. A soft-cover, spiral-bound collection of helpful hints for teaching reading skills.

Schubert, D. G., and T. L. Torgerson. *Improving Reading Through Individualized Correction* (2nd ed.). Dubuque: Brown, 1968. A soft-cover handbook for teachers. The authors emphasize diagnosis and individualized correction of difficulties through the use of self-directed instructional materials. Useful lists of professional references, tests, materials, and devices for improving reading skills, and publishers' addresses are given. The final chapter deals with the "Reading Improvement Program in Practice."

Schubert, D. G., and T. L. Torgerson. *Readings in Reading: Research, Theory, Practice.* New York: Crowell, 1968. A book of selected readings in which, the senior editor says, the attempt is to offer insights into the historical development, trends, theory, research, and practices in reading instruction.

Smith, H. P., and E. V. Dechant. *Psychology in Teaching Reading.* Englewood Cliffs, N.J.: Prentice-Hall, 1961. The best single source on the "psychology of reading instruction." The coverage is comprehensive through the copyright date, and the presentation is well organized and lucid.

Smith, Nila B. *Reading Instruction for Today's Children*. Englewood Cliffs, N.J.: Prentice-Hall, 1963. A methods text for elementary reading.

Spache, G. D. *Reading in the Elementary School*. Boston: Allyn & Bacon, 1964. A methods text for elementary reading. The author's reviews of the basal reader, individualized, linguistic, and language experience approaches to teaching elementary reading are worth careful examination.

Stauffer, R. G. *Directing Reading Maturity as a Cognitive Process*. New York: Harper & Row, 1969.

Stauffer, R. G. *Teaching Reading as a Thinking Process*. New York: Harper & Row, 1969. The two books by Stauffer are offered as companion volumes; the focus of the former is upon process and theory, while that of the latter is upon practices and procedures in teaching reading. The author suggests the latter as an elementary methods text and the former as a text for graduate students interested in examining the teaching of reading as a cognitive process.

Strang, Ruth, Constance M. McCullough, and A. E. Traxler. *The Improvement of Reading* (4th ed.). New York: McGraw-Hill, 1967. A methods text for teaching reading in the secondary school. The coverage is comprehensive.

Tinker, M. A. *Basis for Effective Reading*. Minneapolis: University of Minnesota Press, 1965. The important contribution of this book is its careful presentation of the author's thirty-two years of research on such factors as eye movements in reading, the effect of typography upon efficient reading, and visual functioning and illumination for reading. Related findings of other researchers are also presented.

Tinker, M. A., and Constance McCullough. *Teaching Elementary Reading* (2nd ed.). New York: Appleton-Century-Crofts, 1962. A methods text for elementary reading.

Veatch, Jeannette. *Individualizing Your Reading Program*. New York: Putnam's, 1959, 1967. This is a source book of ideas and procedures directed to the individualization of reading instruction through self-selection, self-pacing, and pupil-teacher conferences.

Vernon, M. D. *Backwardness in Reading*. Cambridge: University Press, 1958. An excellent review of factors related to reading ability/disability ("backwardness" is the term used for "disability" in England, where the book was published).

Wilson, R. M. *Diagnostic and Remedial Reading*. Columbus, Ohio: Merrill, 1967. A methods text for remedial reading. The suggestions are, as the subtitle "For Classroom and Clinic" suggests, appropriate for application in the classroom.

Journals

Reading Research Quarterly, Reading Teacher, and *Journal of Reading*. International Reading Association, P.O. Box 695, Newark, Del., 19711. These journals deal exclusively with reading. All three are publications of the International Reading Association. The focus of the *Reading Teacher* is upon the elementary school; the *Journal of Reading* covers secondary, college, and adult levels; and the *Reading Research Quarterly* is devoted mainly to longer research reports of general interest. A review and summary of the past year's research in reading is regularly published in the Winter issue of the *Quarterly*.

Journal of Reading Behavior. College of Education, University of Georgia, Athens, Ga., 30601. A quarterly journal, sponsored by the National Reading Conference, that places emphasis on the secondary, college, and adult levels but accepts articles dealing with significant aspects of reading behavior at all levels.

Journal of the Reading Specialist. Reading Laboratory, Rochester Institute of Technology, Rochester, N.Y. 14603. Sponsored by the College Reading Association, the journal is devoted to articles of general interest to persons interested in the methodology of teaching reading.

Reading Newsreport. P.O. Box 63, Wethersfield, Conn. 06109. The journal features timely reviews and interviews in a highly readable format.

Journal of Educational Research and *Journal of Experimental Education*. Dembar Educational Research Services, Box 1605, Madison, Wis., 53701. These journals do not have a specific reading focus, but they regularly carry research and/or discussion articles dealing with reading. A review and summary of selected research studies in reading is regularly published in the February or March issue of the *Journal of Educational Research*.

American Educational Research Journal and *Review of Educational Research*. American Educational Research Association, 1201 Sixteenth Street, N.W., Washington, D.C., 20036. Both journals are publications of the American Educational Research Association. Reading-related research in various areas is reviewed on regular cycles in the *Review of Educational Research*.

Elementary English and *English Journal*. National Council of Teachers of English, 508 South Sixth Street, Champaign, Ill., 61820. Both journals are publications of the National Council of Teachers of English. The *English Journal* has a secondary level focus.

Academic Therapy Quarterly. Academic Therapy Publications, 1543 Fifth Avenue, San Rafael, Calif., 94901.

Journal of Learning Disabilities. The Professional Press, Inc., Room 1410, Five North Wabash Avenue, Chicago, Ill., 60602.

Psychology in the Schools. Psychology Press, Inc., 4 Conant Square, Brandon, Vt., 05733.

Journal of Special Education. Box 7030, Philadelphia, Pa., 19149.

Education. Education, 4300 West 62nd Street, Indianapolis, Ind., 46268.

The Instructor. The Instructor, Danville, N.Y., 14437.

Elementary School Journal. University of Chicago Press, 5835 Kimbark Avenue, Chicago, Ill., 60637.

Clearinghouse. The Clearinghouse, 205 Lexington Avenue, Sweet Springs, Mo., 65351.

Psychological Reports and *Perceptual and Motor Skills.* Box 1441, Missoula, Mont., 59801.

Journal of Abnormal Psychology, Journal of Applied Psychology, Journal of Consulting Psychology, Journal of Counseling Psychology, Journal of Developmental Psychology, Journal of Educational Psychology, Journal of Experimental Psychology, and *Journal of Personality and Social Psychology.* American Psychological Association, Inc., 1200 Seventeenth Street, N.W., Washington, D.C., 20036. These journals carry occasional research and/or discussion articles dealing with reading. All are publications of the American Psychological Association, and they are devoted almost exclusively to the reporting of research studies.

School Review. University of Chicago Press, 5750 Ellis Avenue, Chicago, Ill., 60637. Published by the Department of Education, The University of Chicago.

School and Society. Society for the Advancement of Education, Inc., 1860 Broadway, New York, N.Y., 10023. Published by the Society for the Advancement of Education.

Childhood Education. Association for Childhood Education International, 3615 Wisconsin Avenue, N.W., Washington, D.C., 20016.

Child Development. University of Chicago Press, 5750 Ellis Avenue, Chicago, Ill., 60637. A publication of the Society for Research in Child Development, Inc.

Educational Leadership. Association for Supervision and Curriculum Development, NEA, 1201 Sixteenth Street, N.W., Washington, D.C., 20036. Journal of the Association for Supervision and Curriculum Development.

Exceptional Children. Council for Exceptional Children, NEA, 1201 Sixteenth Street, N.W., Washington, D.C., 20036. Journal of the Council for Exceptional Children.

American Journal of Mental Deficiency. American Association on Mental Deficiency, Publication and Sales Office, 49 Sheridan Avenue, Albany, N.Y., 12210. Published by the American Association on Mental Deficiency.

American Journal of Orthopsychiatry. American Orthopsychiatric Association, Publication and Sales Office, 49 Sheridan Avenue, Albany, N.Y., 12210. Published by the American Orthopsychiatric Association.

Journal of Verbal Learning and Verbal Behavior. Academic Press, 111 Fifth Avenue, New York, N.Y., 10003.

High School Journal. University of North Carolina Press, Chapel Hill, N.C., 27514. Published by the School of Education, University of North Carolina.

Educational and Psychological Measurement. Box 6907, College Station, Durham, N.C., 27708.

Journal of Psychology. 2 Commercial Street, Provincetown, Mass., 02657.

American Journal of Optometry and Archives of the Academy of Optometry. 1506 Foshay Tower, Minneapolis, Minn., 55402. Journal of the American Academy of Optometry.

References

Betts, Emmett A. *Foundations of Reading Instruction.* New York: American Book, 1946.

Dale, Edgar, and Jeanne S. Chall. "A Formula for Predicting Readability." *Educational Research Bulletin,* Ohio State University, 1948, 27, 11–20.

Johnson, Marjorie S., and Roy A. Kress. "Individual Reading Inventories." In *Sociological and Psychological Factors in Reading.* Twenty-first Annual Reading Institute, Temple University, 1964, pp. 48–60.

Lorge, Irving. "Predicting Readability." *Teachers College Record,* 1944, 45, 404–419.

Moffett, James. *A Student-Centered Language Arts Curriculum, Grades K–13: A Handbook for Teachers.* Boston: Houghton Mifflin, 1968.

Spache, George. "A New Readability Formula for Primary-Grade Reading Materials." *Elementary School Journal,* 1953, 53, 410–413.

Yoakam, Gerald A. "Determining the Readability of Instructional Materials." In *Current Problems of Reading Instruction.* Seventh Annual Conference on Reading, University of Pittsburgh, 1951, pp. 47–53.

CHAPTER 6

Public Relations

In the long run, a truly successful school reading program can be sustained only if it has the support of the community. While a good reading program need not cost more than a poor one, long-term financial backing *is* required. Equally important, there is a continuing need for cooperation, acceptance, and moral support. When parents, for example, understand and have reason to esteem the activities of the reading program, their positive attitudes will be reflected by their children and they are likely to support the program. Likewise, the community will come through with the financial wherewithal if the values of the program are known and respected.

The support of the community can be earned through sound public relations efforts. This is not to suggest billboard ads, skywriting, or such razzle-dazzle tactics. A competent school staff can do everything that is required to present a sound program to the public without raising their voices or shooting rockets. If they will *provide information, provide services,* and *answer questions,* they can quietly but effectively tell the story, mainly with actions that speak much more loudly than words. The actions in each category, particularly the answering of questions, should be based upon considered philosophy in order that a consistent, coherent policy may be presented.

In the pages that follow, some means for providing information and examples of services that may be extended to the community are discussed, and several questions regarding reading that come up frequently are given along with examples of the types of answers possible.

Provide Information

Information about the reading program or certain of its aspects can be supplied to the community through varied means. Whether formal or informal channels are employed, the information should represent the facts as they are and as they relate to the total context. A basic requirement, then, is that the entire school staff be kept up to date on philosophy, policy, and current development. This will call for some in-service time, but it is time well spent, for many misunderstandings that arise from misinformation or partial information can be avoided.

Some examples of means that can readily be utilized for disseminating information in virtually any community follow.

Parent Conferences

Parent conferences are one way to get general information regarding the reading program as well as specific facts about children's progress to the people in the community who are most ego-involved. Discussion of the program establishes the context within which individual performance can most meaningfully be considered: Thus there need be no great concern that the general information given out at a parent conference will detract from the focus upon the individual. Of course, some time can be saved by presenting an overview of the program to groups of parents, but program specifics are probably best explained in terms of what is implicit for particular children. The parents of a disabled reader, for example, should see how their child is served by the remedial program and, in turn, how the remedial program fits into the overall developmental program. Similarly, the parents of a college-bound senior should see the function of the accelerated program and its relationship to the total developmental program. When parents understand how the program works for the benefit of their children, they can be depended upon to spread the word.

The Parent-Teacher Organization

Information regarding the total program or specific aspects of the program can be provided effectively through the local parent-teacher organization. Presentations by local teachers and consultants or by resource people from outside the school will be well received if topics with general appeal are chosen. But it is not inappropriate to indulge in a bit of showmanship by having the children take part in demonstrations of special techniques and materials or by displaying children's work. When children participate, care must, of course, be taken to see that no individual is identified as a "poor reader" or as a member of the "low group." Regardless of the type of presentation, adequate time should always be allotted to permit the discussion of questions from the audience. In fact, often the most effective presentations are those deliberately constructed to evoke questions from the audience.

News Media

In many communities local newspapers and television and radio stations are not only willing but eager to run stories on school programs and activities. Too often, however, reports turn out to be negative or distorted for lack of planned, comprehensive input from the schools; there is no focusing of attention at all, or notice is paid only as a result of complaints, justified or not. What is needed is the establishment of rapport between school people and reporters for the media. We are not suggesting any whitewashing, but it is possible to see to it that positive aspects of the program are recognized and understood. At appropriate times representatives of the media can be invited to attend in-service sessions, to observe activities in classrooms, and to cover special programs and presentations. News releases and invited interviews can be employed, too, for getting information out at the right times.

Service Organizations

Information can be disseminated effectively to influential members of the community through service organizations if it is made known that school personnel are available for speaking engagements. Personnel who are effective speakers and have a high tolerance for ham and peas for lunch will be called on frequently once they have shown that aspects of the reading program can be presented interestingly as well as informatively. Adult audiences are likely to be highly receptive to information about adult reading skills — "speed" reading is ever popular — and about innovations that appear to have relevance for their children. A speaker may choose a popular theme and still find opportunities to tell his audience what the schools are doing about reading.

Direct Involvement

Some school systems make good use of the time and services of parents and other concerned adults in the community by drawing them directly into reading program activities. "Reading Mothers," for example, have been organized to read stories to children as part of a pre-reading program. Honorary uncles or grandparents have participated in programs where there is much listening and some tutoring of pupils with problems in reading. In cases of real need, adults have been given minimal training to permit them to do directed tutoring with severely disabled readers. There is talent in every community that can be put to use in a variety of ways. The point here is that once people become involved with the program they also become informed; and once they are informed, they become extremely credible disseminators of information.

Teachers' Social Contacts

Being basically opposed to shop talk, we are reluctant to suggest teachers' social contacts as a means for spreading information. Nevertheless, teachers, like everybody else, do tend to talk about what they know best and they are frequently asked about school programs and policies. Thus, as already pointed out, efforts must be made to keep entire school faculties informed on policies, services, and innovations at all levels of the reading program.

Provide Services

A number of reading-related services that can substantially enhance public relations can be provided to the community without involving great expenditures of time, effort, or money. Some examples of services follow.

Help for Disabled Readers

The parents of children with reading problems often turn out to be the severest critics or the staunchest supporters of the school reading program, depending on how well they understand the problem and whether they are convinced that optimum efforts are being expended on their children's behalf. Provisions are, of course, made for helping poor readers within the regular reading program, and parents should be aware of what can be and is being done. Here, however, we are suggesting that additions to the regular program, offered through or with the joint sponsorship of the school, can be a very effective means of establishing rapport with the community.

Summer reading programs are probably the most widely used to augment the help regularly given poor readers. Such a program is effective if it is adequately staffed, if the participants are carefully selected, and if sufficient resources for diagnosis and instruction are provided. Too often it offers a place to send the kids for the morning, becomes a source of part-time employment for any teacher who happens to be available, and is the last activity to be funded. But there is no need to rely solely on summer remedial programs. Other possibilities are (1) a tutorial service coordinated through the school — the school's function is to identify qualified tutors and recommend them to parents who seek additional help for their child; (2) classes in which parents are given information about reading problems and their correction, and, with caution, some concrete things they can do to help; (3) coordination of cooperative arrangements between the school and local service agencies — medical, psychological, psychiatric, and other services may be available, depending on the community. At least as important as anything else, the school should always be ready to provide the parents of poor readers with understanding, accurate information, and well-considered advice.

Reading Improvement for Adults

In the past two decades thousands of out-of-school adults have taken courses designed primarily to increase reading efficiency. Thousands more intend to and will when they have the opportunity. With a minimum of extra effort the school can offer that opportunity. If the course is reasonably good, the payoff in terms of good feeling will be far greater than the investment.

Most school faculties include at least one or two reading teachers who already have or could quickly acquire the additional skills required to teach an adult reading improvement course. Inexpensive workbooks can be purchased by the participants; pacing and/or tachistoscopic devices are optional; so if modest fees are charged, the course can be completely self-sustaining. In our experience the adults who enroll in such a course are almost invariably highly motivated, and they usually make rapid progress and are pleased with the results.

The following are some of the books on reading improvement that are available. Any one of them could serve as the text and/or exercise book for a course designed to help adults read better.

Mares, Colin. *Rapid and Efficient Reading.* New York: Emerson Books, 1964.
    This is our choice as the best single volume to introduce the adult reader to the techniques and psychological foundations for rapid and efficient reading. A limited number of practice exercises is included.

Brown, James I. *Efficient Reading*. Boston: Heath, 1952 and 1962 (rev. ed.).

Herr, Sylvia. *Effective Reading for Adults*. Dubuque, Iowa: Brown, 1958.

Leedy, Paul. *Read with Speed and Precision*. New York: McGraw-Hill, 1963.

Stroud, J. B., Ammons, R. B., and Bamman, H. *Improving Reading Ability*. New York: Appleton-Century Crofts, 1955.

Adult Basic Education

While reading improvement courses are intended for adults who can read adequately but wish to increase their speed and efficiency, there is also a need to help adults at the other end of the reading proficiency scale. Certainly the problem is not rampant in all communities, but the fact is that more adults read below, say, a fourth-grade proficiency level in our ostensibly highly literate society than we care to admit. (See Chapter 1 for a discussion of "functional literacy." Our concern here is for the adult who does not read well enough to cope with minimal demands or to read with independence.)

In many communities adult basic education courses — which usually include instruction in the several basic skill areas, not only reading — are offered through adult/vocational schools and other agencies not tied to the public schools as such. We feel, however, that the public schools have resources in the form of staff, materials, and expertise that would permit them to take a more active role, either by offering courses directly or by working closely with other agencies. In too many instances the public schools have not been called upon or have not been willing to participate in basic education programs. The problems involved in teaching adults are indeed different in many ways from those involved in teaching children, but when it comes to teaching the reading skills, the public schools have much to offer. To proceed as if it were otherwise is not only absurd but a blatant waste of talent and a gross duplication of effort.

One more word: To assume that semiliterate adults in general cannot read because they have never been taught is to oversimplify the problem. In fact, completely unschooled adults are rare; most have been taught but they have not successfully learned, for reasons ranging from poor and inappropriate teaching to irregular attendance at school to social-psychological problems to physical problems. Therefore, when the semiliterate adult returns to school, his justifiably negative feelings must be dealt with and his specific problems should be diagnosed. Again, the resources for doing an adequate job of diagnosis are centered in the public schools.

The following resources may be consulted for information regarding adult basic education programs and/or adult basic reading.

ERIC Clearinghouse on Adult Education, 107 Rodney Lane, Syracuse, New York, 13210.
   A part of the national ERIC system, the Clearinghouse on Adult Education can be consulted for information regarding adult basic education.
National Association for Public School Adult Education, 1201 Sixteenth Street, N.W., Washington, D.C., 20036.

Among other things, NAPSAE sponsors an Adult Education Clearinghouse (Richard W. Cartright, Director) to provide easy access to information on the education, training, and reeducation of adults and out-of-school youth.

Reading-Discussion Seminars

Aside from courses designed to increase adults' reading proficiency, courses or seminars offering opportunities for the discussion and exchange of ideas gained through recreational reading may be provided. The "great books" courses are widely known, but groups may also be formed around other interest areas or may deliberately be left essentially without focus. Here again the school has the main resources in most communities for leadership in establishing and carrying on reading-discussion seminars.

Taken together, the services we have proposed cover a wide range and would, therefore, reach a large segment of the population in a community. None of them would require a great deal of support; in most instances they could be self-sustaining. Yet they can amount to a demonstration of the school staff's interest in having reading development reach beyond the classroom. The effort expended, we feel, will be well rewarded.

Answer Questions

The school staff should stand ready to answer questions about reading instruction, questions about the total reading program, and a wide variety of questions about personal reading and children's reading problems. Certainly it would be unrealistic to suggest that each staff member ought to have all the answers. He ought, however, to be able to answer general questions about the reading program and specific ones about reading instruction at his particular level; and he should be able to find answers to other questions or make referrals to the appropriate persons. The matter of referrals is particularly important. In an age of specialization, nobody is expected to know all the answers; but everybody resents feeling that the buck is being passed when a series of phone calls must be made to track down one answer.

What is required, then, is that a school staff keep informed about the specifics of reading instruction and about the foundations, special aspects, and current development of the reading program, and that they know where to refer questions they cannot answer personally. A well-informed staff is in a position to reflect established policy and to present answers that are consistent with that policy.

Some frequently asked questions about reading follow, along with some guidelines for providing answers. Actual answers must, of course, be modified to fit local constraints and conditions.

1. *When will my first-grader learn to read?* The implicit question here seems to be: When will my first-grader begin to bring home books that he is able to read? An important point to be made in answering is that not all children are ready to profit from reading instruction at the same time and that not all respond

with equal success to beginning instruction. Therefore, it should be made clear that a general answer is not realistic and that even with regard to a particular child one cannot predict with much accuracy when actual "reading" will begin. The danger in making a specific prediction is that if something occurs to impede expected progress anxieties and pressures are likely to get out of hand. A realistic response will be that most of the activities in the first grade are directed toward reading, and each child is repeatedly given opportunities to begin actual reading.

2. *How is reading taught?* Again, the implicit question usually amounts to: How is *beginning* reading taught? And more often than not it is asked by a person who has a very specific notion of how he thinks it *should* be taught; therefore, any answer that is not in line with his expectations is likely to be unsatisfactory. Perhaps, then, the best way to avoid a quarrel over specifics is to give a fairly comprehensive answer to start with. In well-considered programs, reading is usually taught in a number of ways, depending upon both the strengths and preferences of individual teachers and the characteristics and needs of individual pupils. If that is first made clear, then a discussion of how and where certain specific approaches and materials fit into the pattern may be in order.

3. *Do you teach phonics?* This may be the question that is really being asked when the previous one is actually verbalized. Despite everything that has been said recently about phonics and linguistics and decoding, some people are still hung up on articles they read in women's magazines that say reading is taught by "look-and-say." A response to the query should point out the fact that in some approaches a few words are taught as sight words — which seems to be how the whole look-and-say business got started — but that the sight words become the basis for teaching sound-symbol relationships through an *analytic* approach. On the other hand, some approaches begin with the sounds of letters, which are then put together to form words. This is a *synthetic* approach. Whether one calls it a phonic, linguistic, or decoding approach makes little difference (though, of course, sequences may vary greatly). The point is that virtually every approach in use today teaches sound-symbol relationships; nobody advocates memorizing all the words in the English language as sight words. The main differences are in the rate and the sequence of teaching.

4. *Why aren't my daughter and the neighbor girl, both of whom are in the same class, reading the same book?* Typically the questioner is convinced that his child's book is easier, so he is afraid that the child is (a) a slow learner, (b) a "dyslexic," or (c) the opposite of teacher's pet. The main function of the answer, then, should be to reassure the questioner that none of these is necessarily true. It may be pointed out that children are ready for instruction at different times, progress at different rates, need reinforcement of different skills, and respond better to different materials; and for any of these reasons two children might be reading from different books. One might add, too, that sometimes easy books are read just for fun. Reading need not always be the serious business some parents seem to think it is.

5. *Should my child repeat the grade he is now completing?* Often parents will suggest a retention because *they* feel their child is "immature" or "behind in reading." Depending on the school's position regarding retentions, then, the

response could attempt to convince parents that a retention is or is not advisable. There is, of course, no inherent value in a retention as such; in fact, the repetition of a failure experience ordinarily has little to recommend it. On the other hand, if certain conditions have changed and the repeat will involve a different set of experiences, retention may be defensible. The answer must be made in view of school policy and a careful examination of the facts in the specific case. It is to be hoped that the person, not the policy, will be given prime consideration.

6. *Is my child reading at grade level?* Even when schools are ungraded, the question continues to be asked — not, we think, because parents are any more dazzled by the grade level concept than teachers, but because they want to know how their child is progressing. An adequate answer, then, might be given in terms of (a) the child's performance in comparison to his age-grade peers and (b) the child's performance in view of his own capabilities. The former response might appropriately be given in terms of a percentile band: "Bonnie is reading between the 64th and 83rd percentiles; this means she reads better, according to Test X, than 63 per cent of the children in her grade and 16 per cent read better than she does." (We do not believe that percentiles are too esoteric for most parents.) The latter response can be given in terms of a more global assessment of capacity: "Bonnie's achievement is in line with her capability, which, according to test scores and her achievement in other areas, is somewhat above average."

7. *What about the low group?* Children invariably know when they are in the low reading group, no matter how cleverly the groups are named or manipulated or how many groups are established. If the children know, their parents know, so the question merits a straightforward answer. Perhaps the most important point to be made is that assignment to the low group need not be a life sentence, that groups are constantly being changed and children reassigned as they progress. While he is assigned to a low reading group, however, it should be clear that the child works in many other groups and individually during the course of each school day. And, of course, it should also be clear that a low reading group is not just another name for the slow learners: Children may lag behind at various times during their development, and a reduction in pace can give them an opportunity to consolidate their skills and lay a foundation for their next period of more rapid progress.

Even when reading instruction is almost completely individualized, somebody must always be reading easier material, thinner or fewer books, etc. The basic question, therefore, cannot be evaded. The best approach is simply to stress the positive without attempting to conceal the fact.

8. *What can I do to make my child like reading?* Perhaps the honest answer, when the question is phrased as it is, is: *Nothing.* A child can no more be *made* to like reading than an adult can be *made* to like the opera. Perhaps the basic message of the response must be that all coercion should be removed from the situation. A child comes to like to read mainly because he has had pleasant, memorable experiences through reading. Such experiences cannot be forced, but the stage can be set for them. Reading materials can be made available, trips to the library can be arranged, books can be discussed (not reported on, but discussed spontaneously), a quiet place to read can be available, good examples can

be provided. Children can be made to read, but they cannot be made to like reading. Those who learn to like it are usually those who are exposed to books and then left alone to discover them.

9. *Why do girls usually read better than boys?* Although the person who asks the question may be basing it upon a very limited number of observations, girls' reading achievement scores, as a group, at least in the early grades, generally *are* higher than boys', as a group. Furthermore, more boys than girls apparently have severe reading problems, for boys almost invariably sharply outnumber girls enrolled in remedial reading clinics. The question, then, seems to represent more than idle speculation and it deserves a considered answer.

Several hypotheses are commonly advanced to "explain" the sex difference in reading achievement. While no single one seems adequate, a combination of the factors involved in some or all may account for the difference. The six hypotheses given here are taken from Heilman's (1967) excellent discussion:

1. Boys and girls differ in intelligence at different ages. The problem here is that the intelligence tests available provide no basis for testing the hypothesis.
2. Boys and girls mature at different rates. There is some evidence that girls get ahead on some factors related to reading development; but there is evidence, too, that the difference is really in educational rather than maturational factors.
3. The early school environment and curriculum are more frustrating to boys than to girls. Perhaps the problem is aggravated by ignoring boys' developmental lag, and an interaction between the two would tend to obscure each factor taken by itself.
4. Beginning reading materials are more satisfying to girls than to boys. Inspection of the material would seem to support the hypothesis, but, recently, publishers have been making real attempts to appeal to boys.
5. Primary teachers are women. The basic reasoning is that girls and women teachers are more compatible than boys and women teachers.
6. Boys are less motivated to learn to read.

An adequate answer to the question would include all six hypotheses. As the bases for the sex difference come to be more clearly understood, certain variables — e.g., teacher attitudes and behaviors and materials — can be manipulated to enhance boys' achievement.

10. *What about those machines?* Parents hear about the hardware that has, mainly in the past decade, been thrust upon the educational community in general and reading teachers in particular. Typically, they are thinking of a specific, but unnamed, device and they want to know either: (a) Why *isn't* it being used with my child? or (b) Why *is* it being used with my child? Thus, before an answer is ventured an attempt should be made to identify the device in mind. We feel this is necessary because there is no generalizable statement to be made about "machines" in the teaching of reading: Some are defensible and some are not; sometimes they are sensibly used and sometimes they are abused; some are appropriate for use at certain levels but not at others. There is, then, no point in getting involved in a defense of tachistoscopes in speed reading courses when what the

questioner has in mind is a tape recorder or filmstrip projector in the first grade.

Unfortunately, a straightforward answer may not be forthcoming even after the question is focused. The hardware is often used simply because it is there. If, on the other hand, the rationale for its use is worked out before the hardware is purchased — as it should be — there will be no problem.

11. *What do you mean, "reading" in high school?* To many lay people the notion of extending the teaching of reading upward to all levels is still as alien as it was to many teachers a few years ago. The idea of a reading program that stretches through the high school is one that needs to be developed and, for a time, defended.

To be emphasized here is the fact that the development of reading skills is a continuous process going far beyond the essentially mechanical aspects of decoding. Many of the points made in Chapter 3 regarding maturity in reading can appropriately be brought forward in response to this question.

12. *What special programs do you have for poor readers?* The answer to this question depends, of course, on what is available locally. Whatever the specifics, however, the response should make it clear that disabled readers are provided for within the context of an overall developmental program. The typical expectation is that the child with a reading problem will be given remedial help outside the classroom. Yet special help may be given in or out of the classroom, in accordance with the circumstances and the case at hand, and it must be coordinated with the regular activities in the classroom.

13. *What can we parents do to help our poor reader?* Parents are usually more ego-involved with their children's performance in reading than with their performance in any other area of the curriculum. Failure in any other subject can usually be ignored or rationalized in terms of interest, attitude, or aptitude, but failure in reading is not only blatantly obvious but also seeming evidence of some esoteric defect or plain stupidity. Therefore, parents tend to apply considerable pressure — either explicitly or implicitly — when a child has a problem in reading. Their attempts to help the child will probably amount to more pressure rather than anything worthwhile in alleviating the problem.

In framing a response to the query, then, the focus ought to be upon reducing the pressure on the child and, at the same time, reducing parental anxieties. While the best advice might be to stop trying to help and let the school handle the problem, such a suggestion is not likely to be accepted with much enthusiasm. We have found, however, that most parents are willing to channel their efforts into activities that both they and the child can enjoy, like reading stories aloud to the child, working for brief periods with flash cards, or listening to passages the child has had an opportunity to rehearse previously. They will drop phonics instruction, "helping" with assignments, etc., if they are convinced that the problem is receiving attention at school and that their efforts could be running contrary to the school's.

14. *Does my child have dyslexia?* The term *dyslexia* has been around for a long time, but only recently has it become popular to say "dyslexic" instead of something more mundane, like "poor," "disabled," or "remedial" reader. In our opinion, "dyslexia" has ceased to have any specialized meaning and has become

a label stuck on anybody who, for any reason at all, is having some (not necessarily severe) problems with reading. Rather than redefine the term each time it is used, our inclination is to drop it completely. In its present bastardized state the only function it serves is to terrify parents whose children are said to be so afflicted.

An appropriate response to the question, then, would be neither *Yes* nor *No* but a summary of what has been learned through diagnosis about the child's reading problem and a statement of what the prognosis for recovery seems to be. The implicit question has to do less with what to call the problem than with what can be done about it.

15. *What about that creeping and crawling business?* This question, while disarmingly nonspecific, is quite common and it is clearly a reference to one of the salient features of the treatment for reading disability based upon the Doman-Delacato theory of neurological organization. The theory and treatment, developed at the Institutes for the Achievement of Human Potential (formerly the Rehabilitation Center), have been popularized mainly through articles that have appeared in women's and general feature magazines.

The response to the query must be simply that, although the mass media have reported favorably upon the approach, professionals in the fields of medicine, reading, psychology, and education have not only failed to share the enthusiasm but been openly skeptical. There is not a shred of objective evidence to support the approach. Robbins (1967), for example, concluded on the basis of a careful study that (a) "The data did not support the postulated relationship between neurological organization (as measured by creeping and laterality) and reading achievement. . . ." and (b) "The data from the study did not support the contention that the addition of the Delacato program to the ongoing curriculum of the retarded readers in any way enhanced their reading development . . . when compared to similar children not exposed to the experimental program."

16. *Should I hire a tutor for my disabled reader?* While seemingly straightforward, the question is loaded. A positive answer could appear to bespeak a lack of confidence in the instruction, remedial or otherwise, offered by the school. On the other hand, an arbitrarily negative answer could preclude the provision of needed additional help. Honesty, as usual, seems to be the best policy. If the school is able to provide sufficient diagnostic and remedial services, the nature of the services should be explained and a negative answer given. If the school's resources are limited, the judgment is that additional help would be beneficial (i.e., the prognosis for progress is good), and a qualified tutor is available, then the situation should be explained and a positive answer given. There should, of course, be some assurance that the tutor will be available for a reasonable period of time. As always, consideration for the person must guide the answer.

17. *If my child is having difficulty in reading, shouldn't he be bringing work home?* This question is probably, in most cases, related to Question 13, which had to do with help at home. The assumption seems to be that the best way to overcome a problem is to overwhelm it with hard work. Yet, in reality, more general drill, nonspecific exercises, and pressure are precisely what the poor reader does not need. This should be explained in responding to the question. Furthermore, it

should be made clear that special help is ordinarily best offered during the school day when it will not appear to be a form of punishment. Children with reading problems are likely to have many negative feelings about school and teachers. There is no need to add to them by piling on homework.

18. *Should I be teaching my preschooler to read?* This question picked up impetus when a number of the mass magazines ran articles on teaching infants to read. Apparently some parents with four-year-olds began to feel that they had already waited too long. But the question is not really new, nor can it be answered once and for all. Some children do learn to read before they go to school. There is a certain amount of evidence that reading skills can be acquired almost as easily and naturally as oral language if minimal help is provided. On the other hand, an early start may amount to a handicap if the school is not prepared to cope with the child who knows how to read when he first arrives. Further, the fact that a child *can* learn to read at an early age does not mean that he *should*. And it might as well be recognized that most of the available instructional materials are written for traditional first-graders.

How, then, should the question be answered? Our inclination is simply to say: Do what comes naturally. Do not pressure the child to begin to read, but do show your own enthusiasm for books and do answer questions as they arise. A child who is ready and able to begin to read should be permitted to do so. But there is no definitive evidence that preschool reading experience either enhances or impedes future progress in reading.

19. *How fast should I be able to read?* This question is a manifestation of the popularity of speed reading courses for adults. People who have "had the course" are smug, and those who have not are apprehensive that they may be missing something. The question has little to do with the school's reading program, but an intelligent answer will show that the school is concerned about the end product as well as the instructional process.

It is appropriate to point out that the typical adult reads most material at about 250 to 300 words per minute. This is a habitual rate that is about as fast as rapid speech. Most adults can read much faster if they (a) overcome their tendency to subvocalize while reading silently, (b) practice reading rapidly, and (c) adjust their rate to their purpose. It is possible to skim certain materials for certain purposes at several thousand words per minute; but "reading" that involves actually seeing every word is probably limited to about a thousand words per minute. Flexibility is the key: No single rate is best for all purposes and materials.

References

Heilman, Arthur V. *Principles and Practices of Teaching Reading.* Columbus, Ohio: Merrill, 1967, Chap. 13.

Robbins, Melvyn P. "Test of the Doman-Delacato Rationale with Retarded Readers." *Journal of the American Medical Association,* 1967, 202, 389–393.

CHAPTER 7

Specialized Personnel in the Reading Program

Reading is so important in our culture that we make learning to read the central task of elementary school children and refining their reading abilities a major task of secondary school students. Education in American schools is largely a two-stage process: learning to read and reading to learn.

This emphasis on learning to read and reading to learn places considerable responsibility to teach reading on teachers at all academic levels. Although primary grade teachers have the job of starting the reading process, no teacher is exempt from continuing the development of students' reading abilities. One would think, then, that the education of all teachers and principals would include many courses and field experiences concerned with reading pedagogy and the supervision and administration of reading programs. Such is not the case. Nearly all of the teachers and principals with whom we have worked in many different capacities have agreed that they need more education in the teaching of reading and in the administration and supervision of reading programs.

The first Harvard-Carnegie reading study was undertaken to determine how well prospective teachers are being prepared to teach reading. It was revealed that the pre-service education of elementary school teachers is shockingly inadequate in training them to teach reading. Austin and Morrison (1963, p. 164) summarized the findings of this study as follows:

> . . . (1) Three per cent of the colleges and universities do not require prospective elementary school teachers to enroll in any course work devoted to the teaching of reading as a requirement for graduation, (2) when reading is taught with other related subjects in a single course (for example, language arts), as is done in 50 per cent of the colleges, actual class hours devoted to reading average only 8, (3) when time is a factor, intermediate grade study skills will usually be omitted from the course or, if included, will be treated so cursorily as to be of little benefit to the prospective intermediate grade teacher, (4) little preparation is offered that will help beginning teachers to recognize, diagnose, or treat reading difficulties, and (5) little, if any, guidance is offered in reading research.

The second Harvard-Carnegie study was initiated to answer some questions raised by the first. One of these questions was concerned with the role principals play in improving reading instruction in their schools. Austin and Morrison (1963, p. 204) concluded that "there is evidence that some principals are reluctant to accept major responsibility for instructional improvement because they are unfamiliar with curriculum matters, particularly those relating to the reading program." On the basis of the evidence collected in the first and second Harvard-Carnegie studies it appears that elementary school teachers and principals require the services of specialized reading personnel.

The preparation prospective secondary school teachers get to enable them to teach reading tends to be even less adequate than that of elementary school teachers. Burnett (1966) assessed the pre-service education of secondary teachers and judged that the training they receive in teaching reading is often nonexistent and at best exceedingly general and superficial. Moore (1961) described the position of secondary school teachers in this regard as follows:

> One reason why teachers have failed to embrace the notion that "all teachers are teachers of reading" is that they have not been clear as to why they should be. They have not seen reading related to the basic purpose of the content fields in such a fashion as to make clear the significance of reading problems, nor what they, as content teachers, may do to assist in solving such problems.

Certainly the fact that most teachers and principals do not receive sufficient education in reading pedagogy is at least partly responsible for the weaknesses in the reading instruction many students receive. After a thorough study of elementary classroom practices, Austin and Morrison (1963, p. 2) reported:

> . . . after visits to fifty-one school systems in the original study and fourteen in the supplementary study, observations in about two thousand classrooms, and interviews with approximately twenty-five hundred school personnel, the staff concluded that present day reading programs were mediocre at best and not currently designed to produce a future society of mature readers.

It seems reasonable to assume that under comparable investigation secondary school programs would have fared even worse.

In this chapter we shall look at the need for specialized personnel, not only in the general way presented in the preceding paragraphs, but also according to some areas of weakness prevalent in many reading programs. Next, we shall consider the kind of specialized help needed to maintain a good reading program and the specialized training and personal qualifications required of people who are employed to provide that help. Finally, we will present illustrative job descriptions for specialized reading personnel.

Some Reading Program Weaknesses

Lack of Clearly Defined Subprograms

Every school needs to develop four different reading programs which together comprise the total reading curriculum. In many schools this differentiation is not clearly defined and effectively functional. The programs exist to serve the varied needs of students as these needs were specified in Chapter 1. Harris (1961, p. 18) says,

Surveys indicate that in typical elementary schools, about one third of the children read at their grade level, about one third read one or more years above their grade level, and about one third are retarded in reading one or more years. Of the retarded readers, the majority are dull children whose reading is on a par with their other abilities. A substantial minority, comprising about 10 to 15 per cent of all the children, are cases of mild or severe reading disability.

Harris also points out that certain of the students who are reading at or above grade level may be capable of reading at even higher levels and are therefore "underachievers" in reading regardless of their grade level performance. The four programs needed within the reading curriculum, then, are the following (see Chapter 1 for a detailed discussion):

1. *The adapted* — for students who are disabled in reading because of generally slow mental development. This program requires materials at a lower level of difficulty, modified reading and reading-related assignments, and reduced pupil expectations. It should not be inferred that the adapted program is impotent in improving students' reading ability. To the contrary, much teaching and learning takes place in this program, but at a slower pace and at a lower level of sophistication. If students are properly assigned to this program, it is unlikely that they will ever move into any of the other three programs.

2. *The developmental* — for students with normal or above normal general mental development who are achieving at or above grade level. The pacing in this program is rapid compared with that in the other programs. Students progress in some systematic kind of sequence without encountering undue stress or long-term failure.

3. *The corrective* — for students with normal or above normal general mental development who are mildly disabled in reading. This program is implemented by the regular classroom teacher within the context of the regular instructional program. Special exercises, materials, and instruction are provided according to the students' diagnosed weaknesses. Insofar as possible, the reading weaknesses are treated while the students pursue the same course of study as those who are reading at or above grade level. Obviously, adjustments must be made to avoid overburdening these students. If the corrective reading instruction is doing the job, the recipients will eventually move into the developmental program.

4. *The remedial* — for students with normal or above normal general mental development who have a severe reading disability. It is imperative that students in this program have long-term, out-of-class instruction in reading. The remedial instruction is preceded by a thorough diagnosis, and suitable evaluation measures are applied frequently to determine the effectiveness of the remediation being provided. If students are properly assigned to this program (and if the remedial teaching is productive), they will eventually move to the corrective or to the developmental program.

Three things should be noted: (1) Within each of these four programs, there must be provisions for individual differences. (2) Except for the remedial program, which requires individual or near-individual instruction, it is possible to provide the needed instruction in heterogeneous classrooms. (3) All four programs are needed at both the elementary and secondary school levels; at the secondary school level, it is possible and desirable for all but the remedial program to function within the context of the various content areas.

Lack of Reinforcement in Other Curriculum Areas

Just as reading is important to every subject in the curriculum, every subject is a positive or negative reinforcer of what is taught in reading. The materials to be read in other subject matter areas should be selected with the same care and according to many of the same criteria used in selecting reading curriculum materials. The assignments and the instruction given in the content areas should reflect the same knowledge of each student's ability and interests in reading that is reflected in the reading class. It is unfortunate when a child's rapid development in reading skills is not acknowledged by giving him more sophisticated reading assignments in science, social studies, and other classes. It is perhaps even more unfortunate when a child's slow development in reading skills is not taken into consideration throughout the entire school day.

Every content area offers many opportunities to reinforce reading skills and interests. Often the materials used during the time specified for formal reading instruction are less meaningful to students than those used in the content areas. The latter materials and the purposes for using them present the student with significant reading experiences whereas developmental reading materials are often obviously for "practice" and require transfer of skills learned while using them to the actual functional and recreational materials that students encounter.

Poor Grouping Practices

Schools have generally subscribed to homogeneous grouping for teaching reading skills. At the present time this seems to be the most effective way to meet the needs of the greatest number of students. However, the criteria now used in grouping students is likely to do little more than put all of the low-ability, medium-ability, and high-ability students with classmates who have similar abilities. Then essentially the same method of instruction is applied with all groups. The differences among groups are largely differences in achievement expectancies.

Furthermore, the grouping practices in many schools are employed to meet the students' needs only for skills development. The fact that a student with poorly developed reading skills may have similar reading interests to those of a student with well-developed reading skills is frequently ignored. The ideal would be for each child to belong to an interest group as well as a skills development group. Assigning children to two groups would give each child opportunities to share reading experiences with better and poorer readers than himself and thereby lessen the present tendency to type students as good or poor readers solely on the basis of skills development.

For beginning reading instruction, the ideal would be to place children in groups for learning reading skills according to what learning strengths they possess. For example, children with well-developed auditory discrimination might be grouped together, and children with poor auditory discrimination but good visual discrimination might be placed in a different group. The former would be taught to read with a method that emphasizes phonic analysis; the latter, with a method that emphasizes visual analysis. In this way each child would learn by the method best suited to his strengths.

Unwise Materials Selection and Utilization

The market is flooded with basic and supplementary materials for reading instruction. Most of them are thoughtfully planned, attractively packaged, and helpful if used correctly with certain students. None of them is good for all students and none is good if used in a way or for results not intended by the author. One problem is that teachers and administrators tend to judge materials as good or poor rather than as good for some students and poor for others. Another problem arises when teachers and administrators do not recognize that, to be maximally effective, most materials need to be used in a particular way and to achieve particular objectives.

There is nothing on the market that "does the whole job." Nor is there anything on the market that does not require specific instructional practices to be maximally effective. The key to wise selection and use of materials is knowing the students who will use them, the strengths and limitations of the materials, and the theoretical assumptions upon which they are based. These underlying assumptions dictate how the materials should be used with students for whom they are intended.

An example will illustrate the importance of selecting materials from a background of knowledge that includes the major theoretical assumptions behind the development of the materials. Certain linguistic scholars have applied their knowledge of the English language to reading pedagogy and recommended that particular methodologies be used to teach beginning reading. Programs based on their recommendations have been developed, and currently materials for distinct linguistic approaches for teaching children to read are available. At least one of these linguistic approaches is based upon several assumptions: (1) Learning to read is first of all a matter of establishing grapheme-phoneme relationships. (2) Emphasizing meaning is unnecessary and indeed confusing in the initial learning stage. (3) Instruction should avoid confronting the beginning reader with the irregularities of the language. These assumptions are accompanied by definite prescriptions for the teacher to follow: (1) No pictures should be used in teaching children to read. (2) Library books should not be used until a specified number of basic readers are covered. (3) Letters should not be dealt with singly. There are other assumptions and prescriptions, but the point is that for maximum benefit from this approach some definite "do's" and "do not's" must be followed. Teachers or administrators who select materials accordingly should know all the elements of this teaching-learning system before they purchase the materials. Disappointment, frustration, and, ultimately, poor student achievement may result from lack of teacher and student enthusiasm for materials chosen without thorough familiarity or from failure to follow the prescriptive practices demanded by the theoretical assumptions of the system.

Improper Pacing of Instruction

The case for personalized and individualized instruction was established in Chapter 1. Undoubtedly one of the keys to good reading instruction is providing each learner with the materials and instruction for which he is ready. This requires an ongoing system of student accounting which makes the diagnostic teaching of reading possible.

When reading is taught diagnostically, each student's progress is evaluated frequently. His ability to perform specific reading behaviors is checked and noted. The evaluation, then, is also diagnostic in that it provides information relative to the student's (1) readiness to proceed to a different kind or level of instruction or (2) need for more instruction of the kind he has been receiving.

There are three different means of measuring student progress along a predetermined sequence of instruction: standardized tests, informal tests, and teacher observations of classroom behavior. All are important and should be a regular part of each child's instructional program. The important thing is that they be used systematically and precisely so that the student's pace is determined by his actual achievement and needs, not by a curriculum to be covered in a prescribed period of time.

Specialized Personnel

The reading program weaknesses discussed explicate the need for specialized personnel. Not only are the weaknesses significant and prevalent in many existing programs, but they are also too complex to be strengthened without considerable expertise and time. For the most part, classroom teachers and administrators not specialized in reading instruction have neither the time nor the special knowledge required. Implicit in the reading program weaknesses mentioned above is the need for specialized personnel to make decisions both at the classroom level and at the central office level. Pacing students, for example, requires work at the classroom level while materials selection may sometimes be more efficiently accomplished at the system, or central office level. Whether the same person may effectively serve both system-wide needs and individual classroom needs depends upon the size and overall needs of the school system. It should be made clear at this point that every school system has to assess its own needs for specialized reading personnel. How many specialists are required and how they are employed must be decided individually for each school system. The purpose here is to present a rationale for employing specialized reading personnel and to suggest some appropriate responsibilities for them to assume.

We feel that specialized reading personnel would be more effective in improving reading instruction if they were given more realistic and more clearly defined assignments than they typically receive. At the present time, many reading specialists spend too much time and energy attacking overwhelming numbers of problems or deciding which problems fall within their domain and which belong to someone else. A reading specialist who is responsible for system-wide testing programs, materials evaluation and selection, in-service education for classroom teachers, and other duties cannot also administer diagnostic tests to individual students, confer with parents, give remedial instruction, refer students to special reading laboratories or classes, etc. The key to effective utilization of specialized personnel is specific, realistic job descriptions. If the number of specialists available is too limited to accomplish the many tasks that need doing, then task priorities have to be set and clearly communicated throughout the school system.

Central Office Reading Personnel

Certain services are more efficiently performed at the system level than at the individual school level. Testing programs, for example, are needed to determine the effectiveness of the existing reading program. The selection of the tests, decisions regarding the administration of the different forms, interpretations of the data collected, and suggestions for program modification based on the test results can be accomplished better from a central location than in individual schools. Certain in-service education classes for classroom teachers and building principals are also more efficiently administered and conducted from the central office. Committee meetings for system-wide textbook selections, library policies, supplementary materials purchases, etc., call for central office engineering.

Coordination of the various elements in a school system's reading program is an important function of central office specialized personnel. System-wide as well as individual classroom goals should be established for the reading curriculum. The accomplishment of these goals depends upon some kind of sequential instruction as students progress from kindergarten through Grade 12. The experiences obtained in one school's program should be used to direct other schools' programs. All these services are probably best directed from a central office.

Specialized reading personnel who work at the central office must be meticulous about spending a certain portion of their time in the field. Anyone who has left the classroom for any period of time knows how easy it is to lose the ability to empathize with children and teachers. Consulting with principals and teachers about their daily successes and problems is an appropriate service for central office personnel to perform. Dispensing instructional "tips" while "on the run," however, is not considered adequate consultation. On the basis of our experience, we recommend that central office reading consultants move into a host school for a one- or two-week period of time. During this visitation classrooms may be observed, preferably upon invitation, materials examined and evaluated, children tested, and teachers conferred with individually and in groups. Visitations need to be worked out with the principal and staff beforehand. With careful preplanning they have a much greater impact on the instructional program than short visits to solve specific problems. Visitations to schools by central office staff will be discussed in greater detail in Chapter 8.

Specialized Reading Personnel in Schools

Although certain specialized reading services are best performed by a person or persons working out of the central office, there is a great need for specialized reading personnel to be permanently stationed in individual schools. Because of the importance of reading to the American way of life and because of the difficulties many students have in developing reading maturity, every school should have regularly available at least one person who is more highly trained in the teaching of reading than are most classroom teachers and building principals. He should have time to devote solely to the instructional reading program.

The day is gone, we hope, when the person who is most knowledgeable and enthusiastic about the teaching of reading is assigned a room or laboratory "down the hall" to meet with specially referred or volunteer students. Specialized reading personnel who are assigned to schools should always work as resource persons for the entire school as well as with selected students.

The first responsibility of the reading specialist is to develop and maintain a reading program geared to the individual needs of each student. This means a program in which the prevention of reading disabilities and the expanding of each student's reading according to his total personal growth are emphasized. The second responsibility of the specialist is to provide extra help for children with reading problems sufficiently severe to be classed as disabled readers. The student who is reading at or above grade level but substantially below his intellectual potential (two or more years is suggested in Chapter 1) is considered here to be a disabled reader.

Most of what was said previously in this chapter is pertinent to the role of the person specialized in reading who is assigned to one school. The need for such a person is apparent from an investigation of the educational background in reading most teachers and principals bring to their jobs. The specific weaknesses posited earlier as being prevalent in reading programs are all complex enough to require the expertise of a specialist who can devote full time to eliminating them on an individual school basis. However, some differences in job emphasis may validly be established for specialized personnel in elementary schools and specialized personnel in secondary schools.

In Elementary Schools. Reading instruction is a primary task of the elementary school. Therefore, it is essential that the entire elementary school curriculum contribute to each child's development in reading.

If reading instruction is to be maximally effective, certain conditions must prevail. The particular method used to teach beginning reading should draw heavily on the child's emotional, physical, cognitive, and experiential strengths. The kinds of writing tasks assigned, questions asked, and discussions engaged in relative to reading experiences should be structured to achieve specific objectives. The materials a child uses should match his abilities and interests. The groups to which he is assigned should be the best that can be formed for his needs. Diagnostic and evaluation procedures should be specific enough to assess the effects of completed instruction and to prescribe further instruction. Whether a child will profit most from a developmental, corrective, remedial, or adapted instructional program should be decided on the basis of precise measurements. These and other equally important conditions can usually be upgraded by the cooperative efforts of an elementary school principal, an elementary school staff, and a person specialized in the teaching of reading.

In addition to making the regular curriculum as effective as possible in fostering each child's reading development, specialized personnel in reading are needed in each elementary school to provide individual or small-group instruction for students who cannot profit from instruction in the classroom. In school systems with a central office staff of specialized reading personnel who get out into the schools frequently to consult with principals and teachers, the specialists assigned to individual schools may spend most of their time working directly with students who need special instruction. In school systems with no or extremely limited central office personnel, the specialist in the school will need to divide the school day between consulting with teachers and the principal and teaching students.

For some students the pace, distractions, competition, and group work that are a part of the regular instructional reading program may seriously interfere with their learning to read. They need to have reading taught in a distinctive environment by a teacher trained in diagnostic, remedial, and evaluative techniques. Although the number of students who qualify for this remedial instruction is small, such a program should be available in every school.

We do not favor transporting students to clinics or schools equipped with remedial teachers and materials. Besides the stigma attached to being taken "across town" for "remedial reading," communication and coordination difficulties almost always occur between the specialists "across town" and the children's regular teachers. We also question the effectiveness of summer remedial reading programs. Remedial reading is most effective when it is available as soon as the child needs it, minimally upsetting to the child, and closely coordinated with the rest of the child's instructional program. These conditions can be met best by having a specially trained reading teacher in every elementary school.

If it is impossible for an elementary school to employ a special reading teacher full time, then a specifically trained classroom teacher may be given some released time to perform the specialized reading services that every school ought to have. The Madison, Wisconsin, elementary schools have instituted a program for the development and utilization of "reading resource" teachers. Under the program each elementary school identified a classroom teacher known to be an exemplary teacher of reading who also had the personal qualifications to communicate well with other teachers. The teachers identified were invited to become reading resource teachers in their schools. Those who accepted were required to participate in a training program conducted by central office reading personnel. Upon completion of the training course they were given some released time each week to aid their principals in improving the reading curriculums in their schools. When the program was initiated, it was discovered that there was an abundant supply of classroom teachers with the desire to do some special work with reading in their schools. Many had already taken university graduate courses in the teaching of reading. The central office personnel are enthusiastic about the program because it makes a trained teacher available to participate in system-wide curriculum development. The principals are enthusiastic because the program gives them someone in their buildings to whom they can turn for special services. The other teachers, especially those new to teaching, are strong supporters of the program because they have a specially trained person readily accessible to help them with their problems. Parents have been highly receptive. They recognize the importance of reading in our society, and they are willing to support specialized personnel to maintain reading instruction at a high level.

In Secondary Schools. The role of the reading specialist in the secondary school is somewhat different. There is no doubt that the heart of the secondary school reading program must reside in the content areas. If we agree that (1) all secondary school students can profit from systematic reading instruction, (2) each content area requires different reading skills, and (3) functional reading skills are taught best with functional reading materials in actual classroom situations, then obviously reading instruction must be every secondary school teacher's business. We have already noted that the pre-service education of secondary teachers regarding the teaching of reading is likely to be more limited than that of elementary teachers. Therefore, there is great need for secondary school teachers to receive in-service training to help them incorporate the teaching of reading into their content area curriculums. Specialized reading personnel in secondary schools, then, have an even greater in-service education function to perform than specialized personnel in elementary schools. The particulars of this function are discussed thoroughly in Chapter 8.

Suffice it to say here that the in-service education of secondary school teachers in the teaching of reading has two foci: First, subject matter teachers must be shown that the teaching of reading is a legitimate responsibility of theirs. Second, they must be shown precisely what they can do to improve the reading abilities of their students. Accomplishing these two objectives is perhaps the basic job of a secondary school reading specialist.

In addition to establishing and maintaining a developmental reading program within the content areas, the secondary school reading specialist must also set up reading programs for students with unusual needs. These needs may be remedial (for students who have normal or above normal intellectual ability but who are reading below grade level) or developmental (for students who are reading at grade level but who have the interest and potential to read faster or at a more sophisticated level of comprehension or who should develop more interest in reading. In the secondary school such programs are usually more distinctly specialized than in the elementary school and likely to take the form of special classes, laboratory sessions, or small-group instruction.

Establishing criteria for admitting students to special reading programs and teaching the students who are enrolled are definite responsibilities of the special reading teacher in the high school. The kinds of instruction to be used and the specifics of operation should be decided by the principal, the reading specialist, central office personnel, and the entire teaching staff of the school whenever possible. It is vital for all teachers and administrators to know what special reading programs are available to students and the objectives of each program.

The advisability of having a part-time reading specialist in a secondary school is questionable. It would seem that, except for unusually small high schools, one full-time specialist ought to be able to provide only a minimum program. Although the argument can be advanced that something is better than nothing, there is reason to believe that a poor instructional program in a high school may be worse than none at all. Too often the consultant role of the part-time reading specialist is postponed, and remedial reading classes with questionable benefit to the students enrolled become the compromise program. In this case the whole staff validly dismisses its responsibility for lack of know-how. The reading specialist, then, has not only the frustration of being unable to develop a satisfactory program but also an extra preparation or more in his own schedule. Another factor involved is the willingness of a well-trained secondary school reading specialist to devote only part time to his major area of interest and preparation. Perhaps a secondary school unable to staff a full-time reading specialist would be wiser to invest in consultant help from nearby universities than to hire a part-time specialist.

University Consultants

Most universities have faculty members who are specialists in the teaching of reading and willing to serve as consultants to nearby school systems. These people often make good contributions to schools and school systems that have their own specialists as well as to those that lack them.

The contribution university faculty members are able to make depends upon cooperative specific planning by the administration, teachers, and the university consultant. As a general rule, university consultants are little more than inspirational unless they are engaged for extended periods of time to work with a school system or individual school on a carefully delineated project. Like some of the other areas mentioned briefly in this chapter, the role of university consultants for in-service education will be discussed more thoroughly in Chapter 8, dealing with in-service education for reading program improvement.

Qualifications of Reading Specialists

Obviously, the background experiences a reading specialist should have depend upon the kind of services he is hired to perform. However, it is possible to specify some qualifications that seem essential to anyone who works as a reading specialist.

Personal Qualifications. As we have said, a major responsibility of all reading specialists is consultant or in-service work with administrators, classroom teachers, and other specialized personnel such as guidance counselors. Consequently, whether they work on a system-wide basis or in one school, reading specialists need to be able to establish and maintain excellent interpersonal relationships.

When someone receives help from another person, it is important that both emerge from the exchange with a desire to work together again.

Anyone who has worked in a supervisory or consultant role knows that people who are most in need of specialized help are often also most reluctant to receive it. Therefore, the reading specialist frequently has to initiate communication with teachers and administrators. Only one who can initiate and maintain communication in a nonthreatening manner will be successful in changing the behavior of the person who receives specialized help.

It is also important for a reading specialist to be patient. Teaching concepts and changing behavior are slow processes. The specialist must be prepared for the long periods of time required for people who are not reading specialists to assimilate concepts relative to grouping, diagnosing, evaluating, attitude development, etc. Then to help them modify their behavior accordingly calls for even more time. One of the present writers worked with a school principal nearly a year before the latter understood that referring students to remedial teachers solely on the basis of standardized reading test scores was poor practice. It took another year for more sophisticated referral practices to be instituted.

Not only does a reading specialist need to be patient; he must also be able to accept defeat and not be defeated. Not everyone with whom he works will be helped. Ideally, all conditions can be structured and controlled to contribute maximally to each student's reading development. Realistically, there are always inept or uncooperative people, shortages of funds, lack of space, community pressure groups, lack of enlightening research, etc. Only someone with a personality that subscribes to Browning's philosophy, "Ah, but a man's reach should exceed his grasp, or what's a heaven for?" will be a happy, effective reading specialist.

Unfortunately, rebuffs are still a part of an educational specialist's work life. Some teachers and administrators will resent him and look upon his attempts to improve instruction as interfering or an easy way to make a living. He must realize that this negative attitude does exist and will manifest itself in rebuffs or even open hostility. Such manifestations must be met with calmness and refusal to do battle. The person with a thin skin who works as a reading specialist will be shattered personally before the reading program is improved.

Finally, the reading specialist has to be able to maintain objectivity while working with people. He must empathize with many different personality types in a day's time. He must establish rapport, be sensitive to personalities and problems, offer advice according to his appraisal of the individual to whom he is speaking, etc. All of this demands personal involvement that is physically and emotionally draining. The specialist needs to acknowledge the personalities with whom he works without losing his own identity and without losing sight of the job he has to perform.

The preceding paragraphs focus on the personal qualifications of a reading specialist who acts as a consultant to teachers and administrators. The same qualifications are necessary for the specialist who works with children in need of specialized reading instruction. If he is able to establish good personal relationships with adults, he is probably able to do so with children too. In our experience, the man or woman who has poor interpersonal relationships with adults can rarely if ever establish good interpersonal relationships with children.

Educational Qualifications. The International Reading Association has suggested (1968) minimal educational qualifications for reading specialists. At this writing they are as follows:

Special Teacher of Reading   Complete a planned program for the master's degree from an accredited institution, to include

1. A minimum of 12 semester hours in graduate level reading courses with at least one course in each of the following:
   a. Foundations or survey of reading. A basic course whose content is related exclusively to reading instruction or the psychology of reading. Such a course ordinarily would be first in a sequence of reading courses.
   b. Diagnosis and correction of reading disabilities. The content of this course or courses includes the following: causes of reading disabilities; observation and interview procedures; diagnostic instruments; standard and informal tests; report writing; materials and methods of instruction.
   c. Clinical or laboratory practicum in reading. A clinical or laboratory experience which might be an integral part of a course or courses in the diagnosis and correction of reading disabilities. Students diagnose and treat reading disability cases under supervision.
2. Complete, at undergraduate or graduate level, study in each of the following areas:
   a. Measurement and/or evaluation.
   b. Child and/or adolescent psychology.
   c. Psychology, including such aspects as personality, cognition, and learning behaviors.
   d. Literature for children and/or adolescents.
3. Fulfill remaining portions of the program from related areas of study.

Reading Clinician   Meet the qualifications as stipulated for the Special Teacher of Reading and, in addition, complete a sixth year of graduate work to include:

1. An advanced course or courses in the diagnosis and remediation of reading and learning problems.
2. A course or courses in individual testing.
3. An advanced clinical or laboratory practicum in the diagnosis and remediation of reading difficulties.
4. Field experiences under the direction of a qualified Reading Clinician.

Reading Consultant   Meet the qualifications as stipulated for the Special Teacher of Reading and, in addition, complete a sixth year of graduate work to include:

1. An advanced course in the remediation and diagnosis of reading and learning problems.
2. An advanced course in the developmental aspects of a reading program.
3. A course or courses in curriculum development and supervision.
4. A course and/or experience in public relations.

5. Field experiences under a qualified Reading Consultant or Supervisor in a school setting.

Reading Supervisor Meet the qualifications as stipulated for the Special Teacher of Reading and, in addition, complete a sixth year of graduate work to include

1. Courses listed as 1, 2, 3, and 4 under Reading Consultant.
2. A course or courses in administrative procedures.
3. Field experiences under a qualified Reading Supervisor.

Although the International Reading Association has suggested minimal educational qualifications, there is in fact considerable inconsistency among state requirements for reading specialization. There are also considerable differences in university programs leading to specialization in reading. Austin (1968, p. 372) says, "In reviewing the requirements for teacher certification in reading, the lack of agreement among states concerning operational definitions of 'reading teachers,' 'remedial reading personnel,' and 'reading consultants' is evident." In regard to reading specialists, Austin (1968, p. 380) comments about the university training available to them:

In many instances, their preparation has been too meager to enable them to meet the demands placed upon them. In fact, the availability of those persons who possess the requisite skills is limited, and their training frequently is incomplete or impractical. Consequently, universities should design special programs for training teachers to become qualified, knowledgeable reading consultants.

Because university programs and state certification requirements change frequently, the specifics of the differences among states and universities will not be presented here. Suffice it to say that at this writing, suggestions for state certification policies and university programs for training reading specialists are needed.

We do not believe that national standardization of state certification policies or of university programs for specialized reading personnel is advisable. Different states have different needs and resources, and different universities should have the right to structure their programs according to their philosophies, students, and resources. Therefore, we will suggest courses and field experiences that seem to be highly desirable for anyone who works as a reading specialist. Certainly, the responsibilities of the particular reading specialist position being prepared for would be a factor in deciding the priority of the suggested courses and field experiences for a given student.

We do not mean to supersede the recommendations of the International Reading Association, which presents them as minimal. Our hope is to reinforce and supplement the IRA recommendations. It will be noted that the position of Reading Clinician is not included in any of our discussion, even though the IRA does list it, because we do not regard reading clinics as the best way for elementary and secondary schools to use the resources they have available for reading program improvement at this time.

The following list of courses and field experiences may be helpful to (1) teachers planning programs to prepare themselves as reading specialists, (2) administrators reviewing the credentials of candidates for reading specialist positions, (3) universities interested in developing courses and field experiences for teachers who desire reading specialist training, and (4) state departments of public instruction that want some guidelines for determining course and field experience requirements for reading specialization certification.

Suggested courses
Administration of Reading Programs
Adolescent Literature
Adolescent Psychology
Child Psychology
Children's Literature
Developmental Reading in the Elementary School
Developmental Reading in the Secondary School
Elementary School Curriculum
Individual Intelligence Testing
Learning Theory
Linguistics
Major Approaches to Reading Instruction and Related Materials
Principles of Appraisal and Measurement
Reading Diagnosis and Evaluation
Remedial Reading
Secondary School Curriculum
Statistics for Education
The Psychology of Reading

Suggested field experiences
Internship: Central Office Reading Specialist
Internship: Specialist in Elementary Reading
Internship: Specialist in Secondary Reading
Supervised Remedial Teaching

Experience Qualifications. No one should become a reading specialist without having had successful classroom teaching experience. Teachers and principals are much more willing to work with a specialist who has been a successful teacher than with one who has not. A specialist who has been a classroom teacher is more likely to know the problems of classroom teachers and to offer practical advice. "When I was teaching . . ." are often the words that open minds and classroom doors when they are injected by a reading specialist into conferences with teachers and principals. In addition, a reading specialist needs a background of teaching experiences with students at as many different ability and cultural levels as possible. For this reason it is good for him to have taught in a variety of schools servicing students at various ability and cultural levels.

Because of the differences between the elementary and the secondary school, it is advisable for a reading specialist working at either level to have had successful teaching experience at that level. If he works at both levels, he should have had teaching experience at one level and be thoroughly studied in reading instruction in the other. Elementary school teachers tend to feel that secondary school teachers know very little about teaching in the elementary school, and secondary teachers think that elementary teachers don't fully understand the role of a secondary teacher. These feelings are probably valid because of the major differences in the pre-service education of elementary and secondary teachers. Consequently, to gain the confidence and cooperation of either, it is generally necessary to have taught at their respective levels.

Position Descriptions. Position descriptions are presented to illustrate one way in which a school system may utilize specialized reading personnel. It has already been stated that each system should employ and utilize personnel according to its own needs and resources. These descriptions, then, are merely models to be used in developing local descriptions. They should probably not be adopted as they are given.

Four positions are described: two different central office positions, a position for a specialist assigned to one secondary school, and a position for a specialist assigned to one elementary school. It will be noted that the secondary school position and the elementary school position include working as a consultant or resource person for other members of the staff. This is in keeping with the philosophy presented earlier in this chapter: that reading specialists should influence the entire school curriculum by sharing their knowledge of reading instruction with classroom teachers and principals.

Reading coordinator

Reports to: Director of curriculum development.

Supervises: Central office reading consultants and reading teachers.

Required experience and training: Master's degree in remedial and/or developmental reading; at least six years of successful teaching experience in the areas of remedial and developmental reading; successful experience in leadership roles with teacher groups.

Desired additional experience and training: Ph.D., Ed.D., or Reading Specialist degree with emphasis in reading curriculum and instruction; successful experience with research.

Desired personal characteristics: Creativity; leadership qualities; ability to work cooperatively with teachers, principals, and central staff personnel; scholarship; ability to communicate orally and in writing at a high level of proficiency.

Position responsibilities:

Designs and directs new development in the instructional reading program, K–12.

Directs the activities of the central office reading consultants.

Provides in-service education for central office reading consultants, teachers, and administrators.

Interprets the reading program to the board of education and community groups.

Assists the pupil-services department in determining system-wide testing procedures and other activities relevant to the reading program.

Advises and cooperates with nearby universities in teacher education and research relative to reading.

Aids in the recruitment, interviewing, and selection of reading program personnel.

Designs and directs research in reading.

Attends and participates in meetings relevant to the school system's reading program.

Disseminates information regarding reading program development throughout the school system at the local, state, and national levels.

Visits classrooms with the approval of school principals to assist in evaluating teachers and improving their capabilities in the area of reading instruction.

Assists the director of curriculum development in the preparation of course outlines and teaching guides.

Assists in the evaluation and selection of textbooks and other resource materials.

Works with the central office reading consultants to coordinate the reading curriculum from kindergarten to Grade 12.

Central office reading consultant

Reports to: Reading coordinator.

Supervises: Reading teachers assigned to individual schools.

Required experience and training: Master's degree with an emphasis in reading; successful teaching experience at the academic level assigned.

Desired additional experience and training: Ph.D., Ed.D., or Reading Specialist degree or active engagement in an academic program leading to one of the above; successful experience in teacher education and in leadership roles with teacher groups.

Desired personal characteristics: Ability to work cooperatively with teachers, principals, and central office personnel; leadership ability; ability to communicate orally at a high level of proficiency; good sense of organization.

Position responsibilities:

Aids school staffs in developing objectives for reading instruction in the schools assigned.

Organizes and conducts in-service education programs for classroom teachers and for reading teachers assigned to individual schools.

Aids the reading coordinator in research relative to the reading programs being conducted in the schools assigned.

Investigates materials for the academic level assigned and recommends their purchase to teachers and principals.

Aids the reading teacher and the principal in developing and evaluating special instructional programs.

Aids the reading teachers in a continual evaluation of each school's reading program.

Studies the latest thinking and research regarding reading instruction at the academic level assigned and communicates this information to teachers and administrators.

Teams with reading teachers for initiating projects that will benefit from a temporary team approach.

Diagnoses and prescribes instruction for seriously disabled readers.

Communicates frequently with central office reading consultants assigned to other schools and other academic levels.

Works with the reading coordinator and other central office reading consultants to coordinate the reading curriculum from kindergarten to Grade 12.

Supervises reading teachers in their work with teachers and students.

Introduces innovative reading programs and materials to the schools assigned.

Serves on textbook and other committees that affect reading in the schools assigned.

Gives classroom demonstrations for teachers.

Conducts in-service meetings and classes for reading teachers, classroom teachers, and administrators.

Special reading teacher (secondary school)

Reports to: The principal.

Supervises: No one.

Required experience and training: Master's degree or active engagement in a program leading to a master's degree with an emphasis in reading; course work in developmental reading in the secondary school, remedial reading, principles of appraisal and measurement, supervised teaching of students in a secondary school instructional reading program; successful teaching experience in a content area in a secondary school.

Desired additional experience and training: Reading Specialist degree or certification beyond the master's degree; successful teaching experience in more than one content area in a secondary school.

Desired personal characteristics: Ability to establish and maintain good interpersonal relationships with high school students, teachers, parents, and administrators; leadership abilities; ability to communicate orally at a high level of proficiency; good sense of organization.

Position responsibilities:

Develops and maintains, with the help of central office reading consultants, a systematic developmental reading program residing in the content areas by helping teachers in all content areas incorporate the teaching of reading into their curriculums. This help may be in the form of in-service meetings, demonstrations, individual conferences, or team teaching.

Develops and teaches special classes, seminars, and workshops, and supervises individualized study projects for students with special reading needs. These special instructional programs should be closely related to the work being done in the content area classes and as often as possible conducted in conjunction with a particular unit of study.

Advises the principal and central office reading consultants regarding desired reading program development.

Implements, with the help of central office reading consultants and guidance counselors, a testing program and communicates information regarding students' reading abilities to their content area teachers.

Administers diagnostic reading tests to specially referred students and on the basis of the test results recommends special materials, assignments, and achievement expectancies to their teachers.

Teams with reading teachers in other schools and with central office reading consultants to conduct short-term projects or in-service work in another school.

Special reading teacher (elementary school)

Reports to: The principal.

Supervises: No one.

Required experience and training: Bachelor's degree with an emphasis in elementary education; graduate courses in developmental reading in the elementary school, remedial reading, and principles of appraisal and measurement; supervised experience with diagnosis, remediation, and evaluation of disabled readers in the elementary school; successful teaching experience in the elementary school.

Desired additional experience and training: Master's degree or Reading Specialist degree or certification; successful teaching experience in both primary and intermediate grades.

Desired personal characteristics: Ability to establish and maintain good interpersonal relationships with children, teachers, parents, and administrators; leadership ability; ability to communicate orally at a high level of proficiency.

Position responsibilities:

Organizes a systematic plan of referral and instruction for disabled readers likely to profit from individual or near-individual teaching.

Diagnoses and gives remedial instruction to students with reading disabilities.

Acts as a resource person for the principal and teachers in regard to the employment of materials, methods, etc., for reading instruction.

Diagnoses and prescribes corrective programs for mildly disabled students likely to profit from corrective help by their classroom teacher.

Confers with central office reading consultants regarding system-wide reading program development in the elementary school.

References

Austin, Mary C. "Professional Training of Personnel." In *Innovation and Change in Reading Instruction*. Chicago, Ill.: University of Chicago Press, 1968.

Austin, Mary C., and Coleman Morrison. *The First R*. New York: Macmillan, 1963.

Burnett, Richard W. "Reading in the Secondary School: Issues and Innovations." *Journal of Reading*, 1966, 9, 322–328.

Fries, Charles C. *Linguistics and Reading.* New York: Holt, Rinehart & Winston, 1963.

Harris, Albert J. *How to Increase Reading Ability.* New York: Longmans, Green, 1961.

Moore, Walter J. "Every Teacher Is a Teacher of Reading." *University of Kansas Bulletin of Education,* 1961, 15, 85–92.

"Roles, Responsibilities, and Qualifications of Reading Specialists," *Journal of Reading,* 1968, 2, 60–63.

CHAPTER 8

In-Service Education and the Reading Program

> The most important educational experience happening to a student is his teacher.—*Virgil E. Herrick*[1]

There is widespread agreement that the pre-service education of both elementary and secondary teachers is inadequate in regard to the teaching of reading. We presented evidence in support of this position in Chapter 4. There is also a general disenchantment with improving reading instruction through in-service education. The disenchantment is largely the result of administrators' and teachers' past experiences with in-service programs that have seemed irrelevant and have been unproductive as far as moving toward the ultimate goal of in-service education, changing teachers' classroom behavior, is concerned.

Much has been written about the need for in-service education, and many suggestions have been advanced for improving it. Generally, the suggestions focus on improving the organization and presentation of the programs, and they center on involving the teachers in planning them, keeping the group small, providing released time for them, using multimedia, and having follow-up activities. These are all good suggestions, and undoubtedly the quality of most in-service programs could be improved. In this chapter we too will present guidelines for effective in-service programs, and in the following chapter we will describe some programs that have appeared to be successful. However, it is imperative to recognize that conditions other than its format are major factors in determining how successful the program will be in changing teacher behavior in the classroom.

Underlying Conditions

Whether in-service education in reading results in better reading instruction for children or not depends as much on the attitudes of the teachers and administrators who participate in the program as on the program itself. Teachers and administrators must acknowledge in-service education to be as important as pre-service education, and they must be ready, if necessary, to make major changes in how reading is taught as a result of in-service education. In-service education needs to be perceived as a means for improving basic instructional practices, such as grouping for reading instruction, differentiating student assignments, pacing instruction, diagnosing student needs, asking questions, and motivating students to

---

[1] *Strategies of Curriculum Development,* selected writings of the late Virgil E. Herrick. Edited by James B. Macdonald, Dan W. Anderson, and Frank B. May. Columbus, Ohio: Charles E. Merrill Books, Inc., 1965, p. 68.

read. Thus it will best serve the reading development of students at all academic levels.

Administrative Commitment

Lack of Emphasis on Improving Classroom Teachers' Instructional Practices. Although the operation of schools is far more democratic than it once was, the board of education and the administrators hired by the board are still the major policy determiners. "Line" officers are the administrators who allocate the budget and who ultimately make the decisions that determine the goals of a school and how they will be achieved. It is the role of people in "staff" positions to function according to "line" decisions. Since line officers hire and evaluate staff, staff people are generally responsive to the desires of line officers. In simple terms, central office staff members follow the direction of the superintendent of schools, and teachers follow the direction of their principals.

Although there has been much verbalization about improving reading education and considerable expenditure of money and other resources for in-service education to effect changes, the same administrative problems appear to persist; and lists of children with reading disabilities lengthen. Martin (1969) investigated the effect of federal aid programs in the establishment or improvement of secondary school reading programs in Minnesota, Wisconsin, Iowa, and North and South Dakota. Although he sees some positive effects, it is difficult to discern major progress in his findings. He reports,

> It must be noted that schools of the Upper Midwest have not in the course of the past five years achieved a theoretically sound reading program. Schools today report their major problem in developing reading programs is the lack of qualified reading teachers. The area of staffing is the one most in need of federal assistance. Budget deficits are a second problem in all strata. These same two concerns were also paramount five years ago.

Although these were secondary schools, it is not unreasonable to assume that elementary schools would submit similar if not identical needs.

That schools continue to cite the lack of qualified reading teachers and budget deficits as the major obstacles to improving reading education is revealing. Neither of these felt needs can be satisfied through in-service education. The latter, then, is apparently perceived by administrators as a compromise to be used until some real help in the form of money and special reading teachers is available.

It is also revealing to note how administrators use qualified reading teachers and money when these two resources are available. In the elementary school, administrators who can afford it often change from one methodological system to another in their basic reading program and purchase more and newer materials for their supplementary program. This is the case even though there is considerable evidence that it is the teacher, not the particular system or materials, that makes the difference in children's reading development. When a qualified reading teacher is hired, he is often assigned to work full time with the most seriously disabled readers in the school instead of to devote at least some time to helping classroom teachers with grouping, questioning techniques, pacing, and other instructional practices. In the secondary school, administrators furnish and staff "reading laboratories," schedule remedial reading classes, require a special unit in developmental reading in all tenth-grade English classes, and support other special reading programs that have not been impressive in the impact they have had on high schools' reading problems. The expenditure of money and the utilization of staff for special reading programs, different methods, or new materials instead of for in-service education to improve teachers' instructional practices indicate either an unwarranted satisfaction with teachers' methods or a lack of confidence in the ability of in-service education to improve them. The fact is that administrators have been committed to using budget and specialized personnel for bigger and brighter patches instead of for in-service education to better the process that weaves a coat with textural weaknesses in the first place. Slow progress in reading program improvement must be attributed in part to a lack of administrative commitment to changing the instructional practices of classroom teachers from kindergarten through Grade 12.

Basic changes have been made in teachers' instructional practices to accommodate team teaching, modular scheduling, nongradedness, independent study, and other innovations. These changes have been successfully undertaken where administrative commitment has resulted in vigorous expenditure of time and money and productive in-service education to bring them about. Teachers have joined their enthusiasm with that of boards of education and administrators, and their combined efforts have given rise to specially designed school buildings, effective organizational patterns, and, most important, improved instructional programs. Unfortunately, this kind of commitment to reading program improvement has been exceedingly rare. In-service education in reading generally suffers from a lack of the kind of administrative zeal shown certain other programs. If line officers were as ardent in their support of reading program development as they are for other kinds of development, in-service education in reading would be sought after, attended to, and productive of better instructional practices in the classroom.

Changing Instructional Practices Through Teacher Accountability. An important manifestation of administrative commitment to the improvement of teachers' instructional reading practices through in-service education is teacher accountability. People are essentially reward-punishment oriented. They work hard to obtain certain rewards and to avoid unpleasantness of one kind or another. They like to be evaluated and found pleasing. With all its faults, the grading system has motivated students to learn useful things which they wouldn't have learned without it. And although it is often a difficult task, evaluating teachers can be beneficial to the development of good instructional programs.

Teachers are usually evaluated on the organization of their classrooms, the techniques by which they motivate their students, how they use instructional materials, their relationships with fellow teachers, and other factors judged to be important to the school's instructional program. However, they are not generally evaluated on whether they are doing these things better following a specific in-service education program than they were prior to the program. Consequently, in-service education in reading is often neither carefully attended to when presented nor carefully applied in the classroom later.

We have conducted and observed what in our judgment were thoroughly planned, skillfully presented, relevant in-service programs. They were sometimes not taken seriously by the teachers who seemed most to need them. In some instances the principal himself was not on hand for the entire program. It was apparent that no teacher would be held accountable for learning and using in the classroom the information presented. We are not dismissing here the need for inspiring, meaningful, practical in-service programs. Rather, we are stating that no matter how good the quality of an in-service program, some teachers will not respond to it unless they know they will be held accountable for learning and utilizing what has been offered.

Teachers should know that they will be expected to improve their teaching as a result of an in-service reading program, and that their ability to accomplish this improvement will be a factor in their professional advancement. Under such circumstances those who plan in-service reading programs will be more concerned with offering a program to effect change in the classroom, and teachers and principals will be properly motivated to put the suggestions they receive to work.

Attitudes Toward In-Service Education

Attitudes Toward In-Service Education in General. Much evidence is available regarding the inadequacies of teachers' pre-service education. Nevertheless, educators and laymen tend to think of a teacher with a bachelor's degree as a nearly finished product. Certainly they are likely to think of a teacher with a bachelor's degree and several years of "successful" teaching experience as a finished product. The fact is that the product is never finished. There is already too much to know about children and how to teach them to be learned in a lifetime. It would seem, then, that in-service education would be as highly regarded by administrators, teachers, and the general public as pre-service education. Such is not always the case. In-service education has gained considerable respectability in the last several years, but it is still sometimes regarded as something of a nuisance and definitely as something extra rather than a basic component of teacher education. The four years a prospective teacher spends taking university courses and the relatively short amount of time given to student teaching are considered by most to be the heart of his preparation, regardless of the number of years to be spent in the classroom subsequently.

The heavy reliance placed on a teacher's pre-service education has been one factor in causing in-service education to be received less enthusiastically than it should be. The apathetic response is a manifestation of a lack of regard for courses in teaching methods that are offered beyond the pre-service stage. Until the notion that "Now I've made it" is removed from the college graduation ceremony, in-service education is likely to remain a promising but not very productive enterprise. The professors who train teachers must emphasize the limited role they are able to play in the education of a teacher. They must present their courses and pre-service field experiences as the beginning, not the end, of a teacher's instruction in how to teach; and they must develop in prospective teachers positive attitudes toward in-service education. Hiring officials must then do their part to maintain these positive attitudes by making it clear at the time they hire a new teacher that in-service education is highly regarded in their school system's operation, and that active participation in the in-service opportunities provided is a necessary part of the teaching contract.

Attitudes Toward In-Service Education in Reading. The preceding comments are addressed to in-service education in general. We feel that in-service education in reading presents special problems in both elementary and secondary schools.

In the elementary school, teaching reading is considered the most important task of teachers at all grade levels. It is the area of the curriculum that parents are most concerned about and, therefore, the area of the curriculum about which teachers are likely to be most defensive. It is a rare elementary school teacher who admits to lacking competence in the teaching of reading. Only after experience and additional education have removed the deficit will some teachers reveal their former inadequacy. Because elementary school teachers share the feelings of others that their ability to teach the important subject of reading should be un-questioned, they hesitate to show too much interest in a program that purports to instruct them in how to improve their reading pedagogy.

In the secondary school the special problems connected with in-service education in reading arise from the feeling of many content area teachers that the teaching of reading should be none of their business at all. In this respect the basic problem in the secondary school is the antithesis of that in the elementary school. Nothing in the pre-service education of secondary teachers has convinced them of their responsibility to be reading teachers as well as subject matter teachers. As a matter of fact, some content area teachers are offended by the suggestion that they must also be teachers of reading. They know their students need reading instruction, but they feel special reading teachers should do the job. The argument that all high school students can profit from reading instruction and that, therefore, the job is too big for special reading teachers often falls on deaf ears. Teachers who do accept the argument may be willing to incorporate some gimmicks into their teaching, but they balk at making major changes in materials and pacing in their instructional programs. Secondary teachers who arrive at a reading in-service program expecting to do some intensive remodeling in their classes are rare indeed.

In summary, the main objective of in-service education in reading is to change teacher behavior in the classroom. To accomplish it certain conditions over and above good format and presentation must be evident. We have discussed the need for administrative commitment to change, the need for holding teachers accountable for improving their teaching, the need for developing a higher regard for in-service education generally, and the need for changing attitudes of both elementary and secondary teachers toward in-service education in reading. When optimum conditions are not present, the likelihood of changing teachers' instructional practices is slight. If optimum conditions do prevail, in-service education in reading is capable of taking on a new image and becoming more dynamic in bringing about reading program improvements that are urgent in both elementary and secondary school.

Guidelines for In-Service Reading Programs

When optimum underlying conditions for change through in-service education are present, it remains to design and install programs that are stimulating, meaningful, and relevant. To be ready to make significant improvements in a reading program and to be without a good in-service program is as frustrating as to have what appears to be a good in-service program and be lacking readiness. Teachers who are ready to make needed changes must have help at the right time, by the right people, and in the right way. This situation requires capable leaders, good program implementation, proper timing, and other elements that bear heavily on the success or failure of in-service education ultimately to improve students' growth in reading.

A poor in-service program may be worse than none at all because it produces negative attitudes toward in-service education and perhaps even toward the teaching of reading. The following discussion is concerned with factors that have to be considered in the planning, implementation, and evaluation of in-service reading programs. Because of our belief that if such programs are poorly designed and poorly presented they may be detrimental to a school's reading curriculum, we recommend that in-service education be postponed until certain standards of quality can be met. It should not be inferred that all the elements must be perfectly tuned before the program is attempted. If that were the case, in-service education would probably remain always in the planning stage. However, all the elements in a particular in-service program must meet the standards discussed, we feel, for the program to be effective in changing the teachers' classroom behavior.

The Need for Specific Objectives

One important factor in the success of in-service reading programs is the careful identification of the objectives that are being sought. A program designed and implemented to change teachers' behavior must be based upon what is desired of the teachers' students and what teachers need to do to cause the desired student behavior. Teaching reading includes the development of many different skills, attitudes, and habits, and one in-service program cannot hope to have an impact on all phases of a school's reading program. Therefore, it is wise for an in-service reading program to focus upon selected abilities it is hoped that students will acquire and specific instructional materials and practices to teach these abilities. If a school is engaged in continuous in-service work with its reading program, it might well concentrate upon a limited number of phases at any one time.

It is tempting for a person with expertise in reading pedagogy to respond to a call for in-service help that does not state precisely what is wanted. This kind of appeal offers the reading specialist an opportunity to draw upon his own pet interests and competencies. However, an in-service reading program directed at too many problems or at problems vaguely defined by the school requesting help often produces disappointing results. If the principal and the staff of a school are unable to identify their problems and specify the help they want, the reading specialist should be employed first to aid in the necessary identification and specification and then to aid in planning and presenting the program.

We have received calls from school administrators along these lines: "Our school has some money to spend on in-service, and the teachers decided to invest it in some help for our reading program. We'll appreciate anything you can do for us." The following illustrative call would be more likely to result in reading program improvement: "Our sixth-grade teachers are not satisfied with their students' ability to read critically. We would appreciate finding out about some materials and classroom practices that might help our students become better critical readers." In-service education that is focused on improving specific student and teacher behaviors will probably be more effective than some general treatment which may be inspiring but not productive of change.

Involving the School Staff

Not only is it important for specific in-service education objectives to be established, but they ought to be established by the teachers and administrators who participate in the in-service program. The need must be a felt need if change is to occur. Having an "expert" tell a staff what their needs are is risky business. Usually a person needs to work in a school as a teacher or a principal before he is able to know the school's problems and which ones can be profitably attacked.

We are not saying that a specialist in reading should not aid a staff in identifying weaknesses in the reading program. There are times when a principal or a principal and his staff sense that all is not well but are unable to pinpoint the specifics of the problem. It is then appropriate and wise to seek the help of an expert. However, when someone from outside the school is brought in to aid in the diagnosis of reading program weaknesses, he should proceed in a cooperative manner to solicit much information and opinion from the teachers and principal. The staff should be guided to a realization of their problems, not be presented with a list of objectives for an in-service reading program after a period of silent observation.

Often a principal and his staff know precisely the kind of help they need. In this case it is dangerous for the in-service leader to tamper with the objectives already decided upon. Unless the objectives set by the group are highly unrealistic or contrary to good instructional practice, more improvement will probably occur by using them, as stated by the staff, than by modifying them to suit the preference of the in-service leader.

An in-service reading program is a highly personal matter for a principal and his teachers. It is not uncommon for a staff to become defensive for a short time during the planning and implementation of the program. If negative attitudes persist, teachers' classroom behavior will be unlikely to improve. Perhaps the best way to replace negative attitudes with positive ones is to encourage teachers to play a major role in planning and conducting their own in-service reading program. They will then understand better what they are trying to achieve, and any evaluation of the existing instructional program will amount to self-evaluation.

The active participation by principals and teachers in identifying weaknesses, planning the in-service program, and implementing it cannot be overstressed. We have conducted programs that were "sprung" on the teachers by their principal, curriculum coordinator, or other supervisory personnel and have suffered the resultant teacher apathy and sometimes even hostility. On the other hand, we have worked as in-service consultants in schools in a team operation with the principal and teachers. We observed teachers working with their students, inspected materials being used, and held dialogues with teachers and the principal. These observations and conversations were followed by informal staff meetings during which we all shared our perceptions of the strengths and weaknesses in the present reading program. As an outgrowth of our discussions the group cooperatively arrived at the objectives to be sought and a plan of action for attaining them. The team approach to in-service planning and implementation is in our opinion more likely to succeed than any other approach. The wise resource person will share the spotlight with the participating principal and teachers. As a matter of fact, he will get to the edge of the spot as quickly as possible and guide the program from that position as much as possible.

Resource People

Another important factor in in-service reading education is the resource person who acts as the program's leader. Communication is the key to any program that has an impact on classroom behavior. If a resource person hopes to change the instructional reading program, he must be able to talk with teachers and administrators clearly and with an understanding of the problems they face. He should also have appealing personal characteristics, a background of successful teaching experience, a knowledge of current thinking about his reading specialty, a knowledge of reading research in his specialty, and a sensitivity to teachers' capabilities and needs. Resource people with these qualifications are difficult to find, but if an in-service program is to reach students and not stop in the auditorium, they must be earnestly sought and persuaded to take part.

Often not all of the qualifications desired of a resource person by a school are to be found in one person. Therefore, schools should consider the possibility of a team of resource persons for in-service reading programs. One might work with the school on grouping, another on materials, and still another on testing. However, it remains vital for every member of the team to be able to communicate his expertise to the principals and teachers in a manner that produces understanding and stimulates a desire to improve reading instruction.

We believe that an excellent resource person is the principal himself. He is in the school every day, he visits all the classrooms while reading is being taught, he knows each teacher personally, he knows the school's resources and needs, and he has a greater influence on teachers' behavior than other resource people are likely to have. Unfortunately, principals are usually not as knowledgeable about reading pedagogy as other available resource people. In some cases it might be wise to have the principal consult with a reading specialist or reading specialists about specific problems and then return to his school to provide his teachers with the in-service education they need.

Because of the importance of employing people with appropriate qualifications for in-service reading education we have prepared some questions that might be asked regarding resource people who are being considered. It is a rare person who would rate an affirmative response to all of them. How many negative responses are acceptable before a candidate is eliminated and which question or questions are crucial must be left to the judgment of the principal and the teachers requesting help. Certain of the questions are probably more applicable to some kinds of programs than to others.

Personal characteristics
1. Does he communicate orally with fluency and enthusiasm?
2. Does he inspire confidence in teachers regarding their ability to improve their teaching?
3. Does he remain poised when an individual or entire group becomes defensive or shows some hostility?
4. Can he offer compliments easily and sincerely?
5. Does he resist the urge to overwhelm teachers with his knowledge or his jargon?
6. Is he willing to listen as well as talk to teachers?
7. Is he sensitive to the capabilities of individual teachers?
8. Does he combine a sense of earnestness with a sense of humor?
9. Does he find good things to say about the present program before citing weaknesses?

Other qualifications
1. Has he taught successfully and recently at the academic levels or in the subject matter areas of the participating teachers?
2. Can he detect program strengths and weaknesses by observing teachers working with students?
3. Is he able to involve teachers in the in-service program?
4. Is his knowledge of research in reading up to date?
5. Is his knowledge of authority opinion in the field of reading up to date?
6. Does he understand the roles of the principal, central office staff, and other specialized personnel in reading curriculum development?
7. Does he understand that public school curriculum development is subject to financial limitations, public sentiment, administrative bureaucracy, and other factors?
8. Does he offer *specific* suggestions for improving reading instruction?
9. Is he able and willing to demonstrate teaching techniques with students?
10. Is he willing to observe what *is* happening in classrooms before telling teachers what *should be* happening?
11. Is he willing and able to demonstrate how to use instructional materials he recommends and how to administer and interpret tests he recommends?
12. Is he available for follow-up activities?

Demonstrating Materials

Teachers are almost always interested in instructional materials. For most teachers the appeal of new materials is greater than the appeal of new theory.

Therefore, materials may be used for motivational as well as other purposes in in-service reading programs.

Developmental reading materials can be demonstrated in such a way as to teach good instructional practices which may be used with reading materials other than those being shown. For example, the questions which follow or precede a particular published selection may be carefully examined and evaluated to indicate their strengths and weaknesses in eliciting certain levels of thinking about the selection. Or the structure of a selection may be examined and the different thinking strategies necessary for comprehending it noted and discussed. Pictures in instructional materials may be analyzed in terms of children's interests, and thus much information about children's interests and the importance of motivating children to read can be disseminated.

Specialized reading personnel engaged in either elementary or secondary school in-service work will find many opportunities to help teachers improve their teaching of reading by demonstrating functional and recreational reading materials (see discussion in Chapter 3). For example, showing teachers how to teach students to survey a chapter in the social studies text currently being used may be of more benefit than demonstrating a commercially published kit that includes practice exercises in surveying reading selections. Too often only developmental reading materials that are sold commercially are utilized in in-service reading programs. While teachers do need to be aware of the many good developmental reading materials on the market, they also have to know how to use their functional and recreational materials to teach reading.

Secondary School In-Service Programs

In-service reading programs in secondary schools present special problems: (1) With some exceptions, secondary teachers want to teach content, not reading. (2) Teaching reading tends to equate secondary teachers with elementary teachers, who are sometimes perceived as having less prestige than secondary teachers. (3) Many secondary teachers think of reading ability in terms of word recognition and word analysis — in their minds a student either can or cannot read. (4) Many secondary teachers don't require much more than factual recall and literal comprehension from their students. (5) Most secondary teachers think of themselves as teachers of a particular subject matter and prefer to become more specialized in that field than to become more skillful in teaching learning skills. (6) Some secondary teachers see only the need for remedial reading in the secondary school, and they have an unwarranted faith in the ability of remedial reading teachers to make good readers out of poor readers. And (7) secondary teachers are often limited in their access to appropriate materials at the ability levels of their students and are consequently using materials that are too difficult for their students to read independently. For these and other reasons, in-service reading programs are often condescendingly tolerated rather than enthusiastically welcomed by secondary school teachers.

Until more is done in the pre-service education of secondary school teachers to convince them that teaching reading at their academic level is not only necessary but a noble and exciting enterprise as well, in-service reading programs will be more difficult to conduct in secondary schools than in elementary schools.

In conducting in-service programs with secondary school teachers we have found the following practices helpful:

1. Working with teachers in content area groupings. Teachers of a particular subject matter tend to think of their teaching and their problems as being different from those of teachers in other disciplines. English teachers don't see what advice given to science teachers has to do with them. Talk that is not directed at teaching their specific subject is often considered of little or no concern to them. Therefore, meetings with teachers from different content areas seem much of the time to be irrelevant to certain teachers.

2. Openly discussing the limitations of remedial reading in the secondary school, and discussing the legitimacy and nature of an adapted curriculum for students who will probably never learn much from reading.

3. Presenting reading as a thinking process that must function in special ways to enable readers to master content with a particular structure.

4. Demonstrating instructional procedures to improve reading with materials currently being assigned to students.

5. Having samples of materials that are below grade level difficulty, related to the teachers' content and not embarrassing for secondary students to read.

6. Assuring the teachers that teaching reading is not an esoteric enterprise reserved for elementary teachers and specialists but is good teaching practice used to improve skills that never reach their ultimate level of sophistication.

7. Taking time, usually at the beginning of the session, to answer truthfully and sincerely the inevitable questions about readability formulas, speed reading, reading machines, and other interesting aspects of reading pedagogy about which teachers are generally curious and often misinformed.

8. Responding to questions with information whenever possible, and admitting without being defensive lack of knowledge when knowledge is lacking.

9. Presenting reading program development as something to be tailored to the unique needs and resources of each secondary school.

10. Approaching the development of the reading program as an experiment to be tried and evaluated, and being specific about how the evaluation will be conducted.

Time for In-Service Education

Once upon a time, in-service education for teachers was conducted without apology and without extra pay — after school, before school, in the evenings, and on Saturdays. Fortunately, in most school systems this is no longer the case. Most school systems now recognize the importance of providing in-service education for teachers during the regular school day or of giving extra pay for attending meetings at times other than the regular school day. To this end extra money is budgeted to pay teachers stipends for in-service participation, or children are released from school so teachers can attend in-service meetings.

If extra pay or released time is provided, *when* to hold reading meetings does not seem so important as *for how long*. Reading is a subject in itself and basic to all other school subjects. It is also an area of the curriculum about which most teachers have strong feelings and some anxiety. Therefore, in-service reading programs that are to change teachers' classroom behavior require weeks, not hours. This does not mean that teachers need to spend weeks attending meetings. Some group sessions are called for, but more time should be devoted to informal contacts with in-service leaders, the principal, and fellow teachers. In addition, in-service programs should include planned classroom activities under supervision that are followed by evaluative conferences.

In other words, in-service reading programs should be planned to operate for a number of weeks, an entire year, or several years, but not for several one-hour or two-hour meetings. The recipe for a good program calls for simmering as well as boiling.

Timing for In-Service Education

In-service reading programs should not be held when a school is undertaking some other project that is likely to interfere with the concentration that can be given to reading. One of the present writers had the experience of leading some in-service work in a school that was undergoing the trials of accreditation. Needless to say, the effect in changing the instructional reading program was not gratifying.

Although generalizations are dangerous, we feel that the beginning of a school term, shortly after the principal and the teachers have their duties organized and under way, is the most advantageous time to initiate in-service work. Enthusiasm and energy for change among the staff are usually at their highest, no one needs to be defensive about what he has been doing most of the year, and there is time to experiment with and evaluate different instructional practices with students.

Ideally, the in-service reading program should be started when the principal and/or teachers express a readiness to improve their reading program and request the wherewithal to do so. Sometimes this readiness occurs within a staff spontaneously because of some common experience. However, it usually has to be prompted by the administrative staff, parents, or a zealous teacher or two. Realistically, in-service work is best started any time the principal and teachers of a school are able and willing to devote serious thought and vigorous action to assessing their present reading program, planning for improvement, and implementing those plans. If the expertise required for assessment, planning, and implementation exists within the staff, there is no need to employ someone from outside. If it does not exist within the staff, the availability of a competent resource person becomes an element in the timing of the in-service program.

Media

It is no longer necessary to disseminate information on upgrading a reading program by face-to-face oral communication. However, in our view face-to-face oral communication is the most effective in-service medium. Television, films, tape recordings, and other media have all added new dimensions to in-service education, but they must be selected and used with care if they are to benefit the instructional program.

When a school staff is contemplating using media other than person-to-person contact, the limitations of those media should be acknowledged. The ego-involvement that comes when the staff plans and implements improvements designed by them and for them cannot be achieved through viewing or listening to programs produced elsewhere for more general consumption. It should not be inferred that television, films, and media other than personal contact are to be avoided. Because they add variety to a program and provide access to authorities who would otherwise be unavailable, they are valuable. They are also valuable because some ideas can be more effectively communicated by audio-visual means. Our position is that these media should supplement an in-service reading program, not serve as its basic component.

Acknowledging Capabilities

It is exciting to dream of what might be, but it is wise to recognize what is. The extent to which a reading program can be made better is limited by the resources that can be assembled to effect the desired improvement. Some in-service reading programs with which we have been involved have been wasteful and disappointing because the plans for improvement far exceeded the ability to implement the plans. Everyone concerned with the planning of improvements should know what financial, personnel, and building resources can be made available.

Some major changes can be made without additional materials, rooms, or personnel. For example, pacing, assigning reading-related tasks, grouping, and asking questions are basic elements in the instructional reading program, and all can be improved with the existing resources. However, some changes require help from specialized personnel, more instructional materials, standardized tests, or other resources not currently present to accomplish what is desired. Knowing the kind and the supply of resources available will aid the in-service leader, the principal, and the teachers in arriving at goals for the in-service program that can be satisfactorily attained.

Follow-up

The Scottish poet Robert Burns said:

> The best-laid schemes o' mice an' men
> Gang aft agley,
> An' lea'e us naught but grief an' pain,
> For promised joy!

Perhaps Burns's philosophical commentary on the gap between making plans and realizing their objectives is too poetic to fit the situation that exists when in-service planning fails to bear fruit in the classroom. However, the gap between planning and classroom implementation certainly demands careful consideration. As was mentioned earlier, a major frustration of in-service work is that it frequently does not go beyond the planning stage.

One reason for cessation of in-service education at the threshold of the classroom is that in-service leaders have been hesitant to accompany teachers into their classrooms where the plans they made together are to be implemented. Resource persons and teachers should be prepared to continue their work together until the objectives they established are attained. This is one key to realizing the benefits in-service education offers the instructional program.

Follow-up, then, from our point of view, is more than meeting to evaluate progress toward goals and to discuss problems which were not anticipated in previous meetings. Follow-up is first of all a team-teaching arrangement whereby a resource person and a classroom teacher exchange teaching and observing roles while directing the learning of students toward specific objectives. When too many teachers for too few resource persons or other conditions make this kind of follow-up activity impossible, the in-service program is in danger of not realizing much of its potential to improve the learning of students.

Follow-up meetings should also identify and solve problems that were unanticipated or only vaguely identified before. These meetings are often more enthusiastically attended by teachers than previous ones because the needs of the teachers are immediate and plainly related to classroom conditions. It is now often possible for resource persons to respond more definitely to teachers' requests than in preliminary meetings because the teachers' requests are more specific and more clearly stated.

Another productive follow-up activity is evaluating progress toward the objectives established in planning meetings. One way to achieve meaningful follow-up meetings is to establish during the planning meetings a timetable for specific kinds of evaluations. For example, the participants might decide that two weeks from the first meeting they will reconvene to study samples of students' written reactions to a particular reading selection, lists of books students have chosen to read, or students' scores on a phonic analysis test. Unless it is agreed that teachers will attend with tangible evidence of success or failure regarding their efforts to achieve certain objectives, the meetings are likely to be a waste of time. After the collected data have been evaluated, problems may be discussed, new objectives set, and, it is hoped, praise and encouragement liberally dispensed.

Participants in an in-service program deserve and need follow-up activities. Good intentions must be transformed to good teaching. The transformation almost always requires guidance and evaluation of progress from the stage of intentions to the stage of classroom implementation. It is the function of follow-up activities to aid in making the transformation.

Reference

Martin, William R. "A New Look at Secondary School Reading Programs in the Upper Midwest." *Journal of Reading*, 1969, 12, 467–470.

CHAPTER 9

Models for In-Service Education

The preceding chapter discussed a number of factors which contribute to the success or failure of an in-service reading program. A successful in-service experience, we feel, is reflected in improved instructional practice with students. Anything short of this is failure.

The present chapter will describe some in-service reading programs which we believe achieved their objectives. Not all of the underlying conditions discussed in Chapter 8 were present when the programs were in effect. However, even without ideal conditions, the programs described resulted in changes in teachers' classroom behavior. The models (1) are all actual case histories and (2) were instrumental in improving instructional practices in reading even though they were conducted under less than perfect conditions.

The models are illustrations of different approaches to improving reading instruction through in-service education. Although the descriptions specify the academic levels at which each program was successful, it is likely that most, if not all, of the approaches could be successful at various academic levels. We urge that the models be modified and combined in ways that will suit them to the needs and resources of individual schools.

Model 1

Grade levels involved: 1–6
Approximate number of teachers involved: 700
Specific objective:
   to help elementary school teachers be more regular and more precise in teaching their students to think creatively about certain reading selections

Educational television was used to achieve the objective of this in-service reading program. Two 20-minute television scripts were written to present information about creative thinking and how to construct questions to elicit creative thinking about a reading selection. Via the local university television station, a reading specialist and a third-grade teacher gave information, engaged in discussions, and demonstrated specific questioning techniques with a group of the teacher's students. All elementary students were dismissed from school thirty minutes early on the two days the programs were telecast to allow teachers to view and discuss the programs.

Creativity was defined according to Bloom's (1956) delineation of the cognitive level of synthesis. The first program pointed out that ideas obtained from a particular reading selection may be combined with ideas acquired elsewhere in a purposeful search for a new product, pattern, or structure. The second emphasized the construction and using of questions to stimulate creative thinking about a reading selection. The following guidelines for the construction of synthesis-level questions (taken from Sanders, 1966) were presented to the teachers:

1. Do your good readers often have their hands raised before you finish asking
2. More freedom is allowed in seeking an answer than in lower thought categories.
3. In answering, the student creates a product or communication.
4. An answer to a synthesis-level question can be evaluated only subjectively.

Questions constructed according to these guidelines were demonstrated with students, who performed naturally even though they were given no rehearsal before being televised.

Prior to the broadcasts every elementary teacher in the Madison, Wisconsin, public schools received an outline of the television programs that included the major points of information to be presented. Immediately following each telecast the principal or a teacher appointed by the principal led the staff in discussing the information that had been presented. The teachers were then urged to fill out a prepared questionnaire to evaluate the program and to tell of their personal experiences with teaching "creative reading." The questionnaires were sent to the reading specialist who presented the program. Follow-up activities were arranged in schools that requested them. Smith (1969a) has reported in more detail the in-service program described briefly here.

Model 2

Grade levels involved: 1–3
Approximate number of teachers involved: 9
Specific objective:
  to help teachers improve their teaching of creative reading

Following the program described in Model 1, the primary grades teachers in one school requested more information about how to teach creative reading than was presented in the two telecasts, and a late afternoon meeting was arranged. The principal and the teachers met with the central office reading specialist who wrote and narrated the television programs for the purpose of asking him some specific questions about teaching creative reading.

Since the television programs had been recorded on audio-tape, it was possible for the teachers to listen again to the definition of creative reading and the characteristics of questions designed to stimulate thinking at the cognitive level of creativity. In addition, the written reactions to the television programs submitted by teachers throughout the school system had been used to construct questions for teachers to ask of themselves:

1. Do your good readers often have their hands raised before you finish asking your question about a story? It was apparent from the television demon-

stration that the participating students frequently raised their hands to answer a question before it was completely asked. Information received from teachers who viewed the programs indicated that this is typical behavior of good readers. Premature hand raising suggests that students are conditioned to expect questions about their reading that do not require higher-level thinking.

2. Do your students understand how to adjust their thinking when you change the cognitive level of your questions about a story? It was observed during the TV programs that the demonstrating teacher had to clarify precisely the limits of the response being solicited before the students took advantage of the freedom available to them. The students tested the limits to which they might go with their answers. As the teacher reacted to their responses, they learned the rules for working at the cognitive level of creativity.

3. Do you experience feelings of discomfort when your questions about a story are followed by silence? A number of teachers who responded to the television programs commented on the lack of time available for teaching creative reading. Teachers who have a positive attitude toward teaching creative thinking will not be uncomfortable about taking the time necessary to permit students to answer higher-level questions about their reading.

4. Do you find yourself answering some of the "best" questions you ask about a story? When teachers do ask questions that call for creative thinking, they often wait too short a time for students to do effective thinking before answering the questions themselves. Students become used to this pattern and wait for the teacher to answer the "hard" questions.

5. Do you feel a twinge of conscience if you don't tell a student that his response to a question about a story is either right or wrong? Teachers are accustomed to rewarding correct responses and withholding rewards for incorrect responses. It was noticeable in the television programs that the demonstrating teacher had difficulty finding language patterns that accepted students' responses without evaluating them as correct or incorrect. Teachers who teach creative reading effectively are likely to have a ready supply of accepting but nonevaluating responses.

These questions and the audio-tape were discussed and left with the teachers to use to improve their teaching of creative reading.

Model 3

Grade levels involved: 10–12
Approximate number of teachers involved: 60
Specific objectives:
   to help content area teachers incorporate the teaching of reading into their instructional programs and to acquaint a staff with the concept of a total-school approach to developmental reading in the secondary school

The principal of a one-year-old senior high school added a reading consultant to his staff to help all the teachers take an active part in improving their students' reading ability. To initiate the total-school reading program they desired, the principal and the reading consultant requested an in-service program from central office reading personnel to help teachers understand the benefits of such a program and to show as many teachers as possible how to incorporate developmental reading instruction into their content area classes.

Five central office reading specialists joined the consultant, the principal, and the chairmen of the departments of English, science, social studies, and mathematics to plan and present the program. Three of the central office reading specialists and the reading consultant each volunteered to study the needs and instructional possibilities for one of these major subjects, by reading, observing classes, and conferring with the department chairmen. They then worked with the individual chairmen to plan a program geared to the needs of the teachers in each department.

Planning sessions and presentations, then, took place in the context of either the English, science, social studies, or mathematics curriculum. The remaining two central office specialists prepared themselves to offer more general and theoretical aspects of a total-school approach to reading in a high school.

One entire day of released time was provided for the in-service program. During this day the teachers studied and discussed specific objectives for a total-school reading program, adjusting materials to student abilities, criteria for distinguishing the mature from the immature reader, and specific instructional practices for developing reading maturity.

Considerable time was devoted to how the following characteristics of mature readers might be developed in students within the framework of the various content area curriculums:

1. The mature reader reads for specific purposes, which he either sets for himself or has set for him by someone else. His purpose may change as he reads, but he is always purposefully directed.
2. The mature reader is aware of the need for precision with words and makes a conscious effort to enlarge his vocabulary as he reads.
3. The mature reader varies the rate and style of his reading according to the nature of the material and his purposes for reading it.
4. The mature reader organizes his reading into major and subordinate units to aid comprehension and retention.
5. The mature reader is alert to the meaning-bearing elements in English sentences (word-form changes, syntactical-function order, structure words, punctuation marks, etc.).

Teachers from the departments of English, science, social studies, and mathematics met with their chairman and the specially prepared central office reading specialist to consider teaching practices to help all their students develop these characteristics. Teachers from other content areas as well as staff concerned with other pupil services either sat in on these sessions or conferred with the other two central office specialists regarding their particular concerns.

The theme of the entire program was *Toward Maturity in Reading for Inde-*

pendent Study. This theme related the program to the high school's commitment to developing an independent study program.

The development of the total-school reading program and the contribution of the in-service program described here to that development are described elsewhere in more detail (Smith, 1969a).

Model 4

Grade level involved: 10
Approximate number of teachers involved: 4
Specific objectives:

to help social studies teachers use writing tasks to teach students how to read for different purposes and to acquaint the same teachers with research techniques for investigating the effects of certain instructional practices on reading outcomes

To accomplish the objective of this undertaking, the team of teachers who taught the tenth-grade social studies course was invited to participate in a research study and use their students as subjects. The study was designed to investigate the effects of writing tasks at different cognitive levels on students' attitudes toward a social studies selection and their comprehension of it. One writing task read as follows:

In the article "The Liberty Ship" the author points out that Liberty Ships were produced and did function in spite of difficulties. When you finish reading the article, write a paragraph in support of the following topic sentence:

The Liberty Ship serves as an example of the old saying "Where there's a will, there's a way."

The other writing task was constructed as follows:

In the article "The Liberty Ship" the author points out that Liberty Ships were produced and did function in spite of difficulties. When you finish reading the article, write a short scene involving two or more people meeting to solve a problem relating to the Liberty Ship. Describe the setting for the meeting, the problem, and the people present. Then write several lines of dialogue for the scene.

The writing tasks were assigned before the students read the selection and were completed after the reading.

The participating teachers aided in the construction of an attitude inventory, a comprehension test, and writing tasks. They also helped assign students to treatment groups, administer the different treatments, and score the students' written products. By participating in the experiment the teachers learned many things about attitudes and reading comprehension and how to measure those variables. They also learned how to construct writing tasks at different cognitive levels relative to a reading selection and how to research instructional practices with their students.

The results of the study, which also served as in-service education, have been reported by Smith and Barter (1968).

Model 5

Grade levels involved: 7–12
Approximate number of teachers involved: 20
Specific objectives:
> to help secondary school teachers develop positive attitudes toward incorporating the teaching of reading into their content area classes and to teach them specific instructional practices to use with their students

A personal reading improvement course for teachers was used to achieve the objectives of this in-service program. All secondary school teachers in the Madison, Wisconsin, public schools were invited to take a course designed to help them improve their reading ability. The nineteen who enrolled were given five 2-hour classes which included exercises to improve vocabulary, rate, and comprehension.

It was hoped that the participating teachers would inductively learn some techniques to employ with their own students and would develop positive attitudes toward incorporating these techniques into their teaching. The inductive approach was adopted to avoid the negative attitudes that sometimes result when a specialist tells teachers how they should teach.

In addition to improving reading rate and comprehension, a questionnaire survey indicated that this particular in-service approach had desirable effects on attitudes and teaching. On the questionnaire, thirteen of the nineteen subjects responded that because of the course they felt more able to improve their students' reading; eleven said that they were more willing to make reading instruction a part of their classes; and seven commented that they were already teaching their students some reading improvement techniques they had learned in the course.

This program is reported elsewhere in more detail (Smith and Otto, 1969).

Model 6

Grade levels involved: 7–9
Approximate number of teachers involved: 9
Specific objective:
> to help the science, mathematics, and social studies teachers in one junior high school improve their students' ability to comprehend the assigned reading

Three central office reading specialists arranged with the principal of a junior high school to spend one week in the principal's school helping content area teachers meet the needs of disabled readers in their classes. Each specialist was knowledgeable about teaching reading in the content areas and an experienced junior high school remedial reading teacher.

Preparatory to the week they were to spend in the school, the specialists met with representative teachers from the various departments to plan activities that would be most helpful to the teachers who most needed help. It was decided that certain of the science, mathematics, and social studies teachers were least able to cope with the disabled readers. Therefore, the three reading specialists agreed to spend the entire week working with a few teachers from each of those three departments, each specialist to work with the teachers in one department.

During the week it was possible for the specialists and teachers in cooperation to give all students with reading problems informal reading inventories. On the basis of the findings, supplementary reading materials with reading difficulty levels below those of the textbooks being used were identified and collected to be assigned in place of long passages in the textbooks. Accordingly, the teachers agreed to reduce the length of each textbook assignment and spend more time preparing students to read all assignments. The reading specialists demonstrated for the content area teachers specific instructional practices for improving students' vocabulary and comprehension. At the end of the week the teachers had more understanding of their students' reading deficiencies and were better prepared with materials and instructional practices to provide for some of those deficiencies.

Model 7

Grade levels involved: 1–6
Approximate number of teachers involved: 30
Specific objective:
    to train a corps of teachers to perform special reading services in their individual schools

Smith (1969a) has reported a successful in-service program that was conducted to train elementary classroom teachers to assume positions of leadership in the development of the reading programs in their schools. Selected teachers volunteered to attend in-service classes which were addressed to such matters as using diagnostic tests with disabled readers, selecting and using reading materials, system-wide reading program objectives, the role of specialized reading personnel, and trends and issues in reading instruction. The teachers received professional advancement credits for attending the after-school meetings. The credits were not applicable to a university degree, but they did enable the teachers to advance on their school system's salary schedule.

Following the initial training program the teachers returned to their schools and were given one-half day a week released time to aid their principals and central office reading personnel in maintaining a strong developmental reading program. Some of them also do limited corrective work with students who have minor reading disabilities. Follow-up meetings, additional classes available only to the cadre teachers, and visits by central office reading personnel to the teachers in their schools are used to help the teachers implement the information they received from the training program and gain additional information.

Much of the success of the in-service training for this program is attributed to the fact that the teachers are volunteers and have been given responsibilities and opportunities for imparting their knowledge to other classroom teachers.

Model 8

Grade levels involved: 7–9
Approximate number of teachers involved: 30
Specific objective:
> to help junior high school teachers properly use films designed to improve the reading ability of their students

All the teachers in a junior high school were given one-half day released time to study three films from the Reading Growth Series from Coronet Films, 65 E. So. Water St., Chicago, Illinois: *Getting the Big Ideas, Adjusting Your Reading Speeds,* and *Reading Creatively.*

Three central office reading specialists had prepared study sheets for each film in order to involve the teachers in discussions of the concepts presented and of how the film might be used in the various content areas so that students would apply the information presented to their reading assignments. After each film was shown, the reading specialists discussed the concepts presented, told of their experiences with the film, and suggested instructional practices and student activities to accompany the film.

At the conclusion of the half-day program, one of the reading specialists arranged to return to the school when classes were resumed to demonstrate how each film could be used to best advantage with students in different content areas. The importance of applying the same concept differently in two content areas was demonstrated when the reading specialist showed one film to students in their English class and to the same students in their social studies class. The reading specialist taught the students to apply the concept in one way with the English textbook and in another way with the social studies textbook.

Model 9

Grade level involved: junior primary (transition grade between kindergarten and first grade for students who lack reading readiness)
Approximate number of teachers involved: 30
Specific objective:
> to help teachers in this relatively new program understand the objectives of the program in regard to reading instruction

All the teachers in the school system who taught junior primary classes were released from their teaching responsibilities for two full days to meet with central office coordinators of mathematics, science, social studies, and reading. The overall purpose of the project was to help teachers understand basic differences between the junior primary program, the kindergarten program, and the first-grade program. Two and one-half hours were devoted to a group discussion between the reading coordinator and the teachers.

As a follow-up procedure the reading coordinator sent a memo to each of the teachers several days after they returned to their classes. He had used this technique following other in-service meetings and found it effective in summing up group discussions and reminding teachers of the plans that were made during meetings. If carefully written, a follow-up memo often communicates ideas more precisely and more clearly than they are communicated in oral discussion. The oral summing-up at the end of a spirited two-and-one-half-hour meeting is often done imprecisely and when fatigue is interfering with concentration.

The following paragraphs are excerpted from the two-page memo each junior primary teacher received when she returned to her classroom after two days of in-service meetings:

To: All junior primary teachers
From: (name), Reading Coordinator
The recent in-service meeting we shared was a good learning experience for me. The group discussion brought to my awareness the many fine things being accomplished in our junior primary classes as well as some of the administrative and instructional problems that accompany the program.

I think all agree that the junior primary program is needed by many children who have completed kindergarten, but who seem to be lacking in readiness for a structured reading program. These students apparently fall into two categories: those with serious and complex readiness deficits and those with relatively minor readiness deficits. The question seems to be for which of these students junior primary classes are most needed or perhaps whether or not one junior primary class should service the readiness needs of students from both categories. How a particular school answers this question seems important not so much in terms of whether or not certain students will benefit — it seems obvious that students in either category will profit from the special advantages the program offers — but rather in terms of the expectancies of parents and future teachers regarding the junior primary graduate's ability to read. The need for precise communication regarding the kind or kinds of students a particular junior primary program services is important. The instructional program and our evaluation of the effects of the instructional program must consider the seriousness of the student's disability when he enters the program.

Unfortunately, our present methods of predicting the advent of reading readiness in a given child are not as reliable as we would like. Some children who are judged to have serious readiness deficits may prove to be less seriously deficient. In these cases, the junior primary teacher should begin the instructional reading process when the child evidences readiness, or in rare cases the child may be transferred to a first grade class.

However, I believe that junior primary teachers should not feel that getting all of their children — or any of their children if they teach the seriously deficient — started in a formal reading program is their responsibility. The junior primary program, I feel, should be a 38 weeks language readiness program, not an instructional reading program that begins in February, instead of September. It is true that given the conditions present in most junior primary classes some children who would not respond to formal instruction in a first grade class can be taught to respond to print. These responses, however, may be short lived and unproductive of the thinking processes that engage a person who is a mature reader.

There is evidence that reading ability correlates positively and highly to general language ability. It would seem that the sole function of the junior primary program might be to provide children who have speaking and listening deficiencies with many and varied speaking and listening experiences. Motor coordination development might also be an appropriate objective for *some* children. Getting a child started in a reading program should be an objective that may or may not emerge as the junior primary program progresses.

Rhythm and rhyming games, creative dramatics, listening to and telling stories, talking about shared experiences, music and art work are representative of activities that may be varied and presented at different levels of sophistication for an entire school year without boring most children and without formal reading instruction. If these activities are presented correctly, children may inductively learn much about reading that will in the long run serve them better than some formal experiences with decoding the language.

It was apparent during our in-service discussion that opinions and procedures regarding the role of reading instruction in the junior primary program vary. This is consistent with our philosophy that every school should have the kind of instructional program it needs. It was also apparent that the nature and objectives of each school's program need to be communicated to that school's entire faculty and to parents whose children are in the program.

The ideas stated in this memo are certainly subject to discussion and argument. They are ideas which I formed during our first meeting. Perhaps they could serve as a base for discussion at future in-service meetings.

Model 10

Grade levels involved: 1–6
Approximate number of teachers involved: 27
Specific objective:

    to help teachers in one elementary school (1) select new reading materials, (2) improve their grouping arrangements, and (3) improve their instructional practices

The key to the success of this in-service approach was the length of time a reading specialist spent in one school helping teachers improve their teaching of reading.

After studying students' scores on a reading achievement test and the students' placement in ability groups for instructional purposes, a central office reading consultant arranged to spend three weeks in the school working with teachers the entire school day. The consultant administered diagnostic tests to selected students, conferred with teachers individually, and held grade level meetings when these could be arranged. In addition, he demonstrated good teaching practices with students while teachers observed. He also arranged for materials different from those the teachers were using to be displayed for a sufficient period of time for teachers to examine them carefully and discuss them with the consultant and other teachers.

When the consultant left after three weeks, many children had been regrouped, the number of groups in some classrooms had been changed, teachers were using improved instructional practices, and new basic and supplementary materials were on order. A special benefit of the in-service education was the improved professional relationship that had been established between the staff of the school and the central office consultant. The teachers and the principal felt satisfied with the service they received and indicated they would not hesitate to ask for further assistance when it was needed.

Model 11

Grade levels involved: elementary school principals
Approximate number of principals involved: 30
Specific objective:
  to help principals administer the primary grades reading program in their schools

A survey of elementary school principals in one school system disclosed that the primary grades reading program was the area of the curriculum that the principals were least prepared to administer. They readily agreed to attend five two-hour classes entitled "Administering the Primary Grades Reading Program" and taught by two central office reading consultants. The classes were held twice a week in a central location from 9:00 A.M. to 11:00 A.M. They were held early in May when the principals were hiring teachers, planning their instructional programs, and ordering materials for the following school year.

The first meeting was devoted to a consideration of the following organizational plans for teaching reading: three groups in one heterogeneous classroom taught by the homeroom teacher; completely individualized teaching; team teaching; homogeneous grouping for reading within one grade; homogeneous grouping for reading between two or among three grades. The principals were given handouts with diagrams and explanations of the various schemes and asked to list the advantages and disadvantages of each. After their deliberations, the principals were divided into two small groups for discussion.

The second meeting was devoted to different theoretical approaches to beginning reading instruction. The following approaches were considered: phonics, linguistics, basal approach, modified alphabets, language experience, and programmed approach. Again the principals were handed explanations and asked to list advantages and disadvantages of each approach. Small-group discussion followed.

The third, fourth, and fifth meetings provided the principals with information about evaluating the total reading program, evaluating a teacher's performance in the classroom, and using financial resources and specialized personnel. All meetings began with a short presentation by one of the instructors and included plenty of time for questions and discussion.

Model 12

Grade levels involved: 10–12
Approximate number of teachers involved: 40
Specific objective:
  to help senior high school teachers learn about the teaching of reading and the implications of a total-school approach to reading instruction

A full-time reading consultant was added to the staff of a senior high school that served mostly college preparatory students. The teachers were not convinced that most of their students could benefit from reading instruction, especially instruction incorporated into their own teaching. They were happy to have a reading specialist on their staff, but they wanted her to utilize her time teaching the most seriously disabled readers in special remedial classes.

To overcome resistance to a total-school approach to reading instruction, the consultant arranged to hold "coffee hours" one day a week in her small conference room. All teachers were invited to stop in during their preparation period for coffee and an informal discussion about some aspect of reading instruction.

Each week the consultant had prepared a different topic for her guests to learn about and discuss. The topics were chosen to be interesting to senior high school teachers and to have application to their own teaching. The following topics are illustrative: readability formulas, standardized reading tests, teaching reading in the content areas, reading machines, reading laboratories, remedial reading.

The consultant had information pertinent to the topic of the day on the chalkboard, on the bulletin board, and on audio-tape. The information that had been prepared was thought-provoking but not likely to cause the teachers to become defensive. It was apparent that the consultant was informing, not selling.

As word of the coffee hours spread, attendance increased; and soon administrators and department chairmen were joining the groups. Some of the teachers requested more information, some wanted achievement testing for entire classes, some asked for special materials to use with their students, and some sought the consultant's help in planning and teaching units.

Model 13

Grade levels involved: 7–12
Approximate number of teachers involved: 15 *teachers and* 6 *secondary school reading consultants*
Special objective:
  to help teachers and reading consultants understand their respective roles in a secondary school reading program

This in-service class, called "Trends and Issues in Secondary School Reading Instruction," was held in a central location from 7:00 P.M. until 9:00 P.M. on five consecutive Monday evenings. All participants received one professional advancement credit for their voluntary participation. The International Reading Association publication *Developing High School Reading Programs* (Dawson, 1967) was used as a text to stimulate discussion. Regular reading assignments were made for each class meeting. Two central office reading specialists acted as instructors and discussion leaders. Topics covered were: the characteristics of a total-school reading program, developing reading maturity, teaching reading as a cognitive process, the affective dimensions of reading, developmental reading materials for high school students, the disabled reader in remedial reading classes, and grouping to accommodate different reading abilities in content area classes.

Each meeting began with a short presentation to the whole group by one of the instructors. The group then divided for discussion. The teachers met with one instructor to discuss the topic under consideration from their point of view, and the consultants met with the other instructor to discuss the topic under consideration from their point of view. Following the small-group meetings, all participants were brought together again for summarization and discussion of the ideas advanced in the small groups.

Several days after the class meeting, each participant received from the instructors a written communication summarizing the information that had been presented in the class and the discussions that had followed. The superintendent of schools, the assistant superintendent of schools, the director of secondary education, and the director of curriculum development also received copies.

As a result of the class several interesting grouping experiments were initiated by teacher-consultant teams, and one of the instructors spent two weeks helping a participating teacher to improve the curriculum for a class of low-ability ninth-graders. Different materials were introduced, interest and ability groups were formed, and the students were taught certain concepts about reading that they could apply to their assigned work.

Model 14

Grade levels involved: 1–6 *and* 7–12 *(two separate programs with the same objective)*

Approximate number of principals involved: 8 *and* 4

Specific objective:

to help principals administer the reading programs in their schools by involving them in long-range curriculum planning

Eight elementary school principals volunteered to serve on a curriculum planning committee with three central office reading consultants. The group met on a school day in a central location for one morning to take up the following agenda (which had been sent to the participating principals previously): (1) future textbook adoption committees, (2) utilization of specialized personnel, (3) development of an improved program for disabled readers, and (4) in-service offerings for teachers. The decisions made by the group on these matters would be written into the long-range curriculum plans to be presented to the board of education.

Discussion on these items moved to subjects which were tangential to the agenda. It was apparent from the discussion that central office consultants and principals had been unaware of their relative positions on a number of issues basic to reading curriculum coordination. Consequently, they were sometimes unwittingly working at cross-purposes. It was also apparent that principals were unaware of some of the newer developments in reading curriculum.

The reaction of all participants was that curriculum planning of this kind should be a continual occurrence, with principals attending on a rotation basis so all would have the advantage of this learning experience.

A similar meeting held with four secondary school principals yielded many of the same benefits. One particularly positive outcome was the drafting of a memo to the director for curriculum development requesting a statement from him regarding the school system's commitment to reading instruction for all students through twelfth grade. The following paragraphs are excerpted from that memo:

> The following items were on the agenda for discussion:
> Allocations for reading consultants
> Best use of reading consultants
> Best utilization of central office staff
> Developing total-school reading programs
> Special reading programs (remedial classes, speed reading classes, etc.)
> Evaluating programs

The consensus of those present was that the Board of Education and the Superintendent of Schools should explicitly inform all secondary school principals of the system's commitment to a reading program embedded in each classroom. Within such a program each teacher would develop the reading skills needed to read the materials of his subject area. The teacher would also select and assign materials that match students' reading abilities. Principals would be expected to evaluate each teacher's ability and willingness to teach reading as well as his particular subject matter. It was felt such an administrative commitment in the form of a directive to the principals is necessary if the reading program is to have the thrust of line officer support and the leadership necessary to make reading instruction an integral part of the secondary school curriculum.

Furthermore, it was the consensus that once such a commitment is made and principals' responsibilities are established, every principal would have need of a reading consultant to aid him by (1) working with content area teachers to help them meet the reading needs of their students, (2) working with librarians and guidance counselors to make reading development an integral part of those programs, (3) initiating action research with the aid of central office personnel, and (4) guiding and supervising supplementary reading programs (remedial reading classes, speed reading classes, etc.).

In summary, the secondary reading program now and in the future should be characterized by:

1. line officers' commitment, verbal and financial, to a total school program,
2. a reading consultant in each secondary school,
3. reading consultants working most of the time with other staff members rather than directly with students,
4. supplementary programs kept at a minimum so as not to give the impression that these supplementary programs are the basic programs.

Model 15

Grade level involved: 8

Approximate number of teachers involved: 1 science teacher and the science coordinator for the school system

Specific objective:

to help one teacher adjust his curriculum to meet the reading needs of his low-ability students

In a conference between the school system's science coordinator and an eighth-grade science teacher it was established that his students' poor reading ability was the teacher's major problem. The science coordinator sought the help of a central office reading consultant, who agreed to assist the teacher in (1) adjusting his curriculum to his students' abilities and (2) helping his students read more accurately.

The reading consultant spent an entire week observing the teacher working with his students, diagnosing the students' needs with informal reading inventories, and studying the objectives and materials of the science curriculum. Another week was spent by the consultant in collecting and constructing reading materials that were pertinent to the objectives of the course and more consistent with the reading abilities of the students than the textbook they were using. The third week the consultant taught the class for three days while the teacher observed, and the teacher taught the class for two days while the consultant observed. Conferences between the teacher and the consultant followed each class period. Although the textbook was not discarded, students were given shorter reading assignments, some sections were omitted, and the students were carefully prepared for any assigned reading in the textbook. For several weeks thereafter the reading consultant periodically visited the teacher and his class to provide continued support.

An outgrowth of this in-service experience had far-reaching effects. As a result of the education in reading both the science coordinator and the science teacher received, the reading consultant was invited to attend the meetings of the science textbook adoption committee. Before new science textbooks were adopted, the reading consultant tested each book being considered with the students who would use it. The consultant reported to the committee on the suitability of the books for the students who would use them and the possibilities each book offered for teaching reading skills necessary for comprehending science materials as well as teaching science content.

Model 16

Grade levels involved: K–6
Approximate number of teachers involved: 21
Specific objective:
> *to help teachers in one elementary school understand the advantages of teaching reading to three ability groups within a self-contained classroom*

The purpose of this program was to prevent major changes in a school's organizational pattern for reading instruction rather than to promote them. The teachers and the principal of the school had read and heard much about individualized reading instruction, ability grouping for reading instruction between grade levels, ability grouping for reading instruction within one grade level, and other organizational patterns for teaching reading. As a result they began to doubt their own pattern, which had each homeroom teacher teaching reading to three ability groups in a self-contained classroom organization.

A reading specialist, not from the system but very familiar with the school's reading program, was consulted. He knew the school was achieving good results with its present organizational pattern and felt it would be wiser to effect minor changes within the existing organization than to adopt a different one. Fortunately, the principal and most of the teachers were not completely uncritical of the glowing reports coming from the schools which had abandoned the practice of teaching reading in a self-contained classroom with three ability groupings.

The reading consultant met with the principal and teachers at one of their regular staff meetings. The approach was to describe briefly the major organizational plans available to the school and have the teachers discover strengths and weaknesses in each plan if it should be implemented in their school. Since the teachers were reasonably familiar with the different plans presented, this was not a lengthy process. The strengths and weaknesses of their present organization were then noted.

The following plan, which fitted into the school's existing pattern, was suggested as best for the school's current resources and needs:

1. Each teacher teaches reading to all of the students in his homeroom (this facilitates the incorporation of the reading instruction needed by a child into the instruction he receives in other subjects and also facilitates the movement of a child into a higher or lower ability group when warranted).
2. In the primary grades each teacher teaches developmental reading to three different ability groups in the morning and teaches functional and recreational reading to an indeterminate number of interest groups in the afternoon.
3. At the end of the kindergarten year, each child is given a reading readiness test. The results of this test are combined with the kindergarten teacher's

observations regarding the child's readiness strengths and weaknesses. Children who appear likely to have difficulty are assigned to a particular teacher who will use a beginning reading method with his low group that emphasizes the sensory modes of learning that seem to match the child's needs or learning strengths. For example, a child with poorly developed oral language might be placed with a teacher who will use a language-experience approach with his low group while a child with good auditory discrimination might be placed with a teacher who will use a phonics or linguistic approach with his low group. The principal coordinates the program so that unless the child is being unsuccessful or can succeed in a higher ability group, children stay in the same basic program for at least three years.

4. There is much individualized supplementation of the basic program at each level of the program. Children are not rushed through the program and do not skip levels because they are able to achieve at a higher level.

5. In the intermediate grades the able students devote more time to functional and recreational reading while the less able students continue to spend at least half of the time devoted to reading on skills development. The number of ability groups each teacher forms at the intermediate grades level is determined by the range of ability in the class. A completely individualized program may be appropriate for some classes while three groups may seem best for other classes.

A discussion of the above guidelines convinced the teachers that considerable individualization of reading instruction could be accomplished in a self-contained classroom.

Model 1 /

Grade levels involved: 10–12
Approximate number of teachers involved: 60
Specific objective:
   to help a reading consultant in a senior high school explain the need for a total-school approach to reading instruction to content area teachers in her school

The reading consultant in a senior high school and her principal requested help from the school system's reading coordinator in planning and presenting an in-service program. They wanted a program that explained the role of content area teachers in a total-school developmental reading program. The consultant had worked in the high school for a number of years as a reading teacher and was changing her role to consultant in keeping with the school system's desire to incorporate reading instruction into all content area classes in the secondary school.

The students were dismissed from school for an entire day to provide the faculty with released time for in-service education. One-half of the day was allotted to in-service education in reading.

Prior to the program, the reading consultant had identified five teachers who were already incorporating considerable reading instruction in their teaching. She worked with them to help them become more systematic and precise in their teaching of reading through the content they taught. She then persuaded them to discuss their teaching objectives and techniques with their colleagues as the major portion of the in-service program. By way of introduction to their presentations, the school system's reading coordinator agreed to present to the entire faculty some basic concepts about reading and its development in the secondary school.

In his presentation the reading coordinator made the following points:

1. Reading includes comprehension and utilization of ideas as well as decoding the language.
2. There is evidence that students who score well on standardized reading tests are not necessarily mature readers.
3. Content area teachers are in particularly good positions to help students engage in higher-level thinking processes about the assigned reading material.

Following the reading coordinator's short presentation the five participating teachers described how they had been incorporating reading instruction in their teaching. One had been helping students develop better vocabularies for social studies reading; one had been helping students set specific reading purposes before beginning a reading selection; one had been constructing and asking questions at higher cognitive levels for students to answer about their reading; one had been helping students see relationships among ideas presented in mathematics textbooks; and the fifth had been helping students analyze the structure of paragraphs in their textbook.

After these presentations the reading consultant, the reading coordinator, and the five teachers met with small groups of teachers to discuss other ways in which all teachers might contribute to their students' reading development.

Teacher training institutions are being criticized for the inadequacies of beginning teachers to teach reading. Administrators of both elementary and secondary schools are deploring their new teachers' lack of knowledge about reading instruction and lack of good teaching techniques. Elementary school administrators who have been in service for fifteen or twenty years recall the days when prospective teachers were taught how to teach reading. The implication is, of course, that prospective elementary teachers today do not receive the same quality of pre-service training in reading pedagogy. Secondary school administrators of some duration recall a past as bleak as the present in regard to their teachers' pre-service education in the teaching of reading.

We have no rebuttal to offer secondary school administrators. To certify a secondary school teacher who has no education in how to teach reading is indeed indefensible. Yet many states continue to do this knowing full well that many teacher training institutions will not require a course in teaching reading in the secondary school until such a course is made a state requirement for secondary school teaching certification. It is difficult to understand why groups of secondary school administrators have not used their political influence in this regard.

We do offer some defense of present elementary school pre-service education. In relatively recent years different elementary schools have adopted different organizational patterns, different teaching methodologies, different materials, and different grouping plans. Frequently the reading program in one elementary school is quite unlike that in a neighboring school. Consequently, it is not possible for a teacher training institution to produce an elementary teacher who is prepared to teach reading in all schools. The frustration of teacher training institutions in this regard is understandable.

The point is that the pre-service education of teachers is only the beginning of their education. On-the-job training has become a necessity. A major task facing educators of teachers at secondary and elementary levels is providing them with quality in-service education.

References

Bloom, B., *et al. Taxonomy of Educational Objectives.* New York: McKay, 1956.

Dawson, M. A. *Developing High School Reading Programs.* Newark, Del.: International Reading Association, 1967.

Sanders, N. *Classroom Questions: What Kinds?* New York: Harper & Row, 1966.

Smith, Richard J. "Questions for Teachers — Creative Reading." *Reading Teacher,* 1969a, 22, 430–434.

Smith, Richard J. "A Reading Resource Teacher for the Elementary School." *Reading Teacher,* 1969b, 22, 696–701.

Smith, Richard J. "First Steps Toward an All-School Reading Program." *Journal of Reading,* 1969c, 12, 569–574.

Smith, Richard J., and Clinton R. Barter. "The Effects of Reading for Two Particular Purposes." *Journal of Reading,* 1968, 12, 134–138, 174–176.

Smith, Richard J., and Wayne Otto. "Changing Teacher Attitudes Toward Teaching Reading in the Content Areas." *Journal of Reading,* 1969, 12, 299–304.

INDEX

Aberdeen (Scotland), study of WISC profiles, 12

Academic Therapy Quarterly, 140

accelerated instruction, 31, 34

adapted instruction, 27, 31–32, 34–37 *passim,* 73, 157

Adler, Mortimer J., 71, 100

adults, reading improvement for, 146–147

Allen, R. V., 137

Allport, Gordon W., 100

American Educational Research Journal, 140

American Journal of Mental Deficiency, 141

American Journal of Optometry and Archives of the Academy of Optometry, 142

American Journal of Orthopsychiatry, 141

Anderson, I. H., 134

Anderson, Paul L., 96

Aschner, Mary Jane McCue, 90

Atkin, J. M., 44

attitudes toward in-service education:
in general, 178–179
in reading, 179

attitudes toward reading, 110–112

Austin, Mary C., 134, 155, 156, 168

Ausubel, David P., 77

Baer, C. J., 21

Bamman, H., 134

Barbe, W. B., 134

Barnhart, C., 135

Barter, Clinton R., 101, 194

basic reading skills, scope and sequence of, 40–46, 121

Belmont, Lillian, 12

Bereiter, C., 135

Bernstein, Margery R., 90

Betts, Emmett A., 128–129

Birch, Herbert G., 12

Bloom, Benjamin S., 71, 189–190

Bloomfield, L., 135

Bond, G. L., 34–35, 135

Brown, James I., 147

Brueckner, L., 135

Burack, Boris, 101

Burnett, Richard W., 156

Buros, O. K., 135

Bush, C. L., 135

Carhart, Raymond, 21

Carroll, John B., 94, 95

Carter, H. J., 135

central office reading consultant, 161–162, 171–172

Chall, Jeanne S., 126, 135

Child Development, 141

Childhood Education, 141

Clearinghouse, 141

Cleland, Donald, 96

Cohn, J., 135

Cohn, S. M., 135

comprehension, in reading skills statement, 41–47 *passim,* 54–60

Cooperative English Test, 125–126

Cooperative Test of Reading Comprehension, 99–100

corrective instruction, 30, 37, 73, 157

creative skills, in reading skills statement, 41–47 *passim,* 68–69

Cromer, Ward, 17–18

Cruickshank, W. M., 135

Dale, Edgar, 126

Dallman, Martha, 135

Dawson, M. A., 135, 201

Dearborn, W. F., 134

DeBoer, J. L., 135

Dechant, Emerald V., 21, 22, 136, 138

deHirsch, K., 136

Delacato, C. H., 20

Della-Piana, G. M., 35, 136

developmental instruction, 29–30, 34, 37, 157

developmental reading, 72–74, 87

144006